To Anthony Chorley

The Final Crash

Addictive Debt and the Deformation
of the World Economy

HUGO BOULEAU

Best wishes

[signature]

October 2009

HUGO TOBY BIRCH
AKA
HUGO BOULEAU

pendula
press

First published 2007 by Pendula Press
PO Box 666, Clarity House, Smith Street,
St Peter Port, Guernsey GY1 3SL
Tel/Fax 01481 248578

www.finalcrash.com

British Library Cataloguing in Publication Data
A catalogue record for this book is available from the British Library

Hardback
ISBN-13 978–0–9555217–0–6

10   9   8   7   6   5   4   3   2

Designed and produced for Pendula Press by
Chase Publishing Services Ltd, Sidmouth, EX10 9QG, England
Printed and bound in the European Union

CONTENTS

PREFACE

WHY I WROTE THIS BOOK

I wrote this book because I had nagging doubts that something was going badly wrong with our economic system, which I had previously so admired. It has become increasingly clear that our consumer culture is actively encouraging ever-greater burdens of debt and speculation; for the very people who could not afford to take such risks. While benefiting the banking system and corporations alike, it leaves the public on a treadmill of wage-slavery with an ever-poorer quality of life. Not in terms of the number of short-lived techno-gadgets that may be accumulated and disposed of soon after, but in terms of longer working hours, commuting and a lack of social cohesion.

On a purely selfish level I am also fed up with buying imported goods that appear to offer value but instead provide just a fraction of the longevity, compared with quality items that used to be made closer to home. This sham of chrome-plated shininess, with its built-in decay and obsolescence, prompted a parallel in my mind with the coinage of the Roman Empire. At its peak, the coins carried real value in the form of precious metals and were used to portray the image of the Emperor far and wide. As the Empire waned, this was reflected in the money as gold and silver were substituted with cheap base metals. Although the coins looked the same – with the familiar symbols of the past that implied continuity – they were just a tinny imitation of the real thing. I then began to question whether a similar dilution effect was going on today, not just with household goods but with modern money as well.

In the process of writing, I was also able to unwind three deep-seated frustrations. The first involves my day job as an investment manager in an offshore private bank. While I guide some of the wealthiest people on the planet through the maze of markets, further enriching them in the process, the majority of the public receives a very different treatment from retail banks and 'advisers'. Daytime adverts push little more than mortgages, credit cards or consolidation loans which are the ultimate wolf in sheep's clothing – debt on top of debt with longer servitude. Television programmes abound that encourage property speculation but few realise the risks undertaken thanks to the conditioning of its decade-long success. No one appears concerned that property price inflation leaves the next generation with a lifetime of mortgage debt, simply for a place to live. There can be few other species that squander today at the expense of their offspring.

In this Internet age we would appear to be the best-informed generation since the first symbol was scored on clay. Yet we are also the most heavily bombarded by marketing messages, both visible and subliminal. On one Internet home page, under the personal finance column, one sees headings of house prices, loans and credit cards – in that order. It exemplifies the brainwashing that appears to make debt a normal and acceptable part of our lives. There are many foreign countries and cultures where this is simply not the case. In future, the personal finance column may well read debt-reduction, savings and investment – for they should be our real priority. Britain and America were built on a savings culture, which has all but disappeared. This has not been helped by the mis-selling scandals of banks and insurance companies. Our savings famine is best exemplified when we prostrate ourselves before our widescreen altars. Whenever an antique is auctioned or a quiz competition is won, the owner or contestant is asked the standard question 'What will you do with the money?' The vast majority of answers involve going on holiday or spending it. It is ironic in such cases to see a hand-crafted family heirloom traded in to buy modern furniture, which will barely last five years. The occasional pensioner from a bygone era will give the windfall to their grandchildren but I have yet to hear anyone say they will save the money for a rainy day.

These attitudes provide a clue to the malaise: the Anglo-American culture has become one of instant gratification, satisfied by easy and accessible credit. Our banking industry, so long renowned for its stewardship, is now driven slavishly by sales targets. Such purveyors of debt exploit the weakness of our genetic programming to grab and gorge. This is where our forebears were so much smarter than us as they understood the financial principle of wait and accumulate. Their wise ways were betrayed with the surge of inflation that accompanied the Vietnam War, which benefited borrowers but not savers. This was when the last vestige of financial discipline was abandoned.

The second frustration is related to the first which concerns a conspiracy of silence from business and political leaders. We are skipping down a cliff path where the precipice is hidden by wondrous foliage; the warnings signs are barely visible behind the excess growth. It is not just banks that have a conflict of interest to play down the dangers of debt: scores of superficial service industries have sprung up from the property and consumer binge. Governments have likewise reaped an unforeseen harvest that has promptly been squandered.

It appears that we may be facing a meltdown rather than just a temporary slowdown, perhaps the greatest since the dawn of the Industrial Revolution. Some of its portents have already fallen into place, even in the course of writing this book. One can only hope that its publication will provide enough time to take protective action for we are too far gone for prevention. Yet there is only a minority of authors and articles that give sufficient warning. I will mention these titles along the way and list them in the notes and bibliography. Where this recommended reading is concerned, I am frequently standing on the shoulders of giants. Paradoxically, their expertise as specialists is also their weakness as it focuses on specific bands of the spectrum, without illuminating the entire length of the path ahead. This book goes much further in its forecasts which ultimately opens it up to greater ridicule should they fail to be fulfilled. The outcome may well be one where I am made to look a fool and am shown to be completely wrong. However, should only a portion of these concerns come to fruition then this book will provide vital protection. I emphasise here that it is not an investment – which grows what you have – but an insurance policy that can at best only protect and preserve.

Understanding the worst-case scenario sets aside great investment managers from the average majority. In order to cope with a crisis, they imagine how they would feel in a variety of negative scenarios and determine the best course of action in advance. Should the event occur then they are in full control because they have rehearsed the decisive exit procedures. Napoleon Bonaparte summarised the approach: 'If I always appear prepared, it is because before entering an undertaking, I have meditated long and have foreseen what might occur. It is not genius which reveals to me suddenly and secretly what I should do in circumstances unexpected by others; it is thought and preparation.'

The third frustration relates to the intended audience. When starting out on a book, one is full of high-minded ideals to reach out to as many people as possible. The problem with this approach is that no one likes a party-pooper, especially when everyone is having fun. The purpose of this book is not to lecture the public on how to lead their lives – this will no doubt become apparent when the downturn begins. It is designed instead to highlight the endemic conflicts of interest that have spawned a new generation of debt junkies on both sides of the Atlantic. If people understand that they are being manipulated – and not empowered – then they can make up their own minds whether to continue the charade. This book is therefore not a tender request; it is instead a slap in the face to wake us from the clutches of a twisted hypnotist. While the forecasts it carries are negative for western living standards, the long-term message is one of surprising hope: improved working and communal lifestyles, protection from inflation and a new-found respect for nature. This need not be a Utopian pipe-dream. Sadly, it will take a slump to make us work as one, much as we do in wartime. We will also, unexpectedly, be on the road to reversing our dependence on fossil fuels following a debt-driven dollar and energy crisis. We may yet avert an environmental disaster.

The warnings that I and other commentators have given will only be heard by a minority. They in turn may already understand the problem which will be a case of preaching to the converted. This is a predicament that many authors face when they attempt to reach a large audience. As one canny publisher explained, books for a general readership generally don't get read. When it was suggested that a student market should be included this made absolute sense. For fear of sounding pompous, my aim is to generate debate among a new generation of thinkers, untainted by the selfishness of the baby-boom bracket. In the ultimate form of entrapment, these free-thinkers of tomorrow have had student debts thrust upon them, to catch them in the same wicked system that will ultimately come crashing down around us all. In spite of this early burden, they are as yet unlikely to have been spoiled by speculation. They might still have the chance to free their minds from one-dimensional economics that models mankind's actions on that of a consumption-driven machine, without thought of the social consequences or environment. It would also satisfy a long-held disappointment where my own undergraduate education was concerned, giving me the opportunity to explain how markets work in a manner that I would like to have been taught.

Like professions the world over, many economists feel that a subject must include the maximum amount of mathematics to make it respectable, perhaps seeing themselves as scientists rather than the artists or philosophers they should be. In a jargon-filled language I could barely understand, the first minute of a lecture would be spent explaining the basics of a topic then the remainder of the hour would delve into pros and cons of some complex area. From the army to academia, every institution seems to thrive on acronyms and abbreviations that baffle outsiders who dare to enter their private club. If I can leave just one legacy then it would be this: to be the inspiration for a future leader to learn from past mistakes and implement a new and radical approach. I certainly do not wish to portray myself as some kind of messiah of markets; I am more like John the Baptist, preparing the way for someone greater to come. Much like the prophet, there will be critics and contemporaries that benefit from the current system who will want my head on a platter.

The Final Crash unveils the links between the property boom, stock markets and geopolitics and then explains their connection with the dollar, energy prices and the environment. Unlike previous downturns in the West, where economies have righted themselves over the course of an undulating cycle, the latest cosmetic upturn has made the prospect of eventual recovery even less tenable. A series of botched interventions has artificially stimulated the world economy and left it on overdrive. Like an enzyme or protein molecule subjected to critically high temperatures, our disfigured financial system will never regain its useful form. While our capitalist system appears rosy-cheeked on the surface, its vital organs have been poisoned from within by the drug that is debt. As a consequence, we appear to be in the early days of a rebalancing of our standard of living, with wealth tipping away from the western shores toward those of the East.

In the review stage of this book, I have been accused of a great many things by economists and academics, including lack of scholarship and a populist approach, to mention but a few of the kinder comments. As someone from a scholastic family I would be first to highlight and recognise my failings in this department. However, one should note that two dictionary definitions of the word academic are 'abstract' and 'impractical'. It would likewise be a cheap shot to quote Jean-Paul Kauffmann who said 'the economy depends about as much on economists as the weather does on weather forecasters'. Another parallel is that they are like experts who study the sea but never go sailing – it is only when one commits personal or client money to markets that one's opinions may be put to the test by the ultimate judge. In spite of appearances to the contrary my aim is not to alienate this critical, but credible readership, whose students form part of my target audience. It is instead designed to explain a complex topic in a language that is understandable, with practical applications for the reader. Tables of data have been minimised: they may prove a point but it is words that bring ideas to life, just as good public speakers can communicate without depending slavishly upon Power Point.

Existing books have already achieved the difficult balance between explanation of the historical context and ease of reading. Examples in economics include the likes of Barry Eichengreen's *Capital Flows and Crises*; in financial markets, Robert Shiller's *Irrational Exuberance*, and in politics, Emmanuel Todd's *After the Empire*. Where I can make a difference is in the timing aspect. Unlike economists who can propose theories or make predictions with relative impunity, there is little comeback if their forecasts go off-target, assuming one can even remember what they had originally said. For someone managing money for the world's most demanding clients, one's multi-year performance record regularly appears in black and white, in the form of a portfolio valuation. This means that the theory, application and timing have to be right much more often than not, otherwise the money would move on elsewhere.

So why should today's debt levels be any greater a threat than they were in the past? After all, there have been far worse government deficits as a proportion of the economy in centuries past: the Napoleonic Wars being a good example. The difference today is that debt is utterly endemic throughout western economies: not just at government level but for individuals, corporations and financial markets alike. The sheer volume of speculative money and derivative instruments within the financial system is dwarfing anything seen before, approaching 800 per cent of global GDP (gross domestic product – the standard measurement of economic activity) having stood at barely one third back in 1990. Banking and borrowing dominate so many aspects of our lifestyle, culture and work that we feel utterly dependent and incapable of surviving without them. Debt has not just become the fuel for pointless growth but the end-product also. We will undoubtedly see the situation worsen as deficits naturally compound themselves through high rates of interest: when the crash comes, the usual counter-productive remedy of borrowing yet more will no doubt be administered once again. In time, we will come to understand that debt is as pointless today as leaches were in medieval medicine: like then we only use it because we know no better. There is also a view that economics is a man-made system that will be met with man-made solutions. There is no way that leading powers will simply sit back in the face of financial and economic crises and do nothing. This time around, extreme population growth coupled with the limiting factors of geology and the forces of nature are about to rebound in our face: in the form of energy shortages and global warming. We are dealing here with dynamics beyond our puny control. While our ancestors were humble enough to fear and respect the natural world, our arrogance has fooled us into thinking that we are masters of it. Like the biblical Armageddon, the deformation of the current economic system need not be feared as an end of days, but should be viewed as a new beginning or period of purification.

It must be emphasised that economic slumps and crashes are rare events historically. However, just because they are unusual does not mean that they never occur – like natural disasters, we assume they only happen to someone else. As one who deals in timing, the likelihood of a meltdown is mounting in proportion to the ever-increasing level of complacency. The rampant speculation by banks, hedge funds and leveraged buy-outs is yet another symptom of a financial free-for-all that will all end in tears. I expect to see markets crack before we see the back of 2008, with a full-blown depression in place with the dawn of the new decade. Even if one was able to fix the right day of the right month of the right year, there would still be so much scepticism and uncertainty that most people would neither believe it nor know what to do even if they did. For my money, the downturn began with the new millennium as stock markets peaked. The ensuing manipulation of interest rates that made markets rally just one year after 9/11 is a classic secondary symptom of a system already broken by speculation. We are some seven years into a breakdown phase that will span the length of this decade; the truly painful break-up period is yet to come.

In financial markets one frequently witnesses an upsurge in unloved areas of the market once their strongest proponents have lost faith, having endured so many false dawns and disappointments. This is likely to be the same fate for those who have raised concerns over the relentless rise of debt. Only when the last cautionary critic is humbled and humiliated will the crash commence. For now, it seems like the economy can continue expanding forever, unperturbed by the accumulation of such financial toxicity. Even if a classic slump ensues, the majority of people will cling hopefully to the notion that the good old days are just around the corner and assume that political intervention will save the day. Just when one thinks that capitalism is floored and can take no more, it will no doubt spring back once more in defiance of gravity. Like a mortally wounded animal that lashes out for a final time against its hunters, we cannot assume that the old apparatchiks of western economics and politics will give up without a furious fight.

HOW TO READ THIS BOOK

The message of this book is confined to three key points concerning our indulgence in debt, namely: cause, effect and consequence. Part I, 'Party Time', examines the cause of our apparent boom era. This is the fun bit we have just experienced where it felt like the good times would never cease. Part II, 'Hangover', is the inevitable aftermath of our drawn-out borrowing binge. This has knock-on effects well beyond our shores and for our lifestyles in future. Part III is called 'Detox and Rehab' which concerns the consequences of our indulgence which will leave many financially disfigured for life. Like the sensual Siren voices that tempted Odysseus toward the rocks, there will be many smooth-talking salesmen hoping to lure us further into debt. This book will block one's ears to their hypnotic but fatal song and allow a true course to be steered.

The dependence on debt to fund our increasingly extravagant lifestyles bears a remarkable resemblance to the abuse of drugs by an addict. The cycle of occasional use to one of excess and reliance are followed by toxic shock and, one hopes, eventual recovery. The longer the addiction, the worse will be the cold turkey effect when sobering up. For many, it could be too late to act: permanent damage has already been inflicted in the West and living standards may never be the same again. While many believe financial prosperity to be the ultimate aim of our existence, we will rediscover the notion that quality of life and sustainability are much more satisfying goals.

If one is *au fait* with economics then much of the content should cover familiar ground, up until the end pages. Even for those with little financial background it should give a sound summary of where we stand across a diverse – but related – range of current affairs. Anyone with a mortgage or financial investment should most certainly comprehend the potential downside of the global economy which will affect them in the most personal and painful fashion. If the premises of this book prove to be wrong, the worst that can happen is that the reader will have missed out on some future opportunities. They will have reduced their debt, sold some assets too early and built up a cash pile in the process: this is hardly a painful outcome. I have unashamedly used the popular property angle to draw readers into the core of the book. While banner headlines for 'Free Sex' are a cheap trick to make us look at an unrelated advert, the housing boom is in fact a highly relevant part of this study. Although the real estate rally appears to be a bonanza of never-ending wealth, it is merely a mirage. A series of bail-outs has left the developed world in a financial mess where rising house prices are just one of the symptoms of a wider malaise of general asset price inflation.

The content is split between an analysis of the past and a forecast of what may come to pass. This book does not follow the classic two-handed economist approach which provides a variety of probability-weighted forecasts – this is the worst-case scenario only. While there will be tips along the way, the main recommendations will come in the final chapter, 'Puritans and Penitence'. This will collate the ideas and give some investment, business and personal guidelines for the future. As with any project, pre-planning is just as important as the final execution. It is therefore vital that the preparatory work is carried out in today's apparently benign environment before negative psychology becomes widespread. Just as necessity is the mother of invention, so a prolonged period of economic woe will spawn a series of innovations. Although this book can spoon-feed some simple ideas and advice, it will inevitably be down to the individual to pursue their own research: remaining open-minded for the sparing opportunities that lie ahead. There is little point in writing a book on big-picture themes whose conclusions bear little relevance to one's daily life. As highlighted in Malcolm Gladwell's *The Tipping Point*, revolutionary ideas need practical advice and context to spread. While the initial aim is to guide one through a sequence of events, on both a personal and political level, the ultimate goal is to resurrect the idea of monetary reform.

Before embarking on any technical issue I will explain key words and concepts to illustrate their importance. Simplified analogies are also used throughout to explain complicated relationships. While helping the reader to understand the mechanics of a process, where not already understood, they are not intended to be read as exact simulation. I add this comment here in the hope that it will pre-empt the inevitable criticism where, for example in Chapter 3, the flow of water does not exactly mimic and model the flow of financial liquidity: it is simply used to get the general idea across. The final chapters examine the consequences for individuals, financial markets and international affairs. Too often we analyse each of these areas in a vacuum without understanding their role in our three-dimensional human ecosystem, so rarely captured or accounted for in conventional economics.

ACKNOWLEDGEMENTS

My first and most sincere debt of thanks goes to my wife, Anna, who has single-handedly coped with our children in the two years of putting this book together. Without her help, and the aid of some industrial ear defenders, I would never have completed this task. The next thanks are owed to my parents for their lifelong leadership and support.

Having written financial articles for some 15 years, the thought of compiling an entire book had never crossed my mind. When Grant Mellor made this suggestion he arranged for me to meet his friend, and now mine, author Tony Booth. He has been unstinting in his enthusiasm and encouragement from the very first time we met.

The next credit should be offered to those anonymous authors who gave their feedback in the early reviews, albeit brutal at times. After the initial hurt I came to realise that their interest lay not in belittling me but in delivering a bitter but sometimes necessary medicine. Roger van Zwanenberg of Pluto Press has likewise provided paternal guidance, disciplined but reassuring. When I have eagerly taken the wrong course, he has applied restraint. When despondent, he has given me inspiration and assistance.

My thanks for technical guidance go to Daniel Broby, chief investment officer of BankInvest; economic historian Dr Gregory Stevens-Cox; gold expert Frederic Panizzutti, and Dr Norma Birch on energy issues. Jonathan Guillemet and Rick Gomes of East Harbour Consulting have also provided project assistance. My output has leant heavily on authors and researchers, many of whom I have never met. They are acknowledged in the bibliography and notes but especially include the commentator Richard Russell, authors Bob Beckman and Michael Rowbotham and financial strategists at ABN Amro, Morgan Stanley and Brown Brothers Harriman.

Hugo Bouleau
December 2006

INTRODUCTION

DEBT AND THE THREAT TO THE WORLD ECONOMY

Many people in the Anglo-Saxon economies of Britain and America are unaware of the pending debt catastrophe, which will make the crises of the 1970s look like a mild downturn – yet these ordinary people will be the biggest losers. We are on the edge of a 'bust' period where the winners will be those who lose the least. We will look back at the first decade of the new millennium as a period of gross self-indulgence and profligacy in which we put ourselves first no matter what the cost. The communal – though not the financial – quality of life will improve as our values are changed by circumstance.

In H.G. Wells' *The Time Machine*, the inventor 'George' travels far into the future. He encounters a world where beautiful, carefree people known as the Eloi appear to lead an idyllic lifestyle, living just for the day. Every need is catered for such that the past and future have become unknown and unnecessary concepts and long-forgotten books have turned to dust. The reality is that they are nothing but unquestioning human cattle: a subservient food source for underground mutant cave-dwellers known as Morlochs. Every time a siren screams, the people are drawn zombie-like to the caves to be devoured. This seems increasingly similar to our behaviour as consumers, as the call of the shopping mall drags us out day and night to spend like automatons. Like the Eloi, we do not know the source of our food and care little for the future as we brush aside all else to accumulate yet more unnecessary possessions; meanwhile ignoring the deteriorating state of our finances, communities and environment. This appears to be endemic throughout the English-speaking world: as we talk of progress we are actually drifting toward poverty. Payback time

1

for our profligacy is not far away. Only those who emerge from the consumer trance can be saved from the Morloch's cave which in our case is the black hole of debt.

Before summarising the arguments for this book, it is essential to understand how banks multiply debt many times over. There is nothing fundamentally wrong with lending money in a responsible and constrained manner. This is a feature of Islamic banking where borrower and lender share the responsibility. Technically speaking, there is no borrowing or lending of money as this is forbidden by Shariah Law. Instead, the bank matches the depositor with the businessman such that both sides share the profit or loss in a project. In the West, it is the borrower who carries the burden and risks all in the process. In recent decades, self-restraint has been abandoned and loans are foisted on all and sundry, whether they need them or not. The consequence is that money created from bank borrowing – which we will call debt-money – is gradually destroying cash and real wealth. The paradox of swamping an economy with debt-money is that it creates a false appearance of prosperity. As more goods are bought and debt abounds, we find that interest payments steadily siphon off an increasing amount of our earnings. While this is great for banks it is gradually enslaving us and making us dependent on them for life. When oil spreads over the surface of water, it is starved of oxygen and is rendered stagnant. Debt has similarly penetrated and smothered every aspect of our lives. We require a strong detergent to break the interfacial tension and emulsify debt's oily coverage. The way to counteract and dissolve it is with hard cash and debt-free funding, outside of the banking system.

The process whereby good money is driven out by the bad is known as Gresham's Law. In the days when precious metal coins were utilised as legal tender, any that were forged or tampered with would be passed on and distributed, whereas the purest would be hoarded. The quality of the coins remaining in circulation would diminish and therefore devalue. It appears that something similar is happening today whereby the value of our earnings (or purchasing power) is being diluted. By spending beyond our means, we are left with high debts and the lowest level of savings since the 1930s Great Depression, in the case of the US. Debt is like a cuckoo in the nest that pretends to be a friendly sibling, meanwhile gobbling up the other chicks' food at their expense and growing faster in the process.

Banks are allowed to lend out money based on the deposits they receive. The system is known as fractional banking. One might assume from its title that perhaps banks just lend out a fraction of their deposits, in their time-honoured conservative manner. However, the system is completely reversed. Loans do not match deposits; they hugely exceed them. For example, if a bank has a reserve requirement, or cushioning of 1/3rd it means that it can lend out £2 for every £1 on deposit. However, when the requirement drops to 1/10th it can lend out £9 based on just £1 deposited. As if this was not bad enough, when that borrowed money hits another bank, it cannot be differentiated from any other deposit so it is regarded as yet another asset that can be lent against. The same magnification is once again applied and before you know it, a mushroom effect has created more potential for lending than could ever be thought possible. Like Hercules fighting the Hydra, every time a head is cut off, two more appear and the problem worsens. While this has briefly explained the mechanics of the lending process, the rest of the book will go on to reveal its misuse. After all, it is not weapons or soldiers that make war but the philosophy of those that direct them.

STRUCTURE OF THE BOOK

Part I – Party Time

The West has been flooded with debt-sourced electronic money as banks, governments and corporations have jumped on the borrowing bandwagon. Every asset from stocks and bonds to property and chattels has swelled and floated on a tide of financial liquidity. Low interest rates and an unprecedented expansion in bank debt have created an unsustainable rise in US and UK property prices. Such bubbles can last longer and fool more people than ever thought possible. We must learn to recognise them to avoid being tempted into their delicious trap. Attempting to hold on until the top of a trend is a recipe for disaster: it will leave the 'investor' as the greater fool at the end of a long chain of speculators.

We are not talking here of some conspiratorial master plan or New Age mystery that hunts for links or plots where none really exist. The property market has indeed been used as a tool of US monetary policy to artificially float the economy when it should really have experienced a full-blown recession. American markets had already been emasculated by the crash in technology shares in 2000, so the Twin Tower attacks of 2001 appeared to be the *coup de grâce*. A mood of 'no surrender' enveloped the country as the Stars and Stripes appeared across the land, fluttering from every flagpole, porch and SUV (sports utility vehicle). An economic slowdown was politically not an option and any talk of recession was deemed to be disloyal. The slashing of interest rates thereafter, coupled with the huge stimulation through tax cuts and government spending, has caused an irreparable fracture in America's finances. Like an earthquake below the ocean surface, these ruptures are not immediately visible, but the effects soon will be. The financial tsunami will bear down in relentless pulses and waves, battering the global economy at each turn.

Before the tsunami struck Asia on Boxing Day 2004, killing many thousands of people, two unusual phenomena occurred. First, domestic animals instinctively headed for higher ground. Second, the shoreline retracted for hundreds of metres, leaving fish flapping on the sand. Curious onlookers were tragically drawn in and stumbled straight into the path of the oncoming water wall. These warning signs bear a remarkable resemblance to two areas that must now be avoided. The first is the 'buy on the dip' mentality that emerges whenever the property market drops then rallies, just prior to a crash. The second is the strength of the dollar seen in 2005, followed by its relative stability in 2006. This implies that all is well with America Inc. These twin traps are enticing investors back to the danger zone just when they should be heading for the hills.

Although the British and American economies seem serene on the surface, a quick inspection of the fundamentals will reveal that all is not well. The clearest example of this can be seen with the American inflation figures which appear to be permanently anaemic and mannequin-like: they look like the real thing but are a crude imitation. It is common practice to strip out food and energy as these are euphemistically deemed to be too 'volatile'. The most worrisome substitution can be seen where almost a quarter of the index is used to represent property: not the booming real estate variety but the cost of renting, which had barely moved until recently. Such problems were not apparent until May 2006, when unexpectedly high inflation figures sent jitters through the markets. The very components that made it look tame are bringing it back with a roar. Rental rates and Asian import prices are on the up. No doubt they will eventually be substituted out of the index for not behaving. Current economic policy resembles a game of poker in which the pronouncements of politicians are a bluff: the concealed cards are worthless and unknown to us; the stakes on the table are in fact the deeds to our homes.

The greatest risk for the US economy is, quite literally, right at home. Consumers make up 76 per cent of economic activity (a record high) and a nation of shopaholics has been on a roll, hence the seemingly strong growth figures. At a time when individuals should be reaping and storing the harvest of growth they are instead spending more than they earn, creating a negative savings ratio. Up to 2006, wage growth had been rather miserable so it was clear that the source of this magic money stemmed from drawing equity out of residential property in the wake of a housing boom. The most important element of a house price is the cost of borrowing. Now that both short- and long-term interest rates have been moving up, it is only a matter of time before the ten-year housing boom draws to a close. The inverse nature of house prices and interest rates has always been there; we are about to see the flip-side. Much like a children's swing at full stretch, the market slows to a standstill at the peak and accelerates back down under the force of gravity. In short, the party is over. In February 2006, new home sales in America slumped to their lowest level in nine years. The number of such homes for sale rose to a record 525,000. This was enough housing stock to satisfy demand for six months – the largest oversupply in a decade. When any market is saturated with a product, it will tend to fall in price, and property is no exception.

While the adrenalin-rush policy of interest rate stimulation worked wonderfully when applied in the late 1980s and early 1990s, it has since been used repeatedly in an increasingly casual manner. We will reveal how the 18-year reign of Alan Greenspan, as chairman of the US Federal Reserve, was one of unprecedented debt creation and interest rate manipulation. Although he was viewed as a benevolent financial maestro, it is all too easy to be popular when you give people what they want. In March 2006 a smart move was made by the US inflation-mongers who ceased to publish the evidence for the source of inflation, in the form of money supply figures known as M3. Equivalent numbers are poured over and analysed in depth by their counterparts in the European Central Bank yet have been conveniently discarded in America. Part I also sheds some light on the elusive world of hedge funds which have gorged themselves in the Bacchanalian environment of low borrowing costs. The excessive reduction of US interest rates to just 1 per cent was an act against nature. It was as though spirits from the underworld had been unleashed to wreak havoc on earth. Like the Titans who battled the Olympians, this race of god-like giants personified the forces of nature. While their modern counterparts in the hedge fund industry are legends in the financial world, their powers can be equally destructive. When acting in unison, this unregulated force is far more potent than any central bank or government.

Part II – Hangover

Having tried and tested every form of financial excess, the day of reckoning finally dawns. Mass-produced electronic dollars have been flooding out of the country for many years to pay for endless imports from Asia and beyond. One ironic commentator has noted that America's biggest export is empty container-ships which then come back fully laden with foreign goods. When importing more than they export, and not receiving enough inward investment to offset the outflow, a country runs what is called a current account deficit. It is rather like a leaky bucket that has to be re-filled from the neighbour's tap – repeated requests for top-ups become tedious and annoying. As individuals there is only a limited time during which one may spend more than one earns and remain solvent. In the case of governments, they may top up the shortfall via the tap of domestic or foreign borrowing. If lenders dry up, they can devalue their currency (not popular for foreign investors) or engineer a slowdown to reduce imports (not good for getting re-elected). A current account deficit of greater than 5 per cent of economic output is often associated with a currency crisis. By the end of 2005 the US current account deficit had expanded to 7 per cent, opening a gaping wound from which dollars continue to haemorrhage. To put this into context, the Plaza Accord was signed in 1985 to restore the imbalance of what was then just a 3.5 per cent deficit for America. Following the Accord, the value of the dollar halved in just two years. With today's deficit now double that of the 1980s, logic would dictate that the dollar is in line for a tailspin from which it cannot pull out. After all, one can hardly imagine a politician calling for the alternative: a recession for the long-term good of the country.

Much like the endocrine system of the human body, which regulates the ebb and flow of hormones in a feedback mechanism, the financial system should likewise work in equilibrium. Along with a budget deficit, or overspend at home, there is also a hefty trade deficit between America and the rest of the world. The outsourcing of its industrial base and the rapid transfer of white-collar work is leaving America with less and less to export. The competitive advantage of technology remains high only as long as everyone plays by the rules and it is not pirated. While trade imbalances and domestic deficits have been reversible in the past, this time almost half of US debt is held overseas, compared with just 5 per cent in the 1950s. It is dependent on the goodwill of foreign governments as investors; the very same countries that are being harangued by US foreign policy. While not in its interest to do so, the fate of America's finances can be crushed like a cockroach at any time by either the Chinese or Japanese, should they choose to dump dollar-based bonds on the markets.

As we have seen time and again with Latin America, the more debt that is created, the more that interest rates must eventually rise. Higher rates are also required to offset the decline in the currency that typically goes hand in hand with this scenario. As the currency weakens, imported goods become more expensive and this contributes to inflation. The process then escalates out of control. The difference in the case of America is that as the leading superpower, its currency is artificially in demand because most commodities are priced in dollars. For decades the dollar was regarded as being as good as gold in its maintenance of value, following the post-war approach of minimising currency volatility. This changed in 1971 with the final abandonment of the anchor of the gold exchange standard. The Nixon Administration was then free to produce debt-derived money unchecked, as the Vietnam War raged. History is repeating itself with the occupation of Iraq which has already cost the taxpayer hundreds of billions of dollars. There is also a confidence issue in keeping dollars as an asset. Foreign central banks are the biggest holders of US Treasuries or dollar-denominated government bonds. As the greenback (dollar) declines, they begin to make foreign exchange losses.

When US assets become distrusted, interest rates must rise to draw in capital and prevent a crisis. This has a direct impact on consumers as their mortgage costs increase and house prices fall. Just as the cash cow dries up from home equity extraction, there will then be another drain on consumers' spending power. The inflationary knock-on effect for food and energy prices – which surge when the dollar devalues – will bring a grinding halt to much industrial and personal activity. Anyone who remembers the 1970s blackouts in Britain will understand. Oil and other non-renewable commodities are becoming scarcer and harder to extract, while skill and capacity shortages exacerbate supply constraints after two decades of neglect. This is another reason why the coming correction is not just a temporary blip. The control of oil is slipping gradually from western hands as the remaining reserves are concentrated in the MENA (Middle East and North Africa) region. It is noteworthy that America's global dominance coincided with the peak of its own oil production. That source has been dwindling since the early 1970s.

Temporary protection against such currency devaluation is also fully explained through the holding of gold and precious metals. Gold has been used as a store of value for thousands of years but is currently viewed with cynicism, in spite of its recent five-year rally, having previously experienced a grinding 20-year downturn. In order to bail out the US economy at the height of the Great Depression, gold bullion was confiscated from the public to allow the government to inflate the economy artificially such that no one could escape with a store of real value. While confiscation is unlikely in future, we can use the lessons of the era to insure ourselves against future economic woe.

US interest rates have been muffled as developing countries have mopped up mass-produced dollars. This has allowed both the American government and its population to live and spend beyond their means. The relentless purchase of US bonds by foreign central banks was enacted to keep their own currencies competitive compared with the dollar. Their purchases prevented the bond yield – better known as the long-term interest rate – from rising. The maintenance of low borrowing or mortgage rates then allowed the US property market to rally unchecked. The continual flow of dollars in and out of America has been a symbiotic circle that suited everyone concerned. However, the Bush Administration is showing greater signs of protectionism, objecting to overseas takeovers of American businesses. It seems to be the case that the Americans are happy for foreigners to buy their mass-produced blizzard of bonds, but don't like it when they start to purchase something more tangible on home shores. US Senators have also dropped unsubtle hints to China that it could be officially branded as currency manipulators. From here it is only short a step to imposing some kind of counter-productive sanction or tariff on Chinese goods, sending prices soaring for domestic consumers.

The pin that pricks the bubble will doubtless be a factor that few have foreseen. After the event, many will wonder why they had not thought of it beforehand. There are plenty of candidates for the job, with foreign weariness of accumulating yet more US government bonds being the most likely. But pricing oil in euros – which unhinges the daily demand for dollars – is a thorny issue waiting in the sidelines. An invasion of Iran or a civil war in Iraq is yet another possibility. With the escalating costs of the Iraq occupation it would seem inconceivable that an invasion of Iran could be contemplated. However, where religion or political idealism is concerned, logic rarely gets a look in. This is a less likely option as growing Chinese and Russian influence provides a protective cloak around Iran. The association of Israel with America is a further agitation within the crucible of conflict that has come to typify the region.

Part III – Detox and Rehab

Like the components of dynamite, the ingredients themselves are stable and inert, even when mixed: it is the detonator that sets off the blast. The explosive mixture that will lead to a depression is that of endemic debts coupled with inflation and soaring commodity prices. It is now just a question of which factor will set the chain reaction in motion. The snap stock market sell-off of May 2006 could just be a mini version of what is to come. Once share prices slump then that will be the key signal for the austerity to come. A decidedly grim scenario will emerge when the debt bubble deflates, dragging down all asset prices in its wake. This will be the payback for a decade of consumer extravagance and a generation of unchecked bank lending.

If ever a worked example were needed, we only have to look at the slump in Japan following its boom and bust of the 1980s. The lending frenzy on the back of rising real estate became all too apparent as the deflation of the 1990s gripped the country. Another parallel that could see America following Japan is that of demographics. The shift in age profile of the Nippon population coincided with the 1989 market peak and mirrors the approaching retirement of the post-war baby-boom generation in America. As recession turned to depression, Japanese consumers stopped spending and saved with a vengeance. Fear of unemployment kept spare cash in the bank while high street sales slowed to a trickle. As we know from the Japanese example, even if interest rates are slashed to 0 per cent, consumers cannot be persuaded to spend or borrow in an environment of uncertainty and insecurity. While the finger of blame is pointed at the hoarding of cash, it is the indissolubility of debt behind the scenes that is the real culprit. As highlighted by Caroline Baum of Bloomberg, the episode was more of a credit crunch than a liquidity trap defined by the Depression-era economist John Maynard Keynes. In spite of Japan's deterioration over many years, the global scene was still supported by growth in Asia and America. This time around, a slump in the West will drag down much of the world with little support from elsewhere. Developing countries will at least have savings and reserves to stave off the slump to some degree. Meanwhile, the world's stock markets are buoyant and banks continue to generate a myriad of financial products. In spite of rising interest rates since 2004, the degree of apathy by professional investors is incredible. Nature shows that when the herd is complacent and at peace, it is most vulnerable to attacks from lurking predators.

Although stock markets have rallied strongly since October 2002, the long-term charts are showing lots of action but little improvement over the last seven years. This should come as no surprise to economic historians. Once stock markets have risen ten-fold, as they did from 1942 to 1966, the following phase consists of lots of peaks and troughs with little net change. This was the case for the 16 years from 1966 to 1982 when the markets were range-bound, having started and finished at the same level on the index. In modernity we have seen more than a ten-fold rise from 1982 to 1999 as the Dow Jones Industrial Average index rose from 1,000 to just shy of 12,000. Some seven years since, it has only just breached its old highs. Even if no crash takes place the market is likely to be stuck in limbo for years to come.

As rising interest rates reverse financial excesses, so the underlying economies will follow suit: expensive shares will become cheaper by the day. Bond yields will initially rise as country after country devalues its currency and creates more debt in a vain attempt to stimulate. Interest rates and yields will later fall once the downturn transforms into a depression. We can then ponder our existence in an era of hardship. Consumer behaviour will undergo an immense turnaround where recycling, parsimony and sobriety will be the norm. Greed and excess will be viewed as shameful and unacceptable in a world where so many will be suffering. Loans, mortgages and debts in general will in future be a source of shame which few will publicly condone or discuss. Periods of economic anguish can have negative spin-offs as political allegiances shift from a crowded centre to extremes of left and right. Feelings of helplessness may in turn rejuvenate an interest in religion as we seek divine comfort. Life still goes on during a slump and frugality may well come to be viewed as chic. On the plus side, a downturn may also bring families and communities closer together. On the downside, there is likely to be a good deal more theft and social unrest in urban settings.

Behind the scenes, the likes of China have been establishing their infrastructure and building up financial strength. China's influence across the developing world is spreading rapidly as it and Russia tie up deals for the supply of oil, gas and other commodities that will be vital for their future prosperity. It is almost as though there is a political game of chess going on where the Americans are not even sat at the same table, let alone appreciating the slick strategy employed by developing nations. By the time the dollar devalues and commodities surge, the supply agreements will already have been sewn up between non-western allies. Meanwhile, the 2008 Beijing Olympics will be a showpiece exhibition: a debutantes' ball for China's emergence and coming of age.

Once-open economies will turn inward as globalisation retracts, like a snail withdrawing into its shell. Protectionism is also a classic response in such scenarios. As the Anglo-Saxon influence of Britain and America wanes, so a new world order will emerge. Trading blocs will polarise into differing spheres of influence while individual countries seek self-sufficiency in agriculture and energy production. We must not forget that there is also a latent instinct that spurs military action in times of poverty and distress. Without the hyperinflation of the Weimar Republic and the misery of the Great Depression, the likes of the Nazi Party would hardly have been contemplated in a civilised country such as Germany. The recent decades of relative peace, albeit dominated by the Cold War, may not last much longer. We can attempt to redraw the lines of power of a new world order. Like the classroom experiment of shaking iron filings onto a piece of paper held over a magnet, we will see how countries will be pulled and aligned across differing poles and spheres of influence. It can only be guesswork at this stage, but some interesting informal alliances are being formed right now, based on cooperation between commodity-producing countries.

We can then fast-forward our thoughts to view the 'State of the Nation' in 2020. Like Charles Dickens' *A Christmas Carol*, an awareness of the outcome of our selfish actions may adjust the way we behave today. We must accept that the apparent prosperity we now enjoy will not be repeated in our lifetimes. The very countries to which we outsourced our dirty work will be consuming a much bigger slice of the cake. As they prosper and consume we will have to relearn their habits of industry and saving. Having denied them access to our markets through farm subsidies and hidden tariffs, the favour will no doubt be repaid in kind. We will also be called to account for the policies of the International Monetary Fund (IMF) that imposed inappropriate western measures that barely worked in fully developed countries, let alone developing ones. This was even highlighted by the ex-chief economist of the World Bank, Joseph Stiglitz, in his book *The Roaring Nineties*.

While the non-financial quality of life may well improve, our pension and medical benefits will only be a fraction of what is available today. This is something that developing nations have endured for decades. The period of hardship will reverse our wasteful habits and spur innovation in everything from energy production to recycling. Conservation will be 'cool', even for members of the establishment. Britain's Leader of the Opposition, David Cameron, has taken a lead in this area by inviting environmental groups to take part in policy-making discussions. The reduced level of manufacturing output and search for alternative energy may also herald a significant reduction of carbon emissions and greenhouse gases into the atmosphere. Although such complex topics are still hotly debated, it makes sense to plan for the worst-case scenario. The battle against global warming could become the binding force that brings us together. The permanent elevation of commodity prices may prove to be a blessing in disguise as we are forced to research and invest in renewable energy, in a meaningful manner.

The final chapter will give a variety of tips on how to approach the forthcoming malaise. As ever, change and opportunity make easy bedfellows and there will be some businesses that prosper. Shares in companies involved with pawnbroking have already performed very well. Many traditional skills and industries are likely to re-emerge, particularly if protectionism inhibits some imports. There are also specific trades that are typically in demand during periods of hardship. We may even come to appreciate the skills of medieval craftsmen who made goods for life, and not just for Christmas.

No book can perfectly predict the sequence of events that the future may hold. However, the preparatory work done now will prove to be a godsend: if we are to adapt then we need to prepare ourselves for a long struggle. We must accumulate money in the years before it becomes scarce; not just the paper variety that so often devalues, but real wealth and assets that will carry an intractable global value, such as gold. While it pays to be sceptical about those who say 'this time it's different' the phrase in this context is an invitation to save and store, rather than to speculate or squander. If the meltdown does prove to be much more damaging than the depressions of the last two centuries then we can make no assumptions about recovery. It could prove to be the final crash for western stock markets as they wither in proportion to the deflating economies they represent. Although the book concludes with a hint of a possible solution, it is probably too radical for consensus opinion to appreciate or consider – at least for the time being.

Part I

PARTY TIME
Fountains of Debt

1

ON THE HOUSE

If the American people ever allow private banks to control the issue of their currency, first by inflation, then by deflation, the banks and corporations that will grow up around will deprive the people of all property until their children wake up homeless on the continent their fathers conquered.
Thomas Jefferson (US President 1801–09)

Many Americans have been given a 'free' dram by Bush the bartender, or to be more precise, it is freely available 'credit' – a euphemism for debt. A property boom has been vigorously cultivated to offset the negative effects of 9/11, aided and abetted by hefty tax cuts. By slashing borrowing costs in its aftermath, US house prices have gone on to exhibit their fastest growth in 25 years and have doubled in some areas since 2000. According to the Office of Federal Housing, average prices rose by more than 13 per cent[1] between mid-2004 and mid-2005. Although such returns are not that spectacular compared with the hotspots of Spain and Portugal, the fact that they have been generated in the world's largest economy has significant ramifications elsewhere. The reason the US is so important to the rest of the globe is that its consumers are gobbling up the world's excess production of goods. Americans are using not just their own money to fund the shopping spree but also the savings of the developing countries that produce them. It may sound too good to be true, but this has been the norm for quite some time.

When King Canute famously ordered the tide to turn, the attempt was not an act of arrogance but a lesson in humility to show his courtiers that he was a mere king and not a god. History likewise shows us that bankers and business people cannot beat a natural economic cycle, much as they would like to. In America, a great gamble has been taken in an attempt to beat off the ravages of a natural downturn. Through tax cuts and interest rate reductions, the Administration is paying out today in the hope of taxing back tomorrow. Such actions may well have postponed a slump but they have not prevented it. Suffice to say, the artificial boost to consumers has worsened the original problem. One cannot court popularity by using stimulants to keep the economy on indefinite overdrive. Soon, like the spiral of addiction, 'normal' functions seem impossible without the drug. Rest and recuperation are required, without which permanent damage is inevitable.

The US housing market appears to have experienced a bubble which is starting to deflate. For many years, no one thought property was risky. The commonly held view was that cash in the bank was wasted as it could otherwise double in a matter of years by investing it in bricks and mortar. It now appears that attitudes to housing are changing, albeit reluctantly. By July 2006 a record level of homes were left unsold, numbering 3.86 million, while a record inventory of 568,000 new houses[2] was up for sale. By September the number of unsold homes had risen to 4.42 million. Having seen mortgage rates at a 40-year low in June 2003 at 5.21 per cent, the same rates hit 6.78 per cent just over three years later. The inverse relationship between house prices and interest costs never went away, and like a bond, rising yields means lower prices (see Chapter 3).

FIZZY BUBBLES

So what exactly is a bubble? There is no straightforward definition and it is rarely something that everyone sees or believes in at the time. One could say a speculative bubble is the purchase of something that is made solely in the expectation of a price rise and not for its inherent value. This is akin to describing the condensation-covered Carlsberg in *Ice Cold in Alex* as just a drink. A dry definition of a bubble does not capture the yearning, or stirring of emotion, when the grip of a speculative fever takes hold: at first it is your mistress but then becomes your master.

One's initial success in speculation will always be the best, and like a drug, one will forever seek but never rediscover the elusive rush and warm glow of self-satisfaction.

Just to confuse matters, the statistics show that booms based on justifiable fundamentals are often confused with bubbles, which are speculative in nature. Looking at 24 asset booms over 30 years in as many as 15 different economies,[3] only three ended with a crash. To aid their identification, John P. Calverley's *Bubbles and How to Survive Them*, provides an 18-point checklist.[4] Some examples include rapid price appreciation, overvaluation relative to history and increased debt-funding, to name but a few. For our purposes we can describe how a bubble operates to see if it bears comparison with what we see today.

The basic pattern begins with an idea that sets off a craze, usually in an economic upturn, with easy access to borrowing. The theme could be useful, as we saw with American railways in the nineteenth century, or could be rather bizarre, such as the tulip bulbs in seventeenth-century Holland. After the burst, those who borrowed to buy are left with a big debt and an asset worth a fraction of its cost. Whereas many bubble items fall by around 80 per cent from their peak, tulip bulbs shrivelled by 99 per cent. The lesson from these affairs is that prices may rise and fall like fireworks, but debt has a habit of refusing to fade.[5]

Most bubbles go through a lifecycle of cynicism, popularity and feverish accumulation followed by eventual revulsion. In the final stages of the up-wave, investors borrow to buy more of the same product or use financial instruments to magnify the effect. When caught up in a frenzy the mind plays wonderful tricks, such that bubble disciples confuse mirages with visions of the future. At the peak of a price move in any asset or investment, the positive arguments seem utterly compelling and the evidence incontrovertible: press coverage and ownership is widespread. With no buyers left to peddle the process, the trend folds under the force of gravity. If one has nagging doubts that a bubble is in place, then it is wise to heed this subconscious safety mechanism. If something seems illogical, yet everyone else is revelling in it, then welcome to the club of common sense. The trick is always to look at fundamentals and this is where ratios are so helpful in comparing past experience with hearsay.

In the nineteenth century there were regular scenes of panic as depositors rushed to empty their bank accounts at the slightest hint of trouble. To save the day and restore confidence during such events, the bank's owners would make a grand entrance by bringing in sacks of what appeared to be fresh coins and cash. They would then go straight out the back door with the very same sacks and repeat the process to make it reassuringly clear that a never-ending source of funds was at their disposal: appearance is everything when it comes to restoring order. While banking panics may act as a catalyst for a general downturn, it is often the change in their lending behaviour that turns a recession into a depression. The bursting of the 1980s property bubble hamstrung the Japanese financial system as banks became completely risk averse and ceased to lend money: activity ground to a halt. This is the key weakness of a debt-driven economy where constant new loans are required to continue the charade whereby growth is not organic but artificial. When financial institutions lend money to companies or individuals and a recession means they can no longer pay back the interest or capital, then this becomes known as a bad debt. Like bad cholesterol in the bloodstream, where the coronary arteries become blocked and stiffen, the heart is starved of oxygen as the arteries lose their elasticity. In a similar manner, more of a bank's reserves have to be set aside for bad debts. With a shrunken asset base they become less flexible and far more cautious when offering loans.

In Japan, the sins of the fathers came back to haunt the current generation as past lending excesses cut off the fuel for future funding. This is the reason Japan has been stagnating since 1990. Fortunately for the Japanese, they have been carried on either side, like a wounded casualty, between the consumer boom in the West and the industrialisation of the rest of Asia. Any country experiencing a burst property bubble like theirs in future will no longer encounter such two-pronged support. The severity of the Japanese situation has been closely watched by America's central bank, serving as a painful worked example of how the West could unravel in years to come.

The most recent bubble burst was the stock market boom in TMT (Telecom, Media and Technology) shares. Initially spurned by the then chairman of the US Federal Reserve, Alan Greenspan, he later heralded it as a key component of the much-acclaimed productivity miracle. He was responsible for setting US interest rates both before and after the event. The subsequent crash from April 2000 caught out many wealthy investors, investment institutions and businesses. Even those Americans who took no part in the speculation saw a third of their pension funds evaporate, with years of retirement savings wiped out in the space of just two. The public also experienced concomitant cutbacks in spending and reduced employment in its aftermath. Two million US workers lost their jobs and the unemployment rate cranked up from 3.8 per cent to 6 per cent[6] by the close of 2001. However, the recession was not that severe compared with those in preceding decades. For some citizens the century's first boom and bust may as well have happened on another planet for all the effect it had on them.

This time round the majority of the American population is caught up in a housing racket that leaves both them and the financial system dangerously exposed. The mortgage-related element of US banks' earning assets has roughly doubled in the last two decades. In 1987 they made up just a third, in 2000 a half and by 2005 they accounted for over 60 per cent.[7] Banks are taking a huge bet on the health of the mortgage market. There is likewise an overwhelming view among the public that their biggest asset is truly 'as safe as houses'. This pro-property sentiment has been reinforced by the post-2000 bear market in shares, which has concentrated household wealth, quite literally, in the home. Where such consensus and complacency leads, a crash soon follows.

It is foolhardy to use timing from past cycles as a guide to the future as every economic peak and trough will differ in its elongation or contraction. Every time an investor thinks that they have found a pattern that works, one can guarantee that the correlation will cease when it is put to the test with hard cash. Each economic cycle is like a game of cards: the general rules remain unchanged but the hand will vary with each deal. By looking at the formation of bubbles in the past, it is important to understand that they materialise in both a primary and a secondary wave. The primary bubble is one where professional insiders in the relevant business make money during the boom. Its inevitable crash hurts a minority, but they tend to be the more wealthy and vociferous. During the ensuing weak spot, the government is lobbied to stimulate the economy. A period of relief follows, allowing a sentiment of 'business as usual' to resume. The false prosperity it cultivates then sets off a secondary bubble in a different area which forms a precursor to a widespread slump. In America's case, the counter to the TMT crash has spawned a bubble in property with some 69 per cent of the population[8] directly involved. Sadly, it is this secondary wave that pulls in a wider and more vulnerable audience than the first. The attempt to suppress the after-effects of the first bubble has created an even greater one. Similarly, in Tom and Jerry cartoons, the hapless feline Tom frequently receives a ringing blow to the head. A large lump appears and he forces it back into his skull, only for a more painful protrusion to pop out elsewhere. Perhaps we have likewise received some brain damage in the process, believing that the property boom is in some way permanent.

The swing in US interest rates from 1 per cent to 5.25 per cent in the space of two years has already hurt the housing market. American mortgages (up until the boom times) were predominantly based on fixed long-term interest rates. This provided a certainty for monthly outgoings. In an unusual move by a central banker, Alan Greenspan suggested in 2004 that home-buyers should switch to a short-term, adjustable rate mortgage[9] (ARM), instead of choosing the more traditional long-term fixed interest version, which offered constancy. Such variable rate mortgages are far more volatile than fixed-rate borrowing. ARMs were very cheap at the time because they were based upon interest rates of 1 per cent, but only for a limited lock-in period, which would later revert to higher prevailing rates of interest. The temptation to ease cashflow for a couple of years was simply too great. It also sat well with the post-9/11 'only live once' attitude of pushing risk and debt into the future in exchange for a good time in the present. Greenspan's advice coincided with the first round of rate increases, which made it all the more strange. It appeared as though he was trying to keep the property pot bubbling just as the cooking fire was about to be extinguished.

His intervention to encourage a switch was playing a dangerous game that would lead some – such as the famous hedge-fund manager George Soros – to highlight Greenspan's Republican sympathies as a reason for keeping rates so low in an election year.[10] Encouraging consumers to choose a cheaper option in the short term with open-ended liabilities in the long term would appear atypical for a central banker. Surely the security of a fixed deal was the safer option, particularly for those who could barely afford the record-low rates in the first place. Greenspan of all people should have known that interest rates set below inflation could not last much longer and that their elevation was only in its infancy. His comments came in the wake of some very mixed messages about the economy which routed the inflation-sensitive bond market in mid-2004.

In spite of their name, implying variable mortgage rates, ARM loans can initially have their interest rates fixed for one to three years. Although they carried low rates at the time, there will soon be a reality check as the lock-in periods have expired. Cashflows all over the country are being hit given that one fifth of old mortgages are structured this way and one third of new mortgages[11] are following this floating or variable course. Typically, as the brakes begin to bite, one sees a surge in house-buying which builds into a climactic peak. This appears to have been the case as 2005 drew to a close. The behaviour is often driven by the realisation that higher interest rates are on the way, so there is a scramble to remortgage or take out a bigger loan to lock in the low rate. Builders also rush to complete their projects to avoid being left in the lurch with unwanted stock. The demand and hype push up prices at just the wrong time, after which the house of cards begins to tumble. There is an old saying that 'the candle's flame burns brightest before it gutters'. Just as the final piece of wick is about to burn out for good, one sees a last burst of energy. This appears to have been the case for property prices too.

This ultimate expansion is a familiar theme in market bubbles. Having been propelled almost vertically up the chart in what is called a parabolic curve, a final fling is witnessed. The price then fades and falls without support from new buyers. It is very similar to Mount Vesuvius where the power of the eruption pushed red-hot dust and debris directly upwards to form a cloud of menacing proportions. Eventually, the column collapsed under its own weight and formed a deadly ground-hugging avalanche that charred and buried Pompeii. By the middle of 2006, it was becoming all too clear that anything property-related was falling off its perch. US home sales, mortgage applications, home-builder shares and housing market sentiment indicators were nose-diving off their highs. Like Britain and Australia – which are both ahead of America in the economic cycle – the prices will doubtless perk up once more, just in time to pull in the last remaining suckers, before commencing the final descent.

There is still a good deal of debate as to whether there is indeed a housing bubble. The case can be made that it does exist in some states and not in others. To clear away the background noise and find a clear line of sight where property is concerned, ratios can be consulted to put price moves into perspective. After all, if personal earnings surge then perhaps it is not unreasonable that house prices can do the same and more as the cost of a bigger mortgage is easily affordable. Instead of saying that houses have doubled and are therefore expensive, a context is set to confirm whether a move is in line with other related fundamentals. In this case we can compare a straightforward ratio of house prices to personal income. Although simplistic, it does have a startling brutality to it, much like price–earnings ratios for shares (see Chapter 8). In California, the house price to personal income ratio has gone well beyond what can be considered normal. The data for Los Angeles and San Diego[12] show a staggering 10:1 ratio of prices to income, which is well beyond previous peaks. Although California is an acknowledged hotspot, New York is still pricey at 6:1 while the national average is 4:1.

Away from low interest rates, adding fuel to the fire has been the proliferation of financial products such as interest-only mortgages. It is difficult to comprehend how the average person is suddenly going to come up with hundreds of thousands of dollars at some nebulous point in future. It implies that a mortgage will be hanging around borrowers' necks until the day they die. Their relatives can only hope that the life insurance will indeed clear the debt, otherwise there will not be much of an inheritance left for the offspring. Yet otherwise prudent people would continue to put all their faith in the property market, as if wishing for the best possible outcome – eternally rising prices – will make it happen.

In California, half of all mortgages in 2004 were interest-only compared with just 2 per cent[13] in 2001. It should come as no surprise that house prices in that state rose by 17 per cent in 2003 and 22 per cent in 2004 on the back of this cheap source of financing. Every bubble creates its own obscenities and this one is no exception, with what has to be the most counter-productive mortgage product ever. As if the interest-only versions weren't bad enough, we now have negative amortisation products: the ultimate form of servitude. As rates go up, the borrower's payments remain unchanged but the unpaid interest is heaped onto the original loan. If interest rates stay high it is hard to see how the new negative amortisation loans will ever be paid off – like bailing out a sinking lifeboat with a small tin can. Just when one thought that the depths of usury had already been tested, the British appear to have gone one step further, or perhaps one step too far. In August 2006 it was announced that so-called 'deathbed' mortgages would be introduced. The capital is never paid such that the property is never fully owned and the debt is left to the children. This is a shameful legacy for the next generation.

House prices in Los Angeles over the last 30 years have tended to peak[14] before a wider US recession ensues. This would appear to make sense given that the Golden State is roughly equivalent to the sixth largest economy in the world. Alan Greenspan glossed over these localised hotspots by saying that the overall housing market was not problematic. However, ownership is not just confined to one state but is interlinked across America, so any problem in one area will impact throughout. It is not just California that is getting high. A rippling of price rises was evident down both the East and West Coasts, with Florida up 25 per cent and Arizona scorching at 30 per cent[15] in the year to December 2005. The National Association of Realtors declared that a full 40 per cent of residential property purchases in 2005 were for investment and holiday homes,[16] and not for primary residence. If the economy worsens one can only imagine the damage if just a fraction of investment property was forced onto the market. Glut does not even begin to describe it. Meanwhile, US builders' permits in 2005 were running at their highest levels since 1973, implying that future supply will be plentiful.

WITHDRAWAL SYMPTOMS

As rising house prices decouple from personal incomes, the temptation becomes too great for home-owners to withdraw equity from their property, thereby increasing the loan size. This process is almost inevitable because when prices rise there is greater scope to borrow as a percentage of the asset. The lax lending standards and great eagerness by banks to hand out loans is a further fuel for the surge. While this inflates the amount of money in the economy, it should never be forgotten that this has been borrowed and is not a sustainable source of wealth. Much as we would like the proverbial leprechaun to grant our wish of a never-ending glass of ale, this thinking belongs with the fairies.

An overextended property market requires intense activity to keep prices bubbling at such elevated levels. To see how quickly a property boom can grind to a halt, a look at Britain and Australia is once again instructive. House-price rises in Sydney and London have been as steep as those in Los Angeles and have closely tracked each other since California's trough in 1995. In both Australia and Britain (see next chapter) increased interest rates brought the equity-withdrawal game to an abrupt halt in 2005.

As their property markets began to tread water, albeit temporarily, consumer spending in both countries slowed significantly as a result. Optimists counter this argument by saying that as long as jobs are plentiful then people feel secure enough to borrow and will continue to treat their houses as a giant bank account. However, we have seen strong job growth in both Australia and Britain, yet retail sales still suffered in 2005. Any weakness in US property prices is likely to have a major impact on consumer spending, both at home and abroad, because of the import boom that the property bubble has inspired. Much of the equity extraction has been spent on consumer items and house improvements: a case of throwing borrowed money after bad. Should consumers stop spending and start accumulating cash then this is very ominous for the economy. Every recession over the past 40 years has been accompanied by a big rise in household saving.

In the relay race of finding easy money, the baton has been handed on from straightforward equity withdrawal to a phase where equity is extracted when trading up into the next property. It is not just a case of increasing debt to buy a larger house but expanding it yet more to buy all the other 'essentials'. As with any relay race, it requires momentum and a smooth handover to make it work. The consumer is holding the baton and looking increasingly exhausted. As interest rates rise, spending will be further hit as interest costs devour earnings. Household spending on mortgage payments now averages 23 per cent[17] of disposable income: a level not seen since the dark days of 1990.

FLACCID INFLATION

One element that has nurtured a benign interest rate environment has been the apparently low level of inflation. It is measured at different points in the pipeline before goods reach consumers. The most commonly watched inflation statistic is the core rate, which takes out the 'volatile' components such as food and energy (these are included in the headline rate). If one did not eat food, seek warmth or drive a vehicle then that would be great because these activities are not in the index. However, in the biological world which we humans inhabit, prices have risen significantly for the food and energy that we use every day. These are not included in the core rate, which make it somewhat anaemic – yet it continues to be a marker upon which major policy decisions are made. Even the headline rate appears remarkably contained compared with the experience of ordinary Americans.

In September 2005 the headline US inflation rate was 4.7 per cent year-on-year, yet the core rate without food and energy was just 2.0 per cent. Many analysts mistakenly brushed the former figure aside – which was the highest since the early 1990s – as being a one-off. They received a rude shock in May 2006 when the same rate breached 7 per cent and the core rate hit 3.2 per cent, in excess of expectations. Inflation is becoming punitive for ordinary people and the evidence is all around us; yet the inability of all but a few canny commentators to question the official figures defies belief. It appears that George Bernard Shaw's quote still holds true today: 'If all the economists were laid end to end, they would never reach a conclusion.' The data are further massaged to ignore that other essential in life: the roof over one's head. A good example of this was seen in the February 2005 US Commerce Report[18] which showed that new home sales had risen by an impressive 9.4 per cent. Given that sales activity and prices go hand-in-hand, it came as no surprise that new house prices had similarly shot up by 9.6 per cent. Such substantial increases in the cost of living do not show up in the inflation numbers. Instead, we are given the cost of renting rather than the house-price rise itself. This is measured by the 'owner's equivalent rent' (OER) which rose by a very modest 0.2 per cent over the same period that house prices rose close to 10 per cent. Given that OER rental costs make up a quarter of the Consumer Price Index (CPI) then it is no wonder that the inflation Americans have to live with is very different from the official figures they are fed.

In the past, rents used to move, to some extent, with the value of property, albeit in a more muffled manner. However, this relationship has broken down as low interest rates and new financial products have made owning real estate – or more correctly speaking, partially owning it – much more accessible than in the past. With the market tumbling in 2006, rental costs are creeping up as potential buyers opt for renting instead. We may well see an initial squeeze in the availability of rental stock as house-sellers cling to the hope that they will still be able to offload their overpriced properties. If the OER continues to escalate, perhaps it will be swapped with falling house prices. After all, it is not the done thing to include inflationary items in an inflation index. There is a duel going on where core inflation figures include a large dose of items whose prices are deflating, but our daily reality is dominated by prices that are inflating. Those index components that muffled America's omnipresent inflation over the last decade are starting to wane or reverse: namely, productivity improvements, low oil prices and cheap Asian labour.

FLORIDA FLIP

The housing boom witnessed over the last decade is unlikely to be repeated. There will no doubt be many who soon suffer serious losses, particularly if they have mortgages on several homes. The stock of property on the books that is waiting to be sold is mounting in California. Developers have spent their money, but refuse to sell at a discount in the hope that things will improve and they will get a better price. Having seen 17 increases in US interest rates since the bottom of the cycle, this optimism appears to be misplaced. As more people wait for prices to recover, the glut of available housing will swell, like the build-up of cars behind a traffic jam. The chances of renting or selling dwindle in proportion to the number of new houses waiting in the queue. Eventually a fire-sale mentality sets in and there is a rush to undercut prices just to get some or any money back. Many people will come to bitterly regret their decision to become involved in property development which at the time had seemed to be a no-brainer.

Such behaviour has of course been seen before. Florida was the destination of choice in the boom times of the 1920s. The trend for vacations in the region took off after the Great War, given the warmth of its winter climate, while the rest of America froze.

As the economy recovered from the 1920–22 recession, brash New Yorkers soon came to town with cash to burn. As ever, the surge in prices was driven by an easy availability of credit and, much like today, a property could be purchased with a minimal 10 per cent deposit. As the craze grew, the stories of flipping (or selling-on the option to buy a property before it was built) became legendary. An example of this mania is no better illustrated than a plot of land that cost $1,500 in 1914 being sold for $1.5 million in 1926.[19] Such practices closely resemble investor behaviour in the late 1990s, where hot new technology shares known as IPOs (Initial Public Offerings) could double in days and would then be sold on. It is a sobering reminder that the NASDAQ technology share index fell by almost 80 per cent from peak to trough in the following few years.

If you believe this cannot be replicated in real estate, then think again. After the Florida boom climaxed in 1925, prices were little changed a year later, but properties were not selling. In typical fashion, an army of vested interest developers were describing the period as a consolidation phase where prices would soon resume. We are hearing similar comments today. In 1926 the property market inevitably crashed. The sell-off was triggered by a spate of bad hurricanes which should hardly have been a surprise to anyone familiar with the region. As global warming appears to be extending the hurricane season, then history may well repeat itself. Even by the 1960s, some 40 years after the crash, prices had still not recovered to their past peaks. For many top-of-the-market buyers, this limbo would have represented the balance of their natural lives.

Like all speculative bubbles, the pin that pricks them is often unexpected and improbable; that also goes for the timing. Forecasters tie themselves in knots attempting to second-guess the likely catalyst. All one needs to understand is that a bubble is in place. We must not be drawn into the frenzy or be persuaded by the self-supportive words that those around us utter to justify their own ill-considered actions. Few will ponder the negative scenarios before buying that just-affordable property, thereby forgetting the lessons of Florida. Just as the roaring 1920s sent pensioners flocking to the Sunshine State, so today's baby-boomers are being drawn back as retirement beckons. The surge in demand has pushed developers further into the swamps and wetlands, much to the annoyance of displaced alligators who frequently return to their home territory. Another returning beast is the property speculator. Deeply submerged within the human psyche, but never extinct, the 'flippers' emerged from an 80-year hibernation. This time they are called 'condo-flippers' because they rapidly buy and sell – or flip – condominiums. They came back in force in exactly the same spot where their forebears flourished then later foundered. This pattern has been repeated. At the time, one could get credit, purchase an option to buy a house and sell it on at a profit before it was even built: and all online. These properties used to change hands up to eight times before the building was complete. Following the slump in demand in 2006 the flippers are submerging once more.

This behaviour was not just a Florida phenomenon but one which became apparent in the Middle East property hotspots such as Dubai. Like many inexperienced speculators, they get a taste for making money and take on bigger bets with bigger risks until one day they lose more on the way down than they ever made on the way up. It has slipped most people's minds that numerous investors gave up work in the late 1990s to trade shares for a living. Needless to say, they are no longer doing so and the same will come to pass for the legions of amateur property developers whose number has blossomed with the bubble. Television programmes abound with tales of successful development where going out on a limb financially has always paid off. This daily diet of property porn is giving the impression that everyone else is out there making money and doing it better than you. During a bubble phase, the media has little choice other than to give widespread coverage to the latest craze, simply because that is what their audience and advertising customers demand. Contrary voices may be ridiculed as their views don't sell newspapers or advertising space. While some may be perennially negative, just occasionally there will be a few trying to save the unwary from the communal madness.

We have already mentioned wage growth as a possible justification for underpinning property prices. In America, this figure had been running at a miserable 2 per cent per annum for some years, although it moved higher in 2006. There was obviously a major disconnect in 2005 when property prices had been rising at more than six times the rate of wage inflation. Whenever you get ratios like this moving out of kilter then it is a clear sign that something is wrong. Unless a corresponding explosion in wages is in the pipeline then it is likely that the ratio will be brought back into line with a loud thud in property prices. We will look back on the post-2000 period and gasp at our naive expectations that such trends would continue.

To summarise the American situation, there have been three factors at work to push both property prices and mortgage borrowing to ever-dizzier heights. First, higher prices in their own right encourage further investment and activity. Second, the turnover (rate of buying and selling) has boosted the level of participation and willingness to take more risk. Third, lower interest rates make it easier to borrow more for the same cost as before. The upturn has created a virtuous circle. House prices rise, so people borrow more; prices rise again, and people borrow yet more. While it is pleasant to think that this can go on forever, albeit at a reduced pace, life and markets are never like that for long. This begs the question as to what will bring the juggernaut to a halt. Historically, a rise in long-term interest rates, or long-dated bond yields, pushes up mortgage rates, which then choke off the boom. There is a tight relationship[20] between mortgage rates and house sales over the last 20 years. These rates are rising thanks to inflation which will evaporate the fuel that drives the engine of the market. The US central bank is doing all it can to verbally manipulate this yield and keep it capped to maintain low mortgage rates. In the logic of desperation, some are even arguing that a recession is good for bonds and therefore good for property prices such that a self-supporting cycle will come into play.

Just as property prices cannot go up indefinitely, the same is true of debt. We cannot continually spend more than we earn, just because house prices have risen. The compounding effect of interest will eventually catch up, just when house prices are falling. While mortgage debt as a proportion of the overall residential housing stock is not too shocking[21] (some 43 per cent), this masks the fact that some have no remaining borrowing at all. The problem lies with those individuals who carry a mortgage, especially those who took one out recently. The average mortgage-holder has only 37 per cent[22] of their house value left as equity. This is the difference between the house price and the size of the bank borrowing. For those with large mortgages, it will only take a small decline in house prices to leave a great deal of latecomers with no cushioning, thereby losing their initial deposit and possibly their house. Any sustained decline could bring on negative equity for many. This is a polite way of saying that the bank owns your house and can repossess it at any time. As an indication of what may be in store, we have seen shares of US home-builders drop by over 40 per cent in 2006. It appears that the insightful warnings of Thomas Jefferson (in the opening quote) may be coming to fruition, some two centuries later.

If ever there was a concern over personal debt and property, it lies as much with the lenders as with the borrowers. Even before the post-2000 property boom swung into action, commercial banks were already dwarfed by mortgage debts of $1.5 trillion against their own book equity of less than $0.5 trillion. The private mortgage indemnity companies (PMIs) would be utterly overwhelmed in a market downturn as they are insuring sums almost 50 times the value of their own equity.[23] To use an analogy, the equity in a house is like seed corn to a farmer. This is the seed that is to be planted for next year's crop, to provide everything that the family needs once some hard work and luck have been added. This precious corn must be protected from rot, rats and robbery. Without it, there will be no crops or food for the following seasons. Home equity is the same: it is not something to be frittered away needlessly. Too many have eaten their seed corn, leaving no spare for emergencies, let alone for the future. The bullish case for continued American prosperity can be compelling, as it always is at the top of the cycle. Such arguments continue to work until they don't, by which time it is too late to act. The 'soft landing' phrase is cropping up once more, just as it did in 2000.

There is one final comparison, this time with a Bible story. An Egyptian Pharaoh consulted his adviser, Joseph, because he was troubled by vivid dreams. He described how seven fat, healthy cows were eaten by seven thin ones. Joseph's interpretation of the Pharaoh's coded revelations was that there would be seven years of plenty followed by seven years of famine. He should therefore store the excess of the bountiful harvests to supply Egypt during the lean years to come. The Pharaoh followed this advice and the country was saved from starvation. In the case of America, instead of putting something aside for the bad times ahead, the fat cows have been slaughtered and barbecued in one sitting.

When the bartender gives you one 'on the house', it is not a charitable act. He knows he will empty your wallet as you go on buying drinks for the rest of the night. Piling one debt onto another does not make for a stable financial structure, it makes for a house of cards, where the winds of change will precipitate a catastrophic collapse.

2

BINGEING BRITONS

A banker is a fellow who lends his umbrella when the sun is shining and wants it back the minute it begins to rain.

Mark Twain

OVERCONSUMPTION

The property bubble in America is not unique: a similar phenomenon has occurred throughout the English-speaking world. As before, the bigger a property's appreciation, the greater the temptation to borrow more money in the form of a mortgage equity withdrawal (or MEW). At its height in Britain, at the end of 2003,[1] this magic money reached an equivalent of 8.4 per cent of post-tax income, similar to levels seen in Australia. It was no coincidence that MEW peaked with house price inflation, which was running at rates of 20 per cent[2] at the beginning of that year. By early 2005, the craze appeared to be wearing off as house prices hit a plateau and the degree of extraction slowed to 3.0 per cent – its lowest level since 9/11. Given the way that houses have been used like cashpoint machines, it was no wonder that the price declines of 2005 led to a slowdown on the British high street. According to the CBI (Confederation of British Industry) retail sales growth saw its worst performance[3] in 22 years. As the market later resumed its ascent, the extraction rate picked up once more to 5.6 per cent as at the quarter ended June 2006.

Following a rough year in 2005, the property market shifted up a gear. By May 2006, mortgage borrowing exceeded £1,000 billion.[4] In theory this should not be a problem as the lending is based on a total retail housing worth of £3,200 billion. However, one should take into account that there are a significant number of retired people with no mortgage or debts. They grew up in the barren aftermath of the Great Depression and World War II. To the older generation, debt is something to be ashamed of and not glorified or advertised on TV. It is therefore likely that these record debt levels are concentrated among the younger generation. If every price rise is met by yet more borrowing then, like the American example, it will leave very little by way of a buffer should the housing market suffer.

The Bank of England Governor, Mervyn King, had been concerned about the inflationary effect of rising property prices and made his thoughts public in the summer of 2004. His implicit threat to hike interest rates in order to cool the property market had the desired effect. Unfortunately, this good work was undermined by the Monetary Policy Committee (MPC), who voted for a rate cut in August 2005 after the market dipped. It was meant to act as a harbinger of troubles ahead whereas home-owners took it as an excuse to carry on the revelry. The mind can undergo bouts of amnesia where temptation is concerned. Through its actions, the Bank of England has given the impression that it will always act to bail out the property market. This is a dangerous game as it reinforces the notion that house prices are a one-way bet. Known as moral hazard, it encourages speculative behaviour as investors think that the powers that be would never allow a downturn to occur. Having been warned by the Bank's Governor about property euphoria, home-owners have no one to blame if they have already extracted their equity.

The upturn in property prices in 2006 should not be mistaken for resumption in trend: it may turn out to be a post mortem twitch. Like the behaviour of many other assets, when interest rates go up, property prices start to stabilise and often fall. Mervyn King is only too well aware of this, having been the Bank of England's chief economist in the early 1990s. He witnessed a doubling of interest rates from 7.5 per cent to 15 per cent to reduce inflation and the property market duly took a hit.[5] He is well aware that the maintenance of low interest rates is a recipe for further indebtedness, high inflation and hence higher rates down the line. It is better to keep them elevated when the economy is operating close to full capacity, such as now. Inflation is a monster that is better kept caged and controlled – letting it off the leash on humanitarian grounds is asking for trouble. A catch-22 situation exists whereby consumer spending is supported by consumer confidence which is supported in turn by higher house prices and home equity extraction. Like bingo balls suspended in mid-air, if the air-pump slows they start to descend under their own weight. If house prices actually fall and the money pump is switched off then the financial balls that we are all juggling in our daily lives will start to plummet, making us wonder how they had ever stayed up at all.

At the bottom of the property pile are the first-time buyers. They are the initial fuel for the market which sets off a chain reaction. The UK's largest lender, Halifax Bank of Scotland (HBOS), announced in 2005 that first-time buyers had been priced out of the market in nine out of ten British towns.[6] The number of these buyers in 2004 amounted to a mere 361,000, which was the lowest since 1982. They make up just 29 per cent of the market compared with 48 per cent in 1998. The average age of a first-time buyer is now 34 years. There is no clearer indication of the declining state of purchasing power in the economy after decades of inflation. As if the price factors were not enough, they are now competing against people sliding down the ladder in the form of downsizing pensioners and divorcees. Much like the food chain, without the primary source of food, the larger species begin to starve.

These first-time buyers should not be overly worried. While contemporaries mortgage themselves to the hilt with all-consuming interest payments, they can rent property in a nicer area for a lower cost. They have no financial risk and are in a position to buy into the market at leisure when prices fall. This is one argument used by those who wish to talk up the sector. They argue that there will be a pent-up demand waiting to buy houses on price declines so this will cushion any downturn. One factor they have not taken into account is the human element. When prices are falling, people tend to sit on their hands and wait for stability before making a decision. Often this buyers' strike leads to a self-fulfilling downturn because of a loss of confidence: Japan in the 1990s is again a prime example of this behaviour.

Many were surprised how swiftly the first interest rate rises took effect in the UK. Normally, when an economy is growing strongly it has a momentum of its own and initially appears immune to higher rates. Although there is typically a long lead time before elevated interest rates take their toll, the impact was clearly visible even by the beginning of 2005. The speed and effectiveness of such tightening is a classic signal that consumers have borrowed too much. Even a small rise in rates has a significant impact on their disposable income. They are living at the edge with very little financial cushioning to cope with any shocks. The same people often turn to credit cards simply to live, which compounds the problem with their exorbitant borrowing costs. Investment bank Lehman Brothers has created a model[7] to incorporate all of the relevant factors and expect prices to fall gently by 7 per cent by the close of 2007. They put the odds of a property crash at just 25 per cent. At worst, they expect a price decline in the order of 17 per cent if the bubble suddenly bursts. The report was of course rubbished by those with vested interest in the property market. This book should convince readers that even Lehman's negative expectations are perhaps optimistic. With tax increases forecast for 2007, the odds are stacking up against British consumers.

According to the National Housing Federation, house prices in England are at a multiple of eight times[8] the average salary. Since 1997, prices have risen by 155 per cent, yet wages have only increased by 18 per cent.[9] If ever evidence were needed that the market has stretched beyond fundamentals, then this must be it. House price affordability has to be related to one's earnings to finance the purchase: one cannot rise forever without the support of the other. Like an elastic band, there is only so much it can stretch before it snaps or recoils. House prices are at a record 60 per cent divergence[10] relative to average earnings, spanning a period of 40 years.

In a new twist, banks have euphemistically come up with a new way to get us further into debt while claiming that they are being more responsible. The latest system measures the so-called affordability[11] of a mortgage. Those with relatively normal wages but less-than-average expenses can now borrow to the hilt. A classic double-income, no-kids couple can borrow more than five times their combined earnings. This flies in the face of traditional guidelines whereby a mortgage should not exceed double that of a couple's joint income or three times that of a single person. This is symptomatic of banks throwing caution to the wind as they chase new business in a cooling market. As we saw at the peak of the Japanese property boom, loans are being granted up to 100 per cent of property values (and beyond), on the assumption that prices will always rise.

Many first-time buyers and remortgagees scrambled onto the debt bandwagon when rates hit their low point in 2003. At that time, a third of all new mortgage applicants opted for ultra-low interest rates which were fixed for two to three years. Like ARMs in America, this special offer period has now expired and household cashflows all over the country are taking a knock as borrowers are forced to pay the going rate. These discounted mortgage applications accounted for some 450,000 households at the time which is hardly an insignificant number.

One would have thought that the UK government would be making preparations for the impending property crisis, but they too are caught in a dilemma. The problem with such cyclical tax inflows is that planners assume they are a permanent feature and spending is adjusted upwards accordingly. Now that we are so disconnected from the cyclicality of nature, the modern human weakness has become one of over-extrapolation. Much like home-owners, the government will have no cushioning for added expenditure once the downturn arrives. It is the beneficiary of the stamp duty tax from property sales. Amounting to some £3.45 billion[12] when Labour came to power in 1997, by 2005–06 it had risen to an incredible £10.2 billion. This revenue is greater than inheritance tax and capital gains tax combined over the same period. With the inheritance tax (IHT) allowance standing at just £285,000, around a third of all households already hold this value in their main dwelling alone. Since coming to power, Labour's IHT receipts have risen from £1.6 billion to £3.3 billion. While many property values in the UK have almost trebled over the last decade, the inheritance tax threshold has risen by just 22 per cent. At first designed for the seriously rich, the allowance has failed miserably to compete with house price inflation. For the wealthy, IHT is virtually voluntary with detailed advice on avoidance available to those who can afford it. While around 37,000 estates paid the tax in 2005, there are now 6 million people who are potentially liable. The worst hit will be the South East of England where some two thirds of households in London will be caught.

In 2005, house prices experienced their slowest growth[13] in a decade. Although some buyers backed away from the market, by the end of that year they were back with bumper mortgages to buy on the dip. For anyone who has experience of stock markets, a sentence that contains words like 'buy' and 'dip' should ring alarm bells. Perceived wisdom is that the housing market will always go up so purchasing on a price fall appears to make sense; at least to the uninitiated who have never been through a crash before.

The lessons of the late 1980s property slump have been all but forgotten. An incredible third of all new UK mortgage applications did not involve checking the earnings of the borrower,[14] as long as their credit history was sound. There can be no clearer sign that the system is close to a peak. Both banks and borrowers will look back to this point and realise how reckless it had all become. Just as Mark Twain indicated that bankers would snatch back their umbrella at the first sign of rain, in the forthcoming downturn they may also be asking for the shirt off your back. We are seeing the largest rise in County Court Judgments (CCJs) since the last recession. The number of people brought before the courts for bad debts has risen for the first time[15] in 15 years. Some 573,000 judgments were made against consumers in 2005, rising by 7 per cent on the previous year, according to the Registry Trust. These judgments force debtors to repay their loans and credit card debts. The Department for Constitutional Affairs announced in October 2005 that county courts were granted 19,687 repossession orders in the third quarter of 2005. This represented an increase of 66 per cent on the year and was the highest figure since 1996 as mortgage lenders appear to be turning the screw.[16] There are also increasing reports of suicides among both students and the elderly who take the threatening letters and telephone calls from banks at face value. The sums involved are sometimes large but they can also be heartbreakingly small. Given that nine out of ten credit cards are issued without verifying customers' earnings, then banks too must share some responsibility[17] for the rise in bad debts. In the three months leading up to Christmas 2005, some 100 million unsolicited credit card applications were sent out to the public.[18]

In a mirror-image move, Britain and America have both witnessed the spectre of mortgages based on interest payments only, so that the capital of the loan is paid back in the future at some unknown point in time. Loans can be even be granted for 125 per cent of the property value over ever-longer periods. Coupled with the growth of self-assessment, it makes for a worrying cocktail of apparently pain-free debt with no questions asked. The best one can hope for is that the overvaluation of property relative to incomes will realign in a genteel manner as wages go up and house prices move sideways. If stock markets are anything to go by, overpriced assets rarely defy gravity.

As those in Britain will testify, there is a ripple effect that spreads out from London. Most British people do not realise that the UK is one of the world's prime tax havens for mega-rich foreigners (known as UK resident, non-domicile). The top end of the market, in areas such as Chelsea and Mayfair, is therefore in big demand and will suffer little in a downturn. Outside of these enclaves, the broader London economy is heavily influenced by the success or otherwise of its financial services sector. The rise in the London market has also been exacerbated by the expansion of the buy-to-let market. Investors have surged into this arena where flats and houses are renovated then let out. As house prices rise, such investors often feel comfortable that they have made capital gains, covered their expenses and may even be netting a nice level of income after costs. So they buy another and another one, until they have a sizeable portfolio of properties.

The clay feet of this structure, or source of financial subsidence, is founded on low interest rates. When the property market stabilises and borrowing costs rise, the sums do not add up. Having had a nice balance between rental incomes and borrowing costs, the scales have tipped away from the income side. This can be lived with if the market is appreciating, but higher interest rates have a negative effect on house prices. They also slow economic growth, meaning there are fewer workers moving around the country. The sudden shortage of tenants leaves other buy-to-let landlords in the same boat, so they compete to cut rents. This in turn reduces property prices as it's a less sure bet for rental income, and so it goes on. We have already seen Britain's third biggest buy-to-let lender – the Portman Building Society – draw away from offering mortgages on new flats now that an excess is becoming apparent.[19]

The rise and fall of prices is a natural phenomenon and is something that should not be feared or fobbed off. It simply reflects a cycle of birth, growth and decay, then rebirth. This was well understood by our ancestors who celebrated both the Winter and Summer Solstices. In our multinational corporate world, we tend to get caught up in the growth bit with no thought for the other stages of the cycle. We may well be entering a retrenchment phase where property prices reflect actual value again. Sadly for some, overbought markets have a tendency to be oversold down to extreme levels. Anyone considering the purchase of a property should first realise that there have been four one-off events that have all coincided and are unlikely to be repeated anytime soon:

1. a huge government spending programme
2. a self-feeding consumer spending binge
3. lax bank lending policies
4. a once-in-a-generation downward shift in interest rates.

If anyone doubts the role of government spending then it is worth remembering that 6 million workers are now employed by the state, which equates to twice the population of Wales and accounts for one in five jobs in the UK.[20]

CARRY ME HOME

If there is one thing that should be learned from this book, it is an understanding of the cost of carry, a common term in financial markets. Before undertaking any investment, the cost of having money tied up needs to be weighed up against the likely returns. Precious metals are a good example, where the added burden of insurance and storage need to be accounted for. If one is developing a property for rental purposes then an understanding of returns versus all costs is vital. Rose-tinted spectacles do not work with any financial undertaking and if anything, the hidden expenses should be overestimated to add a buffer to the project. Before looking at the cost of carry we must first understand that the outlay of owning a property must not exceed the expected yield from the rental income. If it does, one is taking a gamble that prices will always rise to compensate for the time and money spent on the initial construction and ongoing repair. The closest we can come to defining a bubble is when people buy and sell something in the hope of making a profit, regardless of the intrinsic worth of the object. If the annual yield from the rental income of a property is less than the cost of financing, then it is surely a symptom of being in a bubble. Those who trade in such items are better known as speculators: a term most would find insulting, with its overtones of greed. One can guarantee that if someone is trading in a bubble commodity and does not realise that they are speculating, then there is every chance that they are the last in a line of risk-takers. They will be left holding a shrinking asset, having parted company with their cash. Worse still, they could be facing bankruptcy if they have overstretched themselves and conditions change for the worse.

The reader can do their own calculation on the cost of carry but first they must know what elements to include. The most hidden aspect is known as the opportunity cost, which is a measure of what one has foregone to become involved in the project. This is equivalent to the interest one would have received if the house deposit and renovation budget was instead earning interest. Next, all the bills have to be accounted for: mortgage interest payments; property taxes; income tax on the rental income; insurance; structural repairs, plus any other unexpected items not covered on the rental agreement. When all of these are added together then the cost of carry – or the cost of simply owning a building – can amount to anything in the region of 10 per cent of its value. Many 'investors' are going to be shelling out money for the privilege of owning an idle asset that cannot be sold because of negative equity.

Although rental yields will vary depending on the location, in areas where property prices are high, these yields will normally be at or below prevailing interest rates: around 3 per cent in the UK[21] and America and barely 1 per cent in Spain. To break even with the cost of carry, the property price will therefore need to rise by a good 6–7 per cent per annum (or to double every ten years), just to make up the difference. Even then, one is making the assumption that the tenant is perfect and will not default. As property owners in Spain will confirm, year-round tenancies are a rarity. One should always remember that when times are hard, fewer people will be taking holidays to such areas. At home, the number of tenants defaulting on the rent will be on the increase. Unlike the days of the Highland Clearance in Scotland or the Potato Famine in Ireland, they cannot simply be thrown out on a landlord's whim or because they are uneconomic.

PAIN IN ARREARS

To entice customers into buying their product or service, the marketing side of an organisation often offers cheap deals which are called loss leaders. They may lose money for the company initially but act as an enticement for the customer to become conditioned to using the product. Drug dealers similarly offer free samples in the hope of creating a new market of addicts from whom they will recoup their initial outlay and much, much more. Credit card companies are like any other business and use loss-leading techniques to increase the use of the product and to squeeze every ounce of profit from them. They have done this job for years and know every trick in the book to gain an edge over the customer. For those who can afford to pay them off every month the cards provide a great source of interest-free credit, freedom to shop on the Internet and the ability to pay without the bother of writing a cheque. For those who cannot afford to clear them every month they are a potential nightmare.

Just as high rates of inflation whittle away the buying power of your savings, a high rate of interest can likewise balloon your borrowings. Interest rates of 20 per cent will roughly double the size of your debt in the space of just four years. Such compounding has been around and understood for millennia. When Napoleon Bonaparte was shown its expansive power on an interest rate table, he was heard to say after a period of quiet reflection: 'The deadly facts herein lead me to wonder that this monster interest has not devoured the whole human race. It would have done so long ago if bankruptcy and revolution had not been counter poisons.' There is an apocryphal tale from further back in time when a courtier asked his monarch for some grain to be doubled on every square of a chess board, starting with a single grain on the first, and then two on the second followed by 4, 8, 16, 36, 72, and so on. The king was not a mathematician so did not realise that the same process over 64 squares would take away all the grain ever harvested in the kingdom. Such is the power of compounding.

While some play the game of switching between special offers from different companies, this juggling act can soon come crashing down if just one event distracts them. These special offers will only last as long as credit card companies compete for market share. Once the cold wind of credit caution blows through the industry then the cardholder will cease to be feted as a customer but will instead be classed as a risky debtor. The Anglo-Saxon debt culture is never more apparent when comparing the use of credit cards with our continental cousins. There are over 66 million cards in issue in Britain – five times the European average – as opposed to just 3 million in France. Perhaps this is a contributing factor to the *joie de vivre* across the Channel. Now that the UK market is saturated, penalty charges and higher interest rates are being introduced by stealth to milk the profitability from existing customers. Like the devil, debt comes in many disguises and it has never been easier to borrow money via bank loans, overdrafts, credit cards and credit card cheques. It is virtually impossible to stick to a monthly budget on credit card spending or to keep a mental note of the balance. It is therefore no wonder that we are surprised by the size of our bills each month. Debt accumulation is much like dieting: it is so much easier to add the pounds than take them off. We all know what is required but few have the mental willpower to see it through.

In the classic style of all New Year's resolutions, some 49 per cent of people surveyed in the Consumer Sentiment Report[22] in early 2005 planned to cut their borrowings in the first six months of that year. The bounce in equity withdrawal figures that autumn showed how easily such good intentions go out of the window. According to the annual survey by the National Statistics Office[23] – based on 7,000 households over 2004 – a typical family spent 20 per cent more than it earns. The average spend of close to £600 per week is £130 ahead of the average income. The biggest weekly expenditure is on transportation, which does not bode well for them given the impending energy crisis. Although it sounds old-fashioned, we may need a period of saving before we spend, or of doing without until the next set of wages comes in.

Consumers can be just as predatory as banks as debt corrupts all within its corrosive reach. No doubt in years to come the customers who begged for mortgages will turn the tables on the providers and sue them after the property slump. Some will sue banks for 'allowing' them to take on too big a mortgage when they probably begged for one in the first place. They will claim mortgages were 'sold' to them as innocent victims of a greedy corporate machine. Like mushrooms appearing overnight, compensation lawyers will emerge from every patch of mud to sue lenders in the light of their mis-selling of mortgages. Years after the event, adverts are still appearing on television to encourage anyone who bought an endowment policy to pursue compensation. Insurance companies made the mistake of extrapolating past growth trends into the future then turning it into a sales tool – a topic that will re-emerge time and again in this book. In Britain, the Consumer Credit Bill will bring stricter controls on lending, but it is a little late to be updating this area of the law given that it is replacing legislation from as long ago as 1974. It will likely be a case of closing the stable door after the horse has bolted.

It is not just the poor who are becoming debt-trapped. We are now seeing a sharp rise in the number of high-earning professionals who are getting into financial difficulties. According to the Consumer Credit Counselling Service (CCCS),[24] even those who bring home a gross wage of £50,000 per annum are not immune. Perhaps this trend is to be expected given that many more youngsters are staying at home for longer. Almost 60 per cent of men aged 20–25 are still living at home with their parents and 42 per cent of women of the same age are likewise refusing to leave the nest. With the inexorable rise of costs associated with university education, it is not surprising that even the high-flyers are feeling the pain. The CCCS also revealed the shocking fact that the average caller looking for help had roughly £30,000 worth of non-mortgage debts across ten different sources, many of which were built up on credit cards.[25]

In the case of the UK, the public is carrying an average of one and a half times their post-tax earnings as borrowed money. There is an eye-popping total of £1,300,000,000,000 or 1.3 thousand billion of personal or household liabilities. This is more than the external debts of Africa and South America combined[26] and greater than the entire economic output of Britain in 2005. The expansion in debt continues to run at an unsustainable 10 per cent per annum, which is four times the rate of economic growth. Even when the economy is strong, bad debts are mounting. The Department for Constitutional Affairs[27] is planning legislation to make it easier to repossess the homes of such debtors. Banks are increasingly turning to charging orders, whose issuance has risen from 13,000 in 1999 to 45,000 in 2004. It allows the creditors to take money from the proceeds of house, land or share sales once mortgage and credit card debts are cleared. It is effectively removing the distinction between secured and unsecured loans. Perhaps it is only a matter of time before we return to the dark days of debtors' prisons where bankrupts were jailed and fed by their families until the debt was paid.

In many ways, debt is a modern form of slavery, in that it nets the weakest and most vulnerable. Not only do they have no earthly possessions in their own name but they must work for the rest of their natural lives for someone else's benefit. Meanwhile, house repossessions are on the increase. According to the Council of Mortgage Lenders, nearly 5,000 families lost their homes in the first half of 2005, which is an increase of almost 50 per cent on the year before. This is nowhere near as bad as 1993 when the number of repossessions peaked at just over 58,000. The potential for conditions to worsen is all too clear. Some 100,000 households are three months in arrears[28] on their mortgage payments. The scene is possibly set for a re-run of the negative equity period last seen in the early 1990s. At that time the figure for people in arrears was close to 500,000, remarkably close to the number who took out discounted mortgages in 2003. When credit conditions were easy, many first-time buyers borrowed up to five times their salaries. It should therefore come as no surprise that repayments are getting harder since interest rates started their ascent in November 2003. The likelihood of a rate cut continues to diminish as inflation is hitting its highest levels since 1996. With energy costs starting to bite, the Bank of England's target level of 2 per cent inflation has now been exceeded, standing at 2.5 per cent as at August 2006. The surprise move by the Bank to raise rates in the same month came as a shock to City economists and complacent home-owners.

SOLVENCY ABUSE

Another indicator of how much pain is being caused can be viewed when analysing personal bankruptcies. According to the UK government's Insolvency Service,[29] personal insolvencies grew by 10 per cent in the second quarter of 2006, but a stunning 66 per cent year-on-year. In human terms, the number of personal bankruptcies in England and Wales grew by over 26,000. These levels are the highest since records began in 1960. The IMF has pinpointed Britain as an accident waiting to happen in this regard. Around half of the bankrupts were under the age of 30. Part of the increase is attributable to a change in the way that people file for bankruptcy. The Enterprise Act, introduced in 2004, has made it much easier to go bankrupt as it has removed the harshness of the penalties previously imposed on debtors. The so-called Individual Voluntary Arrangement (IVA) scheme allows for a negotiation to reduce debts owed to the lender. It was designed to help entrepreneurs get back on their feet but has been used by individuals as an alternative to full-blown insolvency. Companies such as Debt Free Direct specialise in this area.

One would have thought that banks would have taken some responsibility for the current rash of bad debts given their widescale and indiscriminate distribution of credit cards and loans. Instead, some chief executives have blamed the insolvency practitioners[30] who help clients free themselves from the web. Having sown the seeds of financial servitude in an industrialised manner, banks bemoan the need to set aside provisions for the ensuing harvest of bad debts. As the UK banking sector announced £20 billion record profits for the first half of 2006, analysts are looking behind the headline figures and calculating these impairment charges below the surface. The malaise is starting to show as Barclaycard profits were beaten up in 2006 also. Only now are lending criteria being tightened, with some half of credit card applications being rejected. In responding to banks' criticism of the insolvency industry, Debt Free Direct has highlighted the advertising disparities between the two industries. In 2005, credit card companies spent some £315 million on adverts versus the £3 million of those who offered advice[31] on debt relief: a ratio of more than a 100:1.

While the property boom and availability of debt makes us appear wealthy, these trends are shallow and deceptive. Just as drink makes us cocksure, so our binge on borrowed money is giving us a false sense of our own superiority. The property bubble is a symptom and not the cause of excess lending by banks, but there are many other distributors of debt that are leading us on a course of financial suicide.

3

PUNCHBOWL

Like gold, U.S. dollars have value only to the extent that they are strictly limited in supply. But the U.S. government has a technology, called a printing press (or, today, its electronic equivalent), that allows it to produce as many U.S. dollars as it wishes at essentially no cost.

Ben Bernanke[1]

SPIKING THE DRINKS

A cabal of western party goers has gathered around the communal punchbowl to drink and dole out its debt-laden contents. Surveying the guest list we have already been introduced to the banker and consumer in previous chapters. Their generous hosts are the politicians and central bankers, from whom debt creation and liquidity is never-ending. We will then meet the greedy company executive and gatecrashing hedge fund industry.

For the debt-based economies of Britain and America, a warped system has evolved that has pawned the legacy for the next generation. It encourages us to live beyond our means in the short term at the expense of our long-term financial health. While it is all-too-easy to blame consumers for being a driver of debt creation, many have had little choice. Their loss of purchasing power and dwindling income as a proportion of the economy has led to survival on a life of credit. This has become known as the hourglass economy[2] where the wealthy sit at the top and are distinct from the bulge at the bottom of both low- and middle-income earners.

After technology shares crashed and 9/11 rocked America, both the economy and the stock market shuddered to a halt. To encourage a willingness to spend and foster the so-called wealth effect, one or more of the following needed to occur: a big rise in personal earnings, a stock market free-for-all or a property boom. In that traumatic environment, the first two contributors to wealth – higher earnings and share prices – were completely out of the question. The only alternative left was to maximise disposable income while pushing up property prices. This pincer movement was executed by slashing mortgage costs, through lower interest rates, and cutting taxes. Over the last 200 years, taxes have been reduced with alarming regularity[3] during the secondary bubble phase. The combined approach was no accident but part of a master plan inspired by the US government and the US Federal Reserve: the pilots of financial policy. This is not meant to sound like some bizarre conspiracy theory but is rather part of a decades-old financial engineering process.

We have seen from past and bitter experience how one excess begets another. The knock-on effect of a generational low in interest rates has inflated every asset to the hilt: there is now nothing left to pump up. When the final crash comes, every active participant in the primary and secondary bubble areas will be blown away. A deflationary pin-prick now looms large. All that will be left is a shadow of sludge where once a pretty bubble blew. To continue the revelry theme, consumers' drinks are being spiked and topped up to keep the party going. The hosts need to gain kudos in order to be invited back onto the party circuit. In this sense the Republicans have succeeded, having been voted in for a second term. Similarly, Alan Greenspan was reappointed some five times during his 18-year term of office. The evidence for the mass production of money can be found in the change in money supply over the years. In the 35 years before the discipline of the gold standard was abandoned, money supply merely doubled. In the 35 years since then it has multiplied thirteen-fold. This has echoes from Ancient Rome: the emperors and patricians despised the plebs but to stay in power they dished out free food and sponsored bloodthirsty games to sedate the masses. 'Bread and circuses' was the catchphrase. The modern equivalent in America should be 'easy credit and tax cuts'. Anyone who acts frugally or responsibly by saving is punished by inflation, leading to a loss of purchasing power. Like the snake-oil salesmen of the Wild West, low interest rates are given as a cure for all ills. 'Have you had a banking crisis, a stock market crash or a terrorist attack? Have some cheap debt-money: that will do the trick.' Be warned: such money is a stimulant and an overdose is overdue. Though fun at first, the party excesses eventually become dull and repetitive and the desire to return to normality ensues.

We need to investigate why US interest rates fell so dramatically to levels not seen in a generation. To solve the puzzle, it is essential to understand the workings of the government bond market. This has been vital in reducing the cost of American mortgages and for funding a borrowing binge that is lurching out of control.

Much as we become overdrawn if our costs exceed our earnings, governments experience a budget deficit when their outgoings are greater than their tax receipts. In 2005, the US government spent $2.47 trillion but only received $2.15 trillion: a shortfall of around $320 billion in one year alone. This excludes the 'emergency spending' that has racked up a further $450 billion from 2002 to 2006. The more they spend now, the more that taxes must rise at some point in future to clear the stack of debts. From 2000 to 2005, US government revenue fell[4] while expenditure rose by close to 40 per cent. The picture deteriorated from a position where Federal inflows and outflows were closely matched in 2000, to one where $1 in every $5 spent has been borrowed.

To cover the shortfall, the Treasury raises money from financial markets by offering what are called government bonds. These are parcels of debt packaged into an investment. In return for borrowing investors' money for a fixed period, the government guarantees to return it in future, meanwhile paying attractive fixed rates of interest in the interim (known as coupons). They begin with a nominal value of $100 at outset, and then some years later $100 is repaid on their maturity, which is the end of their pre-set lifespan. Prior to maturity, prices can vary dramatically depending on three main factors which are often interrelated: namely, inflation, interest rates and the number of bonds in circulation. To make life simple we can see how these factors combine to make the price fall, as this may be the initial theme in the event of a currency crisis. Inflation can wipe out the purchasing power of an asset like a bond that matures at a rigid rate. Its price therefore drops because it is unattractive as a store of value. As the coupon is also fixed, then rising interest rates will make bank deposits more attractive and once again the price suffers. Finally, like any product or commodity, when too much is available without extra demand then the price will fall. This may happen when governments are spending excessively on wars and therefore issue more bonds to fund the fighting. Such countries that have too much debt and inflation must also reward overseas investors with a higher return. This is because they face a greater risk of foreign exchange losses.

When prices fall, the future rate of return for a new investor becomes more attractive. They are rewarded in two ways: first they receive the annual income from the coupons; and second, they gain the benefit in a rise in the bond price as it reverts back up to $100. This combination of capital growth and income is called the yield, which is calculated as a percentage return per annum. Another way to think of the relationship is like an old-fashioned set of equal-arm scales whereby one side will fall (the price) while the other one rises (the yield). The point of this exercise is to understand that the interest rate paid on an American mortgage is based upon the yield of US government bonds. To give consumers more spending money the government set out to reduce their mortgage rates by pushing down bond yields. The pivotal rate used for mortgage borrowing is the yield on the 30-year US Treasury bond. The 30-year element refers to the time to maturity of the bond so it is therefore referred to as a long-term interest rate. Given the importance of the US consumer for both domestic and international activity, we should be aware of the reverse process that now faces us. In a dangerous domino effect, when bond yields go up, mortgage costs rise, consumers cut back and the world suffers.

Looking at the future oversupply of bonds, we see that the weight of costs from Social Security, Medicare and Medicaid will come crushing down on the economy as the first wave of the post-war baby-boom generation hits retirement from 2008. According to the Congressional Budget Office[5] (CBO), in the next three decades, the over-65s will double while the under-65s will increase by just 15 per cent. From 8 per cent of the economy now, the spending programmes are projected to crowd out other projects as they expand to 28 per cent by 2050. The CBO described the problem as 'pressure on the budget that economic growth alone will not eliminate'. That is a very polite way of saying the system is bust. Future tax receipts will not cover future expenditure so the Treasury will have to sell yet more bonds, not just to pay these bills but to pay back loans from the past. In practice, they roll old debts into the future once more by issuing yet more debt. In the final death-throws of a debt-finance economy, it will come to pass that bond issuance will become exponential, like the tale of doubling grains on every chess square. Financial suicide is inevitable when borrowing is heaped on borrowing simply to service existing debt. The compound effect of interest on interest drowns the debtor.

So far, the US government has racked up over $8 trillion of debt, attributable purely to its issuance of bonds. However, tens of trillions of further liabilities are built into the welfare system, in the years to come. US Federal Reserve Board member Professor Laurence Kotlikoff has been brutally frank[6] in saying that America is effectively bankrupt. According to his 2006 paper, 'the US government is, indeed, bankrupt, insofar as it will be unable to pay its creditors, who, in this context, are current and future generations to whom it has explicitly promised future net payments of various kinds.' As the baby-boom generation retires, a 'fiscal gap' will turn into a chasm. This difference between all future expenditure and future tax receipts will widen to almost $66 trillion. This is five times the annual US GDP. In order to fill this hole, the government would need to double personal and corporate taxation or cut these benefits by two thirds straight away. Neither option is likely without severe deflationary and political repercussions. Disturbingly, Professor Kotlikoff argues that America's current policies have the potential for hyperinflation: the condition where fanaticism flourishes.

The only reason why yields have not already soared in the face of this future oversupply is because the likes of China and Japan have been mopping up the existing haemorrhage of dollars by purchasing US bonds. Asians are feeding western spending habits while enriching themselves in the process. Until recently, the relationship was symbiotic, but mutual support is now turning into life support for America. This brings to mind the science-fiction film *Alien*, in which a foreign life-form smothered a crew-member's face in a vice-like grip, taking over his vital functions. It maintained his existence solely to serve the purpose of injecting and incubating its eggs. As the mini-monster hatched and burst through the human's belly, a gory death became inevitable. We can only hope that China's treatment of the West will be more benevolent in the years to come.

THE WIZARD

Having encountered the first party host, in the form of the US government, we can now acquaint ourselves with the second: the US Federal Reserve and its previous chairman, Alan Greenspan. In the 1939 film adaptation of *The Wizard of Oz*, Dorothy travels to the Emerald City to seek an audience with the wizard. Through the smoke and fire a green face appears on the wall and his booming commands make her tremble. Whilst berating Dorothy and her friends for their insolence, her faithful dog Toto draws back a curtain. Behind it is revealed an old man whose charade with levers and a microphone has convinced the populace that he is the great and powerful wizard. It turned out that the wizard of her dream was a dubious fortune-teller whom she had met in Kansas before the hurricane.

It would be harsh to use this analogy to compare Alan Greenspan with the green-faced projection. After all, the intent of the original book by Frank Baum was for the Wicked Witch of the East to represent the malevolent bankers on America's Eastern Seaboard. Greenspan has never claimed to possess greater knowledge of the future than anyone else in markets. Nevertheless, during his office he enjoyed the aura that a naive investment community was prepared to bestow upon him, in the same way that the wizard enthralled and dominated the good citizens of the Emerald City. His audience were so-called Fed-watchers who, like love-sick teenagers, would pore over his every word. Their mood-swings varied, depending on their own inter-pretation of what were purposefully innocuous statements. Like the wizard, Alan Greenspan was revered as a demi-god whose all-seeing eye and all-knowing brain protected and nurtured the capitalist world. This might seem a paradox given the frequency of his financial interventions which prevented free market forces from restoring the natural order. Like the curious Toto, we can uncover the inner workings of his interest rate manoeuvres, whose initial applications were warranted to help to stave off two serious crises. However, these machinations have since been applied on at least four more occasions to patch up a round of financial flops both at home and abroad. Unlike Dorothy, we have no magic slippers to click together to end the coming nightmare. Once the property bubble bursts we may well come to despise her spell-like mantra of 'there's no place like home'.

Greenspan has often applied financial levers and amplified words to manipulate bond markets, albeit failing to do so with the stock market. In spite of some initial success, his willingness to offer interest rate cuts has led to bad habits which have turned America from the world's biggest creditor into its greatest debtor. Like empires of the past, superpowers cannot survive for long without sound finances. We must prepare ourselves for a new decline and fall in our own lifetime. Time and again the US economy has been inflated with mass-produced debt to pull itself and the rest of the world out of a hole. While these interventions were once workable, America is now so sodden with borrowed bucks that further stimulation will do little to help consumers. Like addictive drugs, the longer that debt is abused, the greater the dose that must be supplied to achieve the same economic effect. As higher levels of tolerance lead to greater accumulation of toxins, the patient succumbs to the inevitable collapse. Resuscitation will be akin to applying defibrillating paddles to a lifeless body: any resultant activity is purely artificial.

To achieve their aims, central banks use short-term interest rates as their primary tool to steer the economy. It normally takes around 18 months for alterations to affect economic momentum, like turning an oil tanker on the move. They may also use rhetoric about economic growth or recession to raise or lower bond yields to suit their needs. An example of this economic intervention through the back door is the way that the US Federal Reserve can change the money flowing into or out of the economy. Known as 'steepening the yield curve', they can influence the difference between short-term and long-term interest rates. A combination of low rates and higher bond yields is stimulative because it will have the effect of pouring liquidity, or money, into the economy: rather like putting a bottle to one's lips and tipping it up. The Federal Reserve has used this technique to bail out the banking system before by steepening the yield curve on purpose. Central banks can swamp the economy with money in bad times and drain it when inflation is overheating and the brake needs to be applied. Sadly, they have done too much of the former but too little of the latter.

FOUR SEASONS

There were four elements to Greenspan's reign, each entailing a flood of money to save the day:

Winter: Financial famine of the 1987 crash and Savings & Loans crisis
Spring: Seedlings of corporate greed which grew into the dot. com crash
Summer: Growth of the property bubble to dethrone America hegemony
Autumn: Harvest of debt on Greenspan's retirement

To set the scene when Greenspan became chairman, we need to look at the years before he took office. By 1980 the American economy was in a sorry state following years of underinvestment during the inflation-ravaged 1970s. The highly respected Paul

Volcker, as chairman of the Federal Reserve, was in charge of setting interest rate policy. When he was appointed in 1979 the economy was stuck in a quicksand of low growth coupled with high inflation: the worst of both worlds. He famously came out with fighting talk against inflation and backed his words with a severe rise (or tightening) of interest rates which peaked in 1981 close to 20 per cent. Although it was painful and came on the back of a long period of industrial stagnation, it was just the right thing at the right time. The inflation dragon was beaten back into its cave, falling from over 13 per cent in 1980 to little more than 3 per cent by 1983. The environment laid a stable foundation for employment which was beneficial for the stock market. Little by little, a favourable circle of events moved in tandem.

Winter

When Greenspan took over the role in August 1987, the economic landscape looked rosy. The stock market was flying high as the devaluation of the dollar over the previous two years had given a competitive edge to American exports. Having been trampled underfoot by the 'Japanese miracle' of mass production, the currency respite was a great relief. Within months of his arrival, Greenspan was at the helm when stock markets collapsed in October 1987, which was hardly his fault. He had learned the lessons of the 1929 crash and moved quickly to cut interest rates to avoid a depression.

There were other problems that lay latent within the financial system. When Paul Volcker had imposed sky-high rates earlier that decade, it had hidden consequences. Apart from sending the unemployment rate up to 10 per cent, it also crippled the banking system, particularly the smaller institutions known as Savings & Loans banks (S&Ls). While a combination of low interest rates and high bond yields allow liquidity to pour into the economy, the opposite was true in the 1980s. Instead, the yield curve was drawing liquidity out of the economy, like lowering a bottle down from one's lips. Under these conditions banks have difficulty in lending profitably.

To make money under normal circumstances, banks borrow short and lend long, to use the technical parlance. In other words they give short-term depositors a low rate of interest but charge long-term borrowers a higher fixed rate, thereby making a profit margin in the middle. We will ignore the fact that borrowers far exceed depositors for now. With such elevated rates, businesses and consumers suffered so the economy slowed. Besides the increase in bad debts, banks' profit margins were further squeezed from another angle. They had to pay high rates to short-term depositors yet received lower rates of interest from long-term borrowers. This situation is known as an inverted yield curve and is one of the best, but often the least-noticed, methods of forecasting a recession. Needless to say, as US interest rates continue their ascent in 2006, it appears that the curve may once again be inverting.

The Reagan Administration encouraged S&L banks to move into high-risk areas to boost their income when rates were high, only to find that their loss of financial discipline led both them and the wider economy into a major bust. Sensible regulation that was in place for a good reason became 'reformed' in order to cope with a supposedly new era. Just when we forget why the last generation put the hard-learned rules in place, we go and repeat the original mistakes they were designed to prevent. The deregulation of these sleepy banks meant that they were left unfettered to venture into speculative areas where they had little knowledge and even less experience. They jumped on the real estate bandwagon and went into commercial property lending. The S&L crisis is a salutary lesson as to why reasonable credit controls or lending restraints on banks are so important in avoiding recklessness. The directors' drive for profits in a collection of little-regulated organisations cares little for the big-picture damage they are inflicting.

Like moths to a naked flame, banks are drawn instinctively to the brightest-looking areas which will ultimately burn them. In quick order, the speculative property ventures that the Savings & Loans banks had funded were worth only a fraction of their previous value. Hundreds of financial institutions went bankrupt in the worst banking crisis since the Great Depression. It was just a pity that the political idealism for total deregulation was unleashed without restraint, given the way that businesses seem to find a way to exploit, and then ruin, a good idea. It appears that we are caught in a trap whereby we either adopt too little regulation, which results in a bubble, or too much, which kills off innovation. The banking problems of the late 1980s and early 1990s hit home when stock and property markets were already downcast thanks to the first Gulf War. The Federal Reserve then decided to try a financial experiment. It reckoned that the economy was in such a bad state that low interest rates would not rekindle inflation but instead bail out the banking system. If it took no action then the economy stood a very real chance of sliding into depression. Like the Japanese later that decade, US banks had too many bad debts from the S&L crisis and needed to build their financial base. The most important aspect of this period was the way that interest rate manipulation allowed the banks to build up their capital base once more without taking undue business risk.

By the close of 1991, the Federal Reserve had cut rates 18 times until they hit a 27-year low of 3.5 per cent. With bond yields in the order of 8 per cent, the yield curve was very steep, which allowed banks to repair their battered balance sheets. As well as improving their profit margins, they were able to invest their own assets[7] into bonds with a significantly higher yield. This allowed them to feast on the yield difference, thereby netting themselves several per cent per annum on billions of dollars. Banks are compelled to hold adequate amounts of capital as a safety net against bad debts. This would normally be held in the form of cash. However, the rules had been changed to allow US government bonds to be classified as risk-free investments because they have a low risk of default. They can of course be very volatile, but by the use of semantics the banks were able to buy government bonds in lieu of keeping aside hard cash. They were given carte blanche to carry out what was effectively a risk-free trade with an almost guaranteed return – the nirvana of investments. It was not just a case of getting an extra yield pick-up: the effect of buying all these bonds also sent up their price. The expense and risk of the exercise were firmly with the taxpayer but it did the trick at the time. Needless to say, the banks got better through this back-door subsidy. In the space of six years the economy had gone from feast to famine followed by re-nourishment and a balanced diet.

At this stage Greenspan must have felt like the hero of the hour. In Ancient Rome, the returning victorious generals would ride in triumph through the city on a gilded chariot. As the crowds cheered, a slave would hold a golden crown above his head and repeat the phrase 'you, too, are mortal and all glory is fleeting'. This prevented the generals from getting ideas above their station. Sadly, Greenspan had no one to remind him of his fallibility, which is, after all, the hallmark of all human beings.

Spring

By 1994 it was clear that the US economy was getting back on its feet and Greenspan began to raise rates early that year. This was the responsible thing to do and the punchbowl was duly withdrawn so that the party did not get too boisterous. It was a painful year for bond markets as banks and speculators alike reversed their so-called carry trade by taking profits on bonds and going back into cash. As interest rates rose, the rationale for speculation was neutralised as the cost of borrowing was little different from the yield on bonds. As usual, the speculators headed for the same exit at the same time: bonds were widely sold off so prices fell and yields shot up.

In a classic example of unintended consequences, the work that Greenspan had engineered domestically had an unexpected outcome abroad. When rates were low, foreign direct investment (FDI) from multinational companies had poured into Mexico and Latin America to play on the outsourcing theme. Investors' money followed in hot pursuit. Speculators had also swelled the emerging market frenzy by borrowing dollars at low interest rates and placing the proceeds overseas. When rates went up, investors scrambled out of these volatile markets to pay off their dollar borrowing and a meltdown was activated. Many Asian countries suffered similarly as their currencies were linked to the dollar (known as a peg) and were forced to raise their interest rates as well.

In the face of foreign inflows, Latino governments had been spending as though the good times would never end. The emerging market crisis left them with a barrage of bonds coming up for maturity but with no one to buy them. When your debt is unloved, bond prices fall and interest rates rise such that the economy is crushed: currency devaluation becomes inevitable. When the Mexican government – many of whose ministers were Harvard-educated – devalued the peso, this was truly a shock and killed the dream of emerging market investing for years to come. It also meant that America had to bail out Mexico just when domestic taxes were increasing, which further hurt the dollar. As US investors fled home like a defeated army, they stayed in cash to lick their wounds. This money was later recycled back into the American market where they felt more comfortable. While emerging markets languished, stocks on Wall Street started on a positive bull market run which ran until the end of the decade. For those who are not familiar with stock market terminology, 'bulls' are positively-inclined investors who expect share prices to rise, while 'bears' maintain that the outlook is negative.

When Alan Greenspan mentioned in passing that asset prices were suffering from 'irrational exuberance' in 1996, he was guilty only of being cautious. This is not a bad trait for a central bank chairman. Tragically, the derision he received from smart-alecs in the investment community led him to be silent later on, when it really mattered. Like everyone else at the time, he also became a proponent for the productivity-through-technology theory. When the market later slumped, the exposure of various accounting frauds showed that the corporate earnings bonanza appeared to have more to do with fiddling figures than feeding efficiency. The 'goodwill' in accounting proved to be anything but for pension holders impoverished by the bankruptcy of Enron and WorldCom.

Greenspan had done well in the early years, giving the economy some slack then reining it back when discipline was required. In the crises that followed, he found it easy to loosen but harder to tighten. Every time the quick dose of easy money was applied through lower interest rates, Greenspan was seen as the saviour. Like the middle stages of drug addiction, the fix is frequently applied with apparently no side-effects and the user thinks they still have control. A world tour of crises then rocked from Asia (1997) to Russia (1998), with a home finale in New York when the Long Term Capital Management (LTCM) hedge fund crashed and burned (see next chapter). During these bail-outs there were minimal inflationary consequences: investors believed that the miracle of technology would keep it at bay and make money for all. Payback time is fast approaching for these wildly optimistic assumptions as the overdose of dollars is now seeping through every pore. Like track marks on an addict's arm, inflation is apparent in every economic artery and cannot be hidden for much longer.

The process of coming to the aid of all and sundry creates moral hazard, as discussed in the last chapter. It gives risk-taking investors the impression that they can play the prodigal son with a father-figure ready to bail them out when they have been avaricious. Like greedy chicks in the nest with gullets wide open, the speculators cried out for help and the Federal Reserve duly pandered to their needs. It should always hold true that investors who take risks should lose money if their bets turn sour. The tight link between risk and reward is the natural order of the investment jungle. If the rules are broken, the animal spirits of nature will rear up to wreak their vengeance. The bear of the bear market will soon emerge from hibernation.

Although interest rates did rise towards the end of the Internet boom it was too little too late. At his annual economic address at Jackson Hole, Wyoming, in 2002, Greenspan even had to defend his role[8] during the 1990s stock market bubble. He questioned whether it was the job of a central bank to identify and target such asset spikes with higher interest rates because of similar errors in the run-up to the 1929 crash. However, he could have used further rhetoric as he had done time and again with the bond markets, to either cajole or cramp the stock market. Following his high-profile bad call on equities in 1996 he must have felt very wary of speaking out, for the simple reason that as human beings we don't like to be proved wrong in public. As he made clear during a 1996 Federal Reserve Board meeting[9] before his 'irrational exuberance' remarks, there's more than one way to skin a cat, or bash the bull in this case. He could easily have used controls on margin requirements. In America one can buy shares with just a 50 per cent down payment, using credit for the other half. By reducing this facility, a big source of borrowed money would have been pulled from the system and given the message that he was serious about speculation.

In his 2005 Jackson Hole address, he raised the subject of property bubbles and investor complacency toward risk. This warning was rather low-key as the honest truth was too brutal for the public to take. It may have even sparked off an early sell-off, leaving him to take the blame for a property crisis at the end of his tenure. This risk warning was rather galling. As one who oversaw the conditions for speculation to thrive, he can enjoy retirement and sagely look back to his address and say 'I told you so, right at the peak of the property market.' Jonathan Compton, of London's Bedlam Asset Management, compared this speech with the actions of Pontius Pilate: washing his hands of the responsibility while doing little to change the outcome. Greenspan's version of events will no doubt be made clear in his autobiography. With a reported book deal of $9 million with Penguin,[10] it will have to make interesting reading to recoup those costs.

The changeover of central bank chairman is also an ominous sign. When Bank of Japan governor Satoshi Sumita retired in December 1989, the country was at its zenith. Following the Louvre Accord of February 1987, which aimed to reverse dollar devaluation, the Japanese agreed to weaken the yen. While US interest rates were raised to make their currency attractive, the Japanese slashed theirs to do the opposite. As the economy was flooded with borrowed, speculative money, the property and stock market went into rapture. Japanese property prices tripled from 1985 to 1989. In a statement that the new Federal Reserve chairman Ben Bernanke would do well to remember, the incoming governor, Yasushi Mieno, said on Christmas Day 1989 that 'rampant speculation and rising asset prices threaten Japan's long-term economic health'. How right he was.[11] Some 17 years after the handover, Japan is only just recovering after years of stagnation.

Having shied away from calling a bubble a bubble, Greenspan failed to question the exuberance of the stock market in its final, frenzied phase. When individual stocks are doubling in a matter of months then something is wrong – perhaps he did not want to be seen as a spoilsport. A whole series of events combined in the 1990s to create a bubble in stock markets: the misplaced financial incentives of stock options (see next section); conflicts of interest between analysts and corporate financiers; cosiness between auditing firms and their consultancy businesses; an overly accommodative central bank, and a series of foreign crises with debt and speculation at their heart. The final ingredient in this bitter-tasting brew coincided with the peak in the stock market. Not satisfied with the biggest-ever technology bonanza, the IT industry put it about that the dawning of the new millennium would wreak havoc with computers and all things electronic thanks to the date change. Known as the Y2K phenomenon, it was no doubt hoping that all computers would need to be replaced after 2000 to keep the world turning on its axis and to coincidentally boost its profits. To prevent a meltdown stemming from these exaggerated claims, liquidity was, as ever, obligingly supplied to the market.

Summer

The technology collapse deflated the dream that anything was possible in cyberspace. The realisation dawned that the intellectual capital of Silicon Valley could no longer provide an insurmountable American advantage. While artificially boosting the economy, the post-9/11 property bubble will be seen in future as the marker for the beginning of the end of America's superpower status. For the sake of avoiding one recession, a country that has been respected for the best part of a century has begun to waste away.

Just as there was a master plan to save the banks in the 1990s so there was a scheme to create a property bonanza in this decade. It worked as follows:

- Slash interest rates to give more money to indebted consumers and companies
- This punishes savers and encourages spending
- Ramp up the property market through low interest rates
- This promotes a feel-good factor to encourage more spending
- Reduce 30-year bond issues to stimulate pension fund demand
- Bond prices rise, yields decline, mortgage costs fall, and property is propelled
- If bond markets worry about inflation, drop hints about recessions to lower yields

The first sign of an impending recession is evidenced by a stock market crash, like those seen in 1973 and 1987. There is usually a time-lag of one or two years before the property market follows. The exception to this has been seen in the last five years, which makes it all the more worrying. In the aftermath of 9/11 it was seen as un-American to have a recession even though one was in any case in the pipeline. Shares were already tumbling in the summer of 2001 and the attack simply speeded up the process. In spite of the bounce since late 2002, the stock market rally may prove to be just a respite in what is still a long-standing downtrend. All that low rates have done is put off the inevitable crash. The longer that debt creation goes unchecked; the worse will be the outcome.

Autumn

While Alan Greenspan took retirement in 2006, many Americans will not be in a position to share the same luxury. In stark contrast to their political leaders, many will have to work to their dying day just to pay off the mortgage, with much higher taxes and fewer welfare benefits. During Greenspan's tenure, outstanding mortgage borrowing has more than quadrupled, from $1.8 trillion to $8.2 trillion, with a similar figure for the national deficit. George W. Bush's Administration has created more debt[12] than all the prior Administrations since George Washington combined. At this stage in the cycle, the Administration should be reaping a healthy crop of taxation to cover the downturn ahead. Instead it is letting it go to waste on consumer gluttony which is fuelling imports for the benefit of others. When the bad times come, there will be massive cutbacks in government spending which will worsen an already-hamstrung economy.

Like the autumn concerto of Vivaldi's *Four Seasons*, the harvest has resulted in a drunken daze. There appears to be a similar attitude among America's consumers who are too stupefied by the spending spree to think of the consequences. It is no coincidence that the four-season cycle has turned full circle back to winter. With the end of the Greenspan era, a unique situation has occurred that should fuel the rabid minds of future conspiracy theorists. With the appointment of the new chairman, Ben Bernanke, it will bring the number of Bush-appointed Federal Reserve Board members to seven out of twelve – an explainable but unprecedented event. The seven members of the Board of Governors hold the majority of the votes while the remainder are made up of regional presidents who only hold one-year terms (other than the New York president).[13]

Ben Bernanke has not got off to a good start as Fed-watchers are becoming confused by some contradictory comments.[14] He is being accused of 'flip-flopping' – changing from an inflation hawk to an inflation dove and back again.[15] Part of the problem is that his communications are more open and transparent than Greenspan so his words are easier to interpret. The Federal Reserve under Bernanke's predecessor became something of a one-man show, so the transition was bound to be a tough one. In spite of his impeccable academic credentials, Bernanke dropped an infamous faux pas in November 2002 when he let slip about turning on the monetary printing presses to avoid deflation (the quote that begins this chapter). He was guilty only of being honest but he soon learned that the family secrets must not be aired in public. He is well known as a specialist in the study of the Great Depression and its causes. He argued that the Federal Reserve had been overly zealous in using higher rates to cool the stock market in the 1920s, just when the country had been emerging from a mini-recession. He cannot afford to apply this policy, known as asset price targeting, to the modern economy. There are simply too many debt-inspired bubbles dispersed throughout the land. Now that US money supply figures (M3) are no longer being published, he is free to pump up the economy below the surface, all the while appearing respectable by raising interest rates from time to time. Either way, Bernanke has been left with a legacy that surely no one would envy.

EXECUTIVE LUNCH

The final invited guest contributing to our debt binge is the greedy executive. In this section we will see how no effort was spared to ramp up share prices in the 1990s and beyond, to cash in on a share scheme bonanza. This short-term greed not only left scandal in its wake, but also outsourced yet more American manufacturing overseas. Pension fund holidays also added to the earnings mirage as strong stock markets allowed companies to avoid paying funds into their staff schemes. The money was instead portrayed as improved earnings to enhance profits. Needless to say, many directors' pension funds were segregated from the rank-and-file's and subject to much more favourable terms. Such behaviour is now apparent with top US companies tottering under a $500 billion deficit, or shortfall, in their future liabilities. In the final act of financial madness, some have issued yet more debt to plug the gap. It takes a downturn to reveal the hidden excesses of the previous boom, like sewage floating to the surface. When times are good we drop our guard and are mesmerised by rising profits and share prices. With each upturn appears a whole new language of euphemisms or weasel words to bamboozle investors. The fancier they sound, the bigger the con.

Share option scandals were a classic abuse of a sensible system of rewarding success. If a company performs well and earnings improve then the share price should follow suit. A share option gives the executive the right to buy shares at a pre-set price below the market value, thereby making a profit once sold at their higher target level. They were useful for start-ups with little cashflow but lots of growth potential. They avoided the need to drain the precious coffers with a heavy payroll burden.

The rewards were great and could inspire hard work and dedication, but they were dangerous in the wrong hands. By 2001, they accounted for a stunning 80 per cent of executive rewards in America.[16] The temptation was to use any variety of accounting techniques to boost the profit figures to make them look great for the stock market and send the share price higher. Substantial gearing was also applied to artificially enhance returns (see next chapter). Interpretation of accounting rules were stretched to the limit and special-purpose vehicles were created to keep murky dealings out of sight. The inside conflict of interest for holders of stock options was to boost the share price in the short term for their own benefit and not concentrate on the long-term needs of the company. The mantra of aligning shareholders' interests with those of the directors was going awry, only it was never clear until after the event. While there is a clear benefit to shareholders when directors have a significant stake in the business, share options were frequently used to cut and run rather than to buy and hold.

As price targets were hit, the options would be crystallised and turned into real shares. Given that dividends are distributed on the basis of earnings per share, then the more shares that were in issue, the less each shareholder would earn. This is known as the dilution effect. However, no questions were asked because in the 1990s bull market, share prices kept rising. The surprising element of the latter stages of the rally was the way in which insiders were merrily selling their stock while promoting their company to long-term investors. With the post-2002 rebound in markets, the subject has been resurrected in 2006 with further investigations of manipulation, such as retrospectively setting the option award to coincide with a low point in the share price.[17]

OUTSOURCERY

For the majority of commercial enterprises, the biggest expense is the workforce. For option holders, such expensive items could not be spared so their jobs were outsourced or substituted with foreign labour. The greater the cost saving, the more their earnings could be enhanced and share prices could rise. We have been familiar with the crudest form of outsourcing which started on a large scale during the Industrial Revolution. Instead of making household items for ourselves or through cottage industries, Britain was one of the first countries to industrialise and mass-produce goods for both domestic and international markets. Many worked in terrible conditions, much like those in developing countries today. While mass production and outsourcing may well reduce prices, it is often the case that those who make the goods are poverty-stricken.

Today, the zealous mantra that one will hear from capitalist missionaries is that outsourcing is an inevitable part of the process of growth. With increasing education levels in the West, it allows our workforce to concentrate on the production of higher value-added goods and services to keep the developed world ahead of the game. Basic manufacturing can then be handled in poorer areas of the globe where lower labour costs, rather than educational qualities, are paramount. In this way, so the theory goes, everyone benefits in a win–win situation as developing countries move up the ladder. While this kind of cheesiness may sound good with a large helping of port during an after-dinner speech, the reality of the process is less altruistic. Companies want to cut labour costs by having the work done overseas at cheaper rates where there is less regulation and it is easier to dump pollution. The fact that their home country is losing its essential workforce does not raise an eyebrow at home or in the boardroom. In any case, manufacturers are forced to do so or would go out of business. Any benefit to developing countries is likewise overridden by the stranglehold of World Bank lending, whose debts have been repaid many times over in the form of interest, without the capital diminishing. The more they export, cut costs and privatise as per the International Monetary Fund's doctrine, the poorer they become.[18]

Once upon a time employees were the greatest asset. Now they are one of the biggest liabilities thanks to the excessive increase of employment legislation. With the build-up of the compensation racket, onerous regulations and soaring insurance premiums, then perhaps it is no wonder that companies look overseas for labour. Sensible regulation and procedures are vital elements in controlling excess, but there is a limit which has been surpassed. Winston Churchill raised a good point when he said: 'if you have ten thousand regulations, you destroy all respect for the law'. In Britain at least, the statute book is bulging while its urban and suburban citizens live in fear of violence. Every new initiative claims to 'crack down' or 'tackle' the issues while doing anything but.

While the bureaucratic stranglehold is a major part of the equation, there is also the greed aspect. Do you care about the good of your country or your workforce if your share price target is hit? This is where the carrot for one person becomes the stick for another. The ruthless reduction in costs goes beyond what is plain efficiency and becomes an obsessive pursuit of profit for purely selfish reasons. Just because one company or cell is multiplying faster than the others, it does not necessarily benefit the organism as whole: that fast-growing cell may well be cancerous. Karl Marx was not far off the mark when he made the case that capitalism carried the seeds of its own destruction, saying 'a capitalist would sell you the rope to hang him, if he thought it would make a profit'. Globalisation has certainly created economies of scale but it is a perverse system where similar goods cross paths, moving at great expense from one continent to another. Mass production brings its own inefficiencies and polluting effects, so well exemplified by farming and industrial mass production. It also reduces quality in a desperate bid to sell more and more product with less and less lifespan. Worse still, it breaks the justification for capitalism itself; that of more consumer choice. Goods are made by the cheapest, not the best, producer. In a race to survive, the quality players are wiped out and consumers are presented with only limited choice in terms of longevity.[19]

There is another end-game to outsourcing whereby our manufacturing industry is just the start of the hollowing-out process. We are now seeing highly technical projects, such as architectural design and computer programming, being sent to India. Project work can be e-mailed in the evening from the West and returned overnight from the East. The work ethic of many Asians is truly humbling yet frightening at the same time. We may well get to the point where companies that were once household names in the West will only exist on paper in whichever jurisdiction offers the lowest tax rate. By then the building blocks of manufacturing will have been lost for good, with the workforce, middle and senior management being based abroad. While making top executives exceptionally wealthy, it means that we will lose many industries forever, where once we were world leaders. Given that one third of the world's population is once again entering the free market, then this transfer of industry, technology, expertise and wealth may well be the death knell for our living standards. One day the servant will be the master.

In classic economic cycles, companies invest too much money to build capacity for a product just as the economy has peaked. Having seen great demand for their goods or services, they fall prey to the human weakness of extrapolating a trend. Natural cycles are full of feedback mechanisms to prevent such extremes but business cycles seem to exaggerate the highs and lows. In the late 1990s, companies acted much the same as consumers do now by spending too much at the peak. After the spectacular blowout for the likes of the telecoms industry, they later used better conditions and earnings to reduce their debt rather than expand. It is a key reason why employment growth has been relatively lacklustre in the USA.

Like many addicts, a relapse has occurred and abstemious corporate behaviour has now drawn to a close. This is evidenced by bank lending to business, which has surged since 2004.[20] Another more worrying aspect is the way that companies are gearing up once again by borrowing more to magnify their earnings.[21] They are under pressure from hard-nosed private equity funds that threaten a takeover, thereby ousting them from their jobs. To beat them off with a rising share price, directors must once again boost earnings and pull every lever to survive. They have therefore used bank finance for the gearing and have set about buying their shares back. This swells the magical earnings per share, so craved by analysts and investors. This aggressive activity has not gone unnoticed by the likes of the Bank of England[22] which has warned about the risk of leverage or borrowing. This was just one of five areas listed by the Financial Stability Report, including topics we have covered such as household debt and US imbalances.

The steroid-induced consumer has sprinted magnificently but is gasping with exhaustion, as evidenced by the negative savings ratio and debt burdens. Now that they are overstretched financially, companies are expected to step up to the plate and continue growth through investment spending, which is typical in the mature stage of an economic cycle. However, they see little point in increasing capacity because the return on investment will dwindle in an economic downturn. In any case, business investment only accounts for 10 per cent of the US economic output[23] or GDP. It would require a massive spending spree to take up the slack. The last thing companies require is more employees in a highly regulated and declining economy. However, employment growth is the prop for personal income growth. In the absence of low interest rates and further tax cuts, personal earnings provide the last hope for the future of the property market and hence ongoing consumption. In today's cut-throat environment, the chances of self-serving companies altruistically coming together for the benefit of the western world are in any case extremely remote.

A potent punchbowl of debt has been spiked by every participant. Next in line come the hard drugs of hedge funds. These uninvited and uncontrollable guests may well trash the house and spoil the party for everyone.

4

GATECRASHERS

There are two times in a man's life when he should not speculate: when he can't afford it and when he can.

Mark Twain

The allusion to gatecrashers refers to the uncontrollable latecomers in a much-enlarged hedge fund industry. Designed to reduce risk and enhance returns for the wealthy, these specialist investment funds have, ironically, become a time-bomb for financial markets.

GOT ANY GEAR(ING)?

Gearing is an appealing way to describe borrowing. As with the gears on a car or bicycle, it implies that there will be a more efficient ride. Leverage is the American version of the same, implying strength through enhancement of effort. The corporate mindset is forever coming up with such euphemisms to package the unpleasant. Before detailing hedge fund activities, we can witness the basic ingredients of gearing in a business. The principle is quite straightforward. First, one must find a viable project which will earn the investor more than a bank deposit. Further funds can then be borrowed to magnify the earnings from the scheme. As long as the returns are greater than the borrowing costs then a profit can be made.

No gearing
A $1 million project might generate returns
of 15 per cent per annum   = \$150,000

With gearing
We can magnify the return if we gear up by 50 per cent or borrow $500,000. Instead of employing $1 million, a larger sum of $1.5 million can be put to work.

Return on combined $1,500,000 in a project at a rate of 15 per cent p.a.	= $225,000
Cost of borrowing $500,000 at a rate of 7 per cent	= ($35,000)
Return net of borrowing costs	= $190,000

The earnings have expanded from $150,000 to $190,000, or by 27 per cent. In stock market terms, achieving that kind of growth rate is viewed very favourably. Although this example and its assumptions are oversimplified, the basic technique allows a company to change from sleepy to sexy. Even now, investors appear to be impressed by this feat. There is of course a downside. If inflation takes hold then interest rates will increase in response. Let us say borrowing costs rise to 10 per cent. In such conditions the opportunities are not so favourable in the wider economy. The rate of return may then fall to 7 per cent. Putting the figures back into this geared situation we find that the return net of borrowing drops to just $55,000. If the original $1 million project money had been deposited in a bank it would have received a similar rate of return but there would have been no risk. This is why businesses suffer from inertia and cease to invest as a recession unfolds.

Some companies have to use gearing as there is a long lead time between the beginning of a project and the payback. In a growth environment investors take more risks and actively seek such investments with more gearing beneath the surface. Smaller companies often fit this profile and performed well from 2002 to 2005. When risk aversion returns, as no doubt it will, then investors will flee from such indebted companies.

Hedge funds may apply similar techniques to transform a reasonable return into a spectacular one. In the following theoretical example, loan rates have been used that were prevalent in the easy days of 2004–05. By borrowing many multiples of the assets, the magnification can be stunning. Even when the manager has little skill and cannot beat the stock market they can artificially expand what little return was achieved.

- A fund worth $10 million goes to its bankers, or prime brokers, to gear up assets
- They borrow $20 million (not uncommon as a percentage of the assets)
- The total combined funds available for investment now stand at $30 million
- They achieve unspectacular returns of 7 per cent which generate $2.1 million
- The loan interest on the extra $20 million at 4 per cent comes to $800,000
- The overall return net of borrowing costs therefore amounts to $1.3 million
- Investors see $1.3 million profit on $10 million: a creditable 13 per cent return
- Managers take 3 per cent management and 'incentive' fees for beating deposits
- Investors ask no questions as they have received 10 per cent net of all costs

Like our previous example, the process unravels with higher interest rates. In 2006, these expenses rose above 6 per cent. The rationale for gearing evaporates as these costs are virtually the same as the return on the borrowed assets. In the past, gearing was used to enhance what was already a good rate of return. In some cases it is no longer a single weapon but an entire armoury.

THE EMPEROR'S NEW CLOTHES

In the fairy tale by Hans Christian Andersen, a crooked tailor tricked a vain emperor into parting with his money. He told him that the new royal robes were invisible only to fools. On being shown the imaginary material the emperor pretended to admire the cloth for fear of seeming stupid. His courtiers fell into the same trap to avoid being ridiculed. Their vanity and acquiescence held them back from speaking the truth. It took the laughter of an innocent boy in the crowd to expose the sham on the day of a public procession.

In 1998 a spectacular hedge fund crash saw one of the largest and most respected funds atomised in a financial black hole. It was called Long Term Capital Management, or LTCM for short. The emperors were the board of directors who made up the roll-call of the great and good of both academia and Wall Street. The obsequious courtiers were the banks and brokers who bent over backwards to lavish services and credit to generate their fees. The humble peasants were the investors who bought the funds. Sadly there was no mischievous boy to laugh at the situation. Much like a beautiful stranger, the secrecy and mystique of such funds add to the passion and desire of investors. If the manager gives the impression that the fund's activities are so complex and secretive that they will move the market if disclosed, then investors become desperate for a piece of the action.

LTCM was set up by Jon Meriweather who was a star bond trader on Wall Street. The founders and directors included two Nobel Prize economists and other academics. The investment idea behind the fund was quite brilliant and concerned the convergent behaviour of government bonds over the long term. It relied on small yield changes over time which could be magnified through the use of multiple gearing. As with the courtiers who felt that they alone had the ear of the emperor, each bank was willing to lend generously, grateful that such a prestigious fund should give them the business. It transpired that LTCM was using some 75 counterparties[1] (or financial institutions) to source its credit. The list of lenders reads like the *Who's Who* of banking. The fund had borrowed 50 times its capital, leaving the financial system dangerously exposed when it crashed. Billions of dollars worth of derivative and bond investments were due to be unloaded into an already nervous market so the New York Federal Reserve orchestrated a private sector bail-out to prevent an even wider financial crisis.

As ever, if an investment methodology is working well then no one questions it until the first cracks appear, by which time it is too late to act. In the case of LTCM the process worked wonderfully while the market was orderly, but when the Russian government defaulted on $40 billion of its domestic bonds this caused a contagion or panic effect. Investors sold off less liquid foreign government bonds and fled into US Treasuries. This blew apart the two sides of the yield convergence principle and huge losses were incurred. The models had not taken into account that during panics there is a liquidity crunch imbalance where safe assets perform well but illiquid (hard to sell) assets perform much worse.

The lesson from this episode is that hedge funds make some assumptions on risk, which can be difficult to offset or hedge. Value at Risk (VaR) models which stress-test the investments within portfolios cannot cover all the bases. One of the big selling points is that of a low level of correlation to stock markets with absolute returns achieved for a lower level of risk. However, in times of crisis bad events beget others: dirty secrets that were well hidden will suddenly emerge at exactly the wrong time. We are now being told that borrowing among funds is low by historic standards. This does not take into account the possibility that those assets may be invested in derivative products that are already highly geared. When an investment is founded upon multiple layers of leverage it has a habit of destabilising when pressure is applied. Whenever one suggests a possible repetition of LTCM at swanky hedge fund conferences the patronising head-shaking routine begins. 'Our risk models are different this time around.' Perhaps what they are really saying is 'Can we interest you in some of this lovely cloth ...?'

HEROES AND HORRORS

There is some debate over who was the first hedge fund manager. In Barton Biggs' *Hedgehogging* he suggests that economist John Maynard Keynes should be credited with the title.[2] Legendary investor Warren Buffett instead puts forward his mentor Benjamin

Graham as an early example of such operations in the 1920s. Rightly or wrongly, an American called Alfred Winslow Jones is most often cited. He set up a fund in 1949[3] and first came to prominence in 1966 when his skills were brought to light in *Fortune* magazine. Within two years, some 140 similar funds were on the scene. In the distant past, whenever the stock market fell, the majority of investors would suffer as there were few safe havens. Hedge funds can reduce some of these risks by protecting themselves in a process known as hedging, often using derivative contracts. The latter have been in use for over a century in the arena of real goods or commodities, providing protection against falling prices. Speculators take on some of these risks, operating between farmers and food manufacturers, in the hope of making a profit, and provide liquidity in the process.

Hedge funds can take advantage of these insurance mechanisms to reduce their volatility and enhance their potential. Those with proper risk management can provide reasonable upside performance but lose less on the downside compared with conventional portfolio managers. As well as buying stocks they favour, fund managers can also make money from shorting the ones they dislike. 'Going short' means that one can profit from a price decline. It involves selling a share that you do not own then buying it back at (hopefully) a lower price, thereby profiting from the price difference. Before everyone rushes out to become short sellers, there are some cautionary tales to observe. First, if you own something, the price cannot fall below zero so you have limited downside. However, if you sell a stock that you do not own and your judgement is wrong then your losses are unlimited. This is for the simple reason that a price can rise to infinity but can only fall to zero. Second, the most obvious things to sell have already encountered plenty of bad publicity, so the negative sentiment will already be factored into the price. The life of a short seller is a lonely one, requiring intuition, contrarian thinking and a dose of luck. Few investors possess such skills.

Some of the most famous managers, such as George Soros, Jim Rogers, Bruce Kovner and John W. Henry, to name but a few, have shown that skilled investors can and do beat the markets:

not necessarily year-in, year-out, but over reasonable time-frames. Their funds come in all shapes and sizes with a mind-boggling array of strategies. Hedge funds used to be the preserve of the super-wealthy and were often restricted to limited partnerships of fewer than 100 investors. In some cases they are by invitation only. This stemmed historically from exemptions within regulations drawn up by America's Securities Exchange Commission (SEC). They included the Securities Act (1933), the Securities Exchange Act (1934) and the Investment Company Act (1940).[4] By carefully following the rules, it allowed hedge fund managers to invest with very few restrictions compared with their tightly controlled counterparts, the onshore mutual funds. The general partner was also the investment manager and they would place a large portion of their personal wealth into the fund, thereby giving investors faith that monies would be managed responsibly. By domiciling the funds offshore with large minimum investment sizes, they receive much less attention from regulators given that inexperienced investors do not usually get involved. Those who are wealthy enough to buy them should have a good idea of the risks involved and a greater immunity against losses, should they come to fruition.

Hedge funds in their own right have been great investments for many years. Some of the managers are the most interesting, intelligent and insightful people one could hope to meet. They deserve to be wealthy because they have made money for their clients in good times and bad while sharing the risk in the process. However, there are many managers who have been distinctly average, particularly those who have arrived late on the scene. The line between gearing and skill has become blurred, although this can be calculated using the latest quantitative techniques when analysing price moves. With the rise in US rates, gearing's diminished effectiveness is separating the men and women from the boys and girls. Many new funds have chased higher risk markets to boost returns, drifting into areas well outside their expertise, such as sports teams and film production,[5] notorious for their uncertainty. The meltdown of Amaranth (which traded in natural gas futures) is a case in point, losing billions of dollars in September 2006. It appears that the market can cope with individual fund crashes, but it remains to be seen if rescue packages can be worked out should multiple failures occur.

It has not always been an easy ride for these funds. In the late 1960s poor market conditions brought on hefty investor outflows. The assets under management for the largest funds were drained[6] by some 70 per cent. Even in modernity it can be tough to survive. Wall Street legend Barton Biggs points out in his book *Hedgehogging* that some 1,000 funds went out of business in 2004. This was a near-perfect year for accommodative interest rates. Because of their success during the 2000–02 bear market in shares, the popularity of these absolute return funds exploded. From barely a few hundred 20 years ago, their number grew to 600 in 1990 then to 3,300 by 1998. Some 8,800 are now in existence.[7] By 2004, assets under management had swelled to a staggering $1 trillion in value (one thousand billion). This compared with some $7 trillion invested in US mutual funds and around $30 trillion worldwide in conventional pension and investment funds. By September 2005, hedge fund inflows had continued to grow, bringing the overall total[8] to an incredible $1.4 trillion. Their true purchasing power is anyone's guess, given the level of gearing that can be generated from this asset base.

The funds play a significant role in the market and can even reduce risk in illiquid areas when searching for inefficiencies. They also punch above their weight in terms of trading volumes on the stock exchange, reaching up to half of daily turnover[9] in some markets. This is because they are such active traders compared with traditional investment managers who tend to buy and hold investments for longer periods. Because they can have a large variety of assets in their portfolio they are very well spread, or diversified. Instead of just being stuck with traditional shares and bonds they can go short or take on exposure to oil, precious metals and different currencies. If there is an asset that moves in price and a futures market to hedge the risk, then you will find these funds.

In so-called arbitrage they can play both sides of a trend by purchasing a takeover target (whose shares will rise) and shorting the acquiring stock (whose shares will fall when, as usual, the buyer pays over the odds for the company). They have even become major players in the energy market by stepping in when Enron collapsed. The multiple styles and strategies have meant that they have traditionally enjoyed low correlation with conventional investments. In the past, some would actually benefit in declining markets, or at least not fall as much. The layers of different strategies tend to preserve wealth in a downturn in the classic case of not putting all your eggs in one basket.

This is beginning to change. In the past five years, returns have halved to just 8 per cent per annum compared with an average of 16 per cent per annum[10] in the 1990s. We see that greater risks have been undertaken to generate what are lower rates of return than in the past. One piece of evidence for the rise in mediocrity can be seen by examining the rolling returns of the average hedge fund versus the average portfolio manager[11] with 70 per cent in equities and 30 per cent bonds. The returns of both are not only similar but also reveal a striking correlation to the stock market as a whole. Their ability to diversify away from equities appears to be weakening, especially since early 2003. In this unsatisfactory environment of higher risk and lower returns, the management fees have been expanding. In 2005 these fees amounted to a stunning $16 billion,[12] according to Hedge Fund Research Inc.

As alluded to in this section's title, the shrewd and nimble heroes have been crowded out by horrors tapping into their success. The markets are generally efficient so bargains are few and far between. When you have just a few players exploiting anomalies then it is a sustainable situation. It is rather like prospecting for gold where a few pan-handlers make some great finds and the environment is unharmed. When word of a gold strike gets out, there is too little to go round and the hills are ruined by soil erosion and cyanide. By the end of the rush, the only people making money are those who sell the picks and shovels to the hopeful latecomers. Time and again we take a process that works well then abuse it such that it eventually withers on the vine. Our attitude to nature is likewise unrelenting and exploitive. We revel in its fruitfulness yet destroy it by industrialising the production process and polluting the very source of its growth.

This phenomenon appears to be happening with hedge funds now. There are too many players crowding into a limited market like an excess of predators with too little prey. To make matters worse, a new breed of investor has joined the foray. To avoid the risky nature of being exposed to one single hedge fund we now have reams of funds of hedge funds. They are so numerous and similar in nature that they resemble a colony of penguins, looking and sounding the same. As ever, one should be careful to avoid generalisation, as there is a minority of notable exceptions to the rule. Such products typically package between 20 and 100 hedge funds encompassing hundreds of strategies with no doubt a great deal of overlap (and plenty of hidden charges). Instead of picking specialist dishes off the menu, investors are getting every possible assortment mixed into a glutinous porridge. This approach is often bland and uninspiring. They exist because there is too much risk of a single fund going into default so one needs to hold a variety to diversify. The lack of transparency makes due diligence difficult for the ordinary investor so they rely on a fund of funds manager to do it for them. People within the business understand that fraud in a little-regulated area is more likely compared with a listed company which is regularly reviewed by analysts. Although tiny in proportion to the number of funds, the number of civil case actions[13] brought by America's SEC has risen from 10 in 2002 to 29 in 2005.

Perhaps the best sign that the industry is close to maturity is the news that pension funds[14] are looking to increase alternative asset exposure. These retirement funds dwarf every other investment animal, having accumulated huge sums over decades of contributions. If pension trustees allocate even a small percentage into hedge funds it will quash any hope of achieving excess returns. The managers find it difficult enough to invest existing assets effectively: the best have already closed their doors to new money. Some of the areas where hedge funds operate are like meadows of delicate wild flowers. Let in too many ramblers and they will trample the very thing they have come to savour. There have already been several portents of the dangers that lie in wait. Their battering in the spring of 2004, 2005 and 2006 should have been enough to make new investors approach with care. Although there was some reduction in gearing after 2004, it was obvious that there was no wholesale clear-out of leverage. A dollar devaluation or further rise in bond yields would cause chaos for these funds, many of which would be driven to a forced liquidation of illiquid assets across the world. When everyone funnels toward the same narrow outlet, a log-jam ensues leaving little room to escape. Prices can fall spectacularly under such conditions.

Some fund managers had previously complained about the lack of market volatility which had reduced the opportunities. They should have been careful what they wished for. Although interest rate rises had been well-flagged and discounted, it seemed to come as a surprise to many of these managers. In the spring of 2005, markets sold off as hedge funds reduced their gearing in tandem because borrowing costs mounted. Assets had to be sold to pay back the loans. Up until that time the funds had been borrowing in dollars and investing overseas. When borrowing in a weakening currency it is favourable because the size of the debt shrinks when you repay the loan. The realisation dawned that as US rates rose, it would create a suction effect on the world's capital which was then drawn toward America. The dollar began to strengthen and caught many on the hop. For hedge funds the damage came in four uneasy hits to their performance:

- The cost of borrowing increased
- The dollar strengthened leading to foreign exchange losses on non-US investments
- The simultaneous liquidation strategy of so many funds worsened the price declines
- As they all rushed for the same exit, the correlation of unrelated assets began to rise

Borrowing in dollars meant they were 'short' of the currency. When it strengthened, they made losses on overseas investments. Dollars had to be bought back to reduce risky gearing. A 'short squeeze' then followed which drove the currency higher still. Speculators never seem to learn this simple lesson. In early 2006, dollar investors lost around 25 per cent when tempted in by the seductive high yields on Icelandic bonds. As the trapdoor opened, the currency bombed and bond prices followed. High yield bond markets from the Arctic to Africa were ditched in tandem, creating a self-feeding fall.

One selling point of hedge funds is that they are meant to complement your portfolio by reducing the correlation across different assets within it. If investments move in the opposite direction to each other, then that is negative correlation, which is a good thing as it allows one's portfolio to stand firm in a variety of conditions. With too many funds and too few opportunities, the performance of risky investments across the world has started to converge and correlate,[15] thereby negating the diversification benefits of the original investment philosophy. Instead of being strong oaks, many funds have turned into fragile saplings at the mercy of the wind. If evidence were needed of their diminishing opportunities one can look to the stock market for clues. Listed hedge fund companies[16] carry rather dowdy valuations which implies that their performance and business models exhibit low growth potential, which does not sit well with the marketing material.

MINDERS AND BOUNCERS

There is a terrifically difficult balancing act where hedge funds are concerned in attempting to match sensible regulation with innovation. On the one hand, you have the investment banks, known as prime brokers. They act like footballers' agents who pamper the stars and look after their every need. Investment banks make all the arrangements for hedge funds' dealing, borrowing and general banking. They are very well rewarded for their services and in this sense they are the minders.

On the other hand, you have the bouncers who are trying to keep order and prevent the bad apples entering the system; these bouncers are known as financial regulators. They are becoming more and more concerned about the amount of gearing and derivative activity sloshing around the financial system. Much like the Lloyd's insurance market of the 1980s, you may be able to hedge or insure your bets but it is unclear where these risks are accumulating. So what can regulators do to come up with an overall score of hedge fund gearing and risk? The answer is that they cannot do so all along the chain but they can monitor the activities to some degree. Many of the individual managers are based onshore in major capitals such as New York or London. So too are the investment banks that lend them money, as are the dealers with whom the funds place their trades. The problem lies with the fact that many funds are based in offshore jurisdictions. While some have listings on well-regulated stock exchanges such as Dublin, this is done to lend an air of respectability rather than being a guarantee of investor protection.

The Financial Services Authority (FSA), Britain's financial regulator, has been investigating the activities of a high-profile hedge fund with billions under management. The head of wholesale banking regulation, Tom Huertas, summoned the 30 biggest funds for a meeting to warn them against market abuse. Another of their leading officials, Hector Saints,[17] said 'some hedge funds are testing the boundaries of acceptable practice concerning insider trading and market manipulation'. In America, the SEC attempted to increase transparency by making hedge fund managers register as investment advisers in February 2006. The amendment of the 1940 Investment Advisors Act was rejected a few months later in June when a manager called Philip Goldstein took the SEC to the US Court of Appeal and won. Since the Amaranth crash, regulators from both the UK and the USA have wisely called for a borderless control of derivatives. One can only have sympathy for their role, of having to hold a tiger by the tail while blindfolded.

The Achilles' heel of hedge fund transparency goes back to the old chestnut of a potential conflict of interest, which is the curse of every boom. This time around it may well be the incestuous relationship between investment banks and hedge funds. New managers frequently find that they cannot attract money without real performance, yet they cannot establish a performance history without real money. Unless the investment manager is a household name the fund will need initial money, called seed capital. An investment bank may well provide this money as such banks are always looking for opportunities. There is, however, a price to pay. In return for seed capital the investment bank will expect to receive reciprocal business for its largesse. There is always potential for conflict when you have an industry that benefits from selling to itself. Collectively, it would appear that the prime beneficiaries of servicing the hedge fund business are those who are best positioned to spot potential problems. Like so many previous examples, it may be difficult to ask too many questions or rock the boat.

Investment banks earn money from hedge funds in the ultimate example of cross-selling. First, the assets need to be held somewhere so a custodian bank account can be set up to hold the investments – for a fee, of course. Second, when a trade is placed in the market a dealer is provided and commissions will be earned. Third, they provide contractual settlement whereby the hedge fund manager can deal with virtually any broker without having to go through all the usual mounds of paperwork. Fourth, and most important, they provide borrowing facilities to gear up, including stock lending for going short. Every need is catered for by the friendly prime broker.

Having seen a slump in the early 2000s, the investment banking world went through some lean times, but the prime brokerage business proved to be a godsend. Credit Suisse First Boston[18] estimated that hedge funds generated around an eighth of worldwide investment banking revenues in 2004. This figure came close to $19 billion. A further $6 billion was generated from prime brokerage services of granting credit and providing custodial services for trading. Looking at the crude mathematics of the business, it would seem that the prime brokers made $25 billion on $1 trillion of hedge funds, which equates to 2.5 per cent of the total. If investment managers are taking another 2 per cent as performance and management fees, then the funds will have to churn out returns in excess of 4.5 per cent annually just to break even. It is little wonder they use gearing of between 100 per cent and 500 per cent to achieve their aims. No matter how it is dressed up, high gearing is high risk, especially when interest rates are in the ascendant.

PASS THE PARCEL

Having once been the preserve of the very wealthy, being a Name at the Lloyd's insurance market in London was opened up to a much wider audience in the 1980s. By a curious coincidence this was also the period when asbestosis cases started to emerge. These individuals would act as guarantors to the insurance companies. If the claims were no greater than expected they would reap a reasonable reward which could pay the school fees. In the rare event that anything went wrong then there was a danger that they could be called on to contribute towards the insurance claims. Years of apparent success built up apathy and high expectations, rather like the property market today. Much like bookies, insurance companies like to offset their risk. This is where re-insurance companies come in to reduce the potential losses. In the children's game of pass the parcel, when the music stops, the child with the multi-wrapped present must unpeel a layer to see if they are the lucky winner. For insurance companies the parcel is not a prize but a punishment, as they are left to pay out a large claim. By dividing out smaller parcels of risk, the liability is spread around more evenly. It should always be remembered that these risks do not simply disappear as they are always somewhere in the system. For anyone who has supervised a children's party, they will be familiar with the spoilt child who, to stand a greater chance of winning, will not pass the parcel. Insurance risks similarly converge in the wrong areas as speculative re-insurers become greedy and take on too big a share. Like toxins in a food chain, risks concentrate and emerge in the most unexpected of places. As re-insurance syndicates took ever-greater gambles, some did not appreciate how exposed they would be in a disaster. This may provide a parallel with some hedge funds today.

The Lloyd's fiasco was a fine illustration of how risks are not properly estimated and complacency reigns supreme where a 'good thing' is concerned. When it turns sour, there are knock-on effects that reinforce the law of unintended consequences. Names were simultaneously forced to sell their mansions and London maisonettes in the middle of a property slump, thereby creating a glut of similar properties on the market. The inevitable price decline set in and bargains abounded. This is why it is so important to build up cash rather than debt at the peak of a boom. Another unexpected side-effect could be found in the fine art market which was swamped when demand was already thin on the ground. These are usually the first items to go when wealthy families are faced with bankruptcy or inheritance tax. A salutary lesson can be drawn: when a downturn takes hold, from whatever source or quarter, you must not be one of the panicking herd selling assets into a falling market, be it for shares, property, fine art or even fine wine. It is far better to be the bargain basement buyer.

The thorny topic of credit derivatives, or synthetics, has echoes of the Lloyd's insurance market. After the Savings & Loans crisis, we saw how banks borrowed cash to buy higher yielding government bonds to profit from the difference in yield. Hedge funds have gone several steps up the risk ladder using the same method. Instead of buying government bonds they have bought emerging market debt instead. Riskier still, they have acquired bonds from highly indebted companies such as General Motors (GM). To protect themselves against the risk of such companies defaulting, or not meeting interest payments, some funds bought insurance on GM bonds in the form of credit derivatives. Because of its deteriorating financial position, GM's bonds were downgraded in 2005 so the price fell and the yield rose even further. By holding credit derivative insurance, some funds were able to protect or hedge themselves. Judging by the scramble to buy the insurance after the downgrade, it appears that many funds were not properly insured. They had been hoping, as usual, for the best outcome[19] without preparing for the worst.

The concern about credit derivatives is three-fold. First, there has been a massive growth in their use. In 2004 the market increased by 123 per cent, creating an exposure of $8.4 trillion[20] to these instruments of insurance. In 2005 they grew by 105 per cent such that their so-called notional value stood at $17.3 trillion,[21] which is in excess of all outstanding corporate debt on the planet.[22] The total derivatives market across all sectors is worth an incredible $298 trillion. To put this into context, the value of such instruments was equivalent to less than a third of the world economy in 1990 but equates to nearly 800 per cent of global GDP in 2006. Much like the Lloyd's re-insurers, someone somewhere must be exposing themselves to these credit risks. For the second concern, these contracts are traded over-the-counter between banks and do not pass across an exchange where regulators would be able to monitor their activity. Third, the paper-based system for confirming trades is so old-fashioned and snowed under that it is taking up to a fortnight[23] to settle some deals. The problem became so acute that several leading investment banks were summoned in 2005 to see the New York Federal Reserve in order to introduce an electronic system. A year on from this meeting, things have improved but deficiencies remain, particularly with the lack of contract standardisation. Should a corporate default occur, and the credit derivative contract has not been settled, then the party that is meant to pay up may attempt to renege on the deal. Although unlikely in current conditions, in the event of widespread bankruptcies – which are typical in a slump – it may be used as a survival tactic for those who entered the market thinking that underwriting was a doddle.

While we have emphasised hedge fund risks, we should spare a thought for another source of leverage which is growing in the form of private equity funds. They raised $260 billion[24] in 2005, using this capital for substantial leverage. The threat of takeovers from such funds has led the management of many listed companies to gear up and artificially improve earnings; just when the opposite course of action should be followed. Although such funds have been around for two centuries, they are using huge gearing to buy companies, strip costs the bone and sell them on at a profit. These deals are getting out of hand in terms of size and it is likely that a mega-deal will mark the pinnacle of such vulture-like corporate raids. When a large company gets taken over by a small private equity fund with massive gearing then it will be time to back away from these investments. The costly takeover of Germany's Mannesmann by Vodafone in early 2000 marked the pinnacle of TMT (Telecom, Media and Technology). It would be the ultimate irony and top-of-the-market act of hubris should Vodafone in turn be taken out in this manner.

Debt is overwhelming consumers as interest devours disposable income through mortgages, loans and credit cards. Western governments are running up a burden of deficits for both the present and the future. Investment banks and hedge funds have added to the mire. We have had our fun in the boom times: a hangover is now inevitable.

Part II
HANGOVER
Financial Fallout

5
DELIQUENT $

Permit me to issue and control the money of a nation, and I care not who makes its laws.

Amschel Mayer Rothschild, 1838

The quote above from the son of the founder of the Rothschild banking empire carries a chilling clarity that still rings true some two centuries later. Those who feed and foster debt creation will ultimately control the community and country they are meant to serve, just as Thomas Jefferson foretold at the time. While there have been numerous currency devaluations for weak nations over the years, it is also clear that large economies are no less immune. We see that mistakes from the past are repeated time and again as empires wax and wane in their repetitive cycles: starting with insecurity and ending in arrogance.

From occupying a position of trust, the dollar has been defiled into a mass-produced, manipulated currency. We are facing devaluation on an unprecedented scale which will catapult commodities such as fuel and food prices to unbelievable heights. The catalyst for the reaction may well be a reduction in Asian appetite for US bonds which will send short- and long-term interest rates spiralling. In this chapter we will examine the evolution of the dollar and how it came to occupy its dominant position as the so-called reserve currency. We will then see how artificial stimulation of the US economy has led to its overproduction. Its fate now lies with foreign powers that grow wearier of holding it by the day. Having examined the multiple causes of debt's escalation we may also experience its many hangover effects. There are several elements lining up in a classic precursor to an economic slump: excess debt, currency devaluation, price inflation and rising interest rates. The end result is poverty. This was the experience of Latin America in the 1980s and today we see how Third World debt has desiccated its victims in Africa. As its countries are bled dry by interest payments to the West, its people similarly suffer.

As argued by Michael Rowbotham in *The Grip of Death*, inflation is not caused by the classic economic mantra[1] of 'too much money chasing too few goods'. If anything, we have too little money, which is why so many use credit cards simply to survive. As our meagre wage increases steadily lose purchasing power, so we must borrow more to keep pace with prices. It is likewise clear that there is a huge surfeit of manufacturing capacity across the world, which produces too many goods. From couples starting out to companies starting up, all must take on huge burdens of borrowing. The front-loading of debt today means prices must rise in future in a never-ending game of catch-up.

FISTFUL OF DOLLARS

It is no coincidence that in spaghetti western films starring the likes of Clint Eastwood, the hard-bitten bandits would always be on the hunt for gold rather than cash in times of trouble. The modern dollar evolved from two conflicts on home soil: namely, the War of Independence and the Civil War. At the time of the Declaration of Independence in 1776, the Continental Congress issued paper-based money called Continentals to finance the revolution. This had no backing from silver and gold, but the theory went that once the British Redcoats had been sent packing then the notes could be redeemed against the future flow of tax revenues. The Continentals soon became worthless as inflation made its usual wartime appearance. As America's first President, George Washington, once said,[2] 'A wagonload of currency will hardly purchase a wagonload of provisions.' After the currency devalued and went out of circulation, there was a deep distrust of paper money for years to come. Although it briefly emerged during the war of 1812 against the British, it remained dormant for another half-century.

During the American Civil War of the early 1860s, the Southern states issued Confederate currency in paper form with no backing from precious metals. The Confederacy printed more than double the amount of notes compared with the greenback dollars of the North,[3] and inflation was rife. In a smart move by the Yankees, the enemies' currency was counterfeited[4] and liberally distributed in the South: the loss of confidence led to further inflation, from which devaluation and defeat became inevitable. By the 1880s, America's establishment as the world's industrial leader was well under way. However, its industrialisation was not a straight-line progression. Prior to World War I there were frequent financial crises, as seen in 1873, 1884, 1890, 1893 and 1907. Money could only be created in proportion to the amount of gold in circulation, which was in turn a reflection of its supply from fresh discoveries or successful export of goods overseas. During a downturn the lack of gold meant that the economy was gridlocked, although cash could always be found to fund wars. Even during Britain's Industrial Revolution, mass production made goods plentiful but poverty was widespread,[5] leaving little money to purchase them. Any country following a gold standard was constrained because it could not increase money in circulation without extra gold or silver. The Federal Reserve Act was therefore passed in 1913 to allow for a more 'elastic' money supply. Its official role[6] has expanded to promote stable prices, economic growth and full employment while regulating the flow of money and credit. Some commentators say that the Act was unconstitutional because it went directly against the Constitution set down by the Founding Fathers, whereby gold and silver were considered to be the only legal tender. As the great market observer Richard Russell once quipped, the phrase on dollar bills 'In God We Trust' should perhaps be replaced with 'In Gold We Trust'.

The Coinage Act[7] of 1792 was passed by Congress whereby the value of the gold dollar coin was fixed at $19.75 per troy ounce. To buy that same gold ounce would now require $644 (July 2006), some two centuries later. Not surprisingly, the bulk of the dollar's loss has occurred since the establishment of the US Federal Reserve. The greatest dilution followed the abandonment of the final vestige of the gold standard in 1971. Since Alan Greenspan became Fed chairman in 1987 the dollar has roughly halved. It had already devalued in the two years prior to his entering office, thanks to the Plaza Accord (see later in this chapter): shrinkage on such a large scale has gone largely unnoticed. This is because inflation figures are only compared with the previous month or year and not the last five, ten or fifteen years. Reality is about to catch up with these inflation-mongers who have permitted the proliferation of debt-money for the benefit of banks, while allowing our agricultural, industrial and savings culture to decay. It is the younger generation who must pay the price of this profligacy. The sins of the fathers will indeed be visited upon their sons and daughters.

SPIDER'S WEB

While America is the spider, the dollar is the sticky web that ensnares us all: every thread of silk is indirectly linked to another around the world. Should any foreign insect become entangled, its wrath is soon visited upon the lesser prey. Just 20 years after its own civil war, America became the emerging market powerhouse of the Victorian era. While the use of slave labour and government subsidies is often overlooked in the way the West was won, a good deal of success can be attributed to the determination of tough, risk-taking immigrants. They were willing to try their luck in the new world where everyone had the right to better themselves. America's work ethic and access to raw materials allowed it to overtake the arrogant and maturing British Empire, symbolically around the time that the *Titanic* sank.

America dominated manufacturing[8] with reasonable-quality goods that were cheaper than the competition, thanks to low levels of taxation. Americans were also renowned for their frugality and saving, in the finest traditions of their Puritan roots, so there was plenty of money for investment. The behaviour of their modern descendants is in stark contrast to their ancestors, more closely resembling Britain in the hedonistic 1920s. High standards of living are now demanded as a right and not a privilege. When a country is the leader in world trade or is the strongest superpower (the two often go hand-in-hand) then it may achieve reserve currency status, as is the case for the dollar today. Whether voluntary or not, its use is widespread as a conduit for worldwide trade. When that country loses the qualities that made it great in the first place then a decline of the currency is inevitable. We have seen it all before with the Roman, Byzantine and Ottoman Empires, to name but a few. The one-time supremacy of the British pound reflected Britain's military strength and dominance of international trade and finance. By the end of World War II the pound was usurped by the dollar as Britain became utterly indebted to both America and its own colonies. Only one currency will tend to hold reserve status as it is a reflection of a monopolistic position.

In July 1944 the Bretton Woods system was formulated to provide the financial stability that had been so lacking before World War II. As the world's richest country and largest holder of gold, it made sense to introduce a system of fixed exchange rates against the American dollar. By 1946, the US had accumulated roughly $26 billion worth of gold[9] out of a world total of $33 billion. Along with this financial might, America was also the world's leading producer of coal and oil. The dollar therefore provided a mooring to which other currencies could cling. Its value was defined as being $35 per ounce of gold. This was not a true gold standard of the past but what was called a gold exchange standard where foreign countries looked on dollars as a proxy for gold as the two were physically interchangeable. As the decades progressed, America's protective wing allowed the economies of Japan and Germany to expand aggressively. The latter were also willing hoarders of US bonds such that by the 1960s, central banks held twice as many US dollars as British pounds. The Allies had at least learned the lessons of the doomed Treaty of Versailles: it is better to nurture one's defeated foe than punish them and let resentment fester unchecked.

As America's involvement in the Vietnam War became more prolonged and costly, the fixed exchange rate mechanism began to strain at the seams. It was clear that far more dollars were being printed than could be justified by any backing from gold.

A series of speculative and political attacks broke the system as the British pound devalued in 1967 and France put the convertibility of dollars into gold to the test. President Nixon closed the so-called gold window on 15 August 1971, so as to keep a hold on the remainder of America's precious metals. The loss in confidence led to capital flight and Nixon imposed a combination of price and wage freezes, import tariffs and a suspension of the convertibility of dollars into gold. Although the crisis was not as damaging as the break-up of the 1930s gold standard, the dollar once again devalued in 1973. This set a painful backdrop for the rest of the 1970s such that the main currencies became free-floating. Without the firm grip of the golden anchor to restrain its creation, the dollar has since been swept away on an ocean of debt-money.

Rather like a well-maintained toll road, international trade flows down the same convenient route whereby commodities such as oil, precious metals and foodstuffs are quoted in US dollars. America is rewarded with a built-in demand for its currency as global trade supports the demand for dollars. Although it is not a prerequisite for a reserve currency to be a perfect store of value, its continued deterioration could one day see it discarded from common use. Oil- and commodity-producing countries want to be paid with a strong currency and not a weakening one.

Much like President Nixon's Administration, the current Bush regime has fallen into the quick-fix trap of mass-producing dollars through bond issuance, this time to pay for the war in Iraq. It is just one of many items on the government's shopping list of 'must have' projects. Instead of being trustees of the global economy they are selling the family silver and remortgaging the estate. So far they have been able to abuse this blank cheque book status because of the built-in demand mechanism. Foreign central banks are now backing away from placing new money into dollars and are instead looking to diversify elsewhere. Any future world powerhouse will no doubt demand that globally traded commodities are priced using a basket or combination of mainstream currencies. While China has been coy about reducing its overwhelming dollar holdings, others have been more forthright. Arab states are lining up to make their views known. The United Arab Emirates, Syria, Qatar and even Kuwait have declared their intention to divest themselves of some dollar exposure in favour of euros. In the case of Syria[10] they plan to end the currency peg altogether. In April 2006, Qatar's central bank governor said that they may hold up to 40 per cent in the euro. Even Sweden and Switzerland are getting in on the act. Although none of these countries are big players on the currency markets, the sentiment is not helpful. The drip-drip effect of their statements must be cause for concern. While not necessarily aggressive in their intent, the moves reflect a general caution towards US assets and America generally.

In November 2000, Saddam Hussein called for oil to be priced in euros, which did little to aid his popularity in America's eyes. Left-wing President Chavez of oil-rich Venezuela is also believed to be in favour of this approach. In 2005, Iran once again proposed an oil market in euros, although such a move would be unlikely as long as OPEC (Organisation of Petroleum Exporting Countries) maintained its general policy of pricing oil in dollars. This was designed to inflame tensions as America pushes for the abandonment of Iran's nuclear power programme. While linking the repricing of oil with military intervention may be the stuff of conspiracy theories, one should not ignore the symbolic damage to America's prestige. Removing the dollar as reserve currency is a big threat to America's hegemony because for the first time it puts a genuine ceiling on its spending.

We have already mentioned Paul Volcker, who was Alan Greenspan's predecessor as chairman of the Federal Reserve. Professional courtesy has led him to place a five-year timescale[11] on the likelihood of a full-blown dollar crisis. In April 2005 he referred to the economy as 'skating on thin ice'. On the surface, Ben Bernanke, the new Fed chairman, seems to be doing his job by raising interest rates at a reasonable clip. This has supported the dollar as 'hot' portfolios flows are being drawn toward the United States. By 'hot' we mean not long-term money but speculative inflows attracted to a rising interest rate environment.

This money can leave just as quickly as these 'investors' have the loyalty of a head louse. While many investment strategists feel that higher rates are a sign of responsible action, few acknowledge that the economy is being flooded with debt below the surface, like the *Titanic* was holed under the waterline by the gashing iceberg. As we saw with Mexico in 1994, when loans start to mature in ever-increasing quantities and the Treasury looks to renew them, foreign investors get scared by the sheer scale of the obligations. While the likes of Latino governments will always be more vulnerable because foreign debts have to be repaid in a hard currency, Americans can print their own paper to pay off foreigners at will. This situation cannot go on forever, especially if their reserve status is stripped away.

One Congressman has recycled John Connelly's quote from the Nixon era of 'our dollar, your problem' where foreigners are concerned. In fact, a weaker dollar is everyone's problem as we are now ensconced in a world of currency weaklings. To return to the *Titanic* analogy, on a stricken ship the decks may lurch from bow to starboard, or from dollars to euros in this case. The fact remains that the vessel as a whole is still sinking and it doesn't really matter which side of the railings you cling to. In future, we may find that, much like a tiny lifeboat, the only escape route from the domino effect of devaluations is by holding the currencies of small, conservatively run countries with little debt. The likes of the Swiss franc and Singapore dollar spring to mind, but even they cannot exist in isolation. As many survivors swim to the few remaining life-rafts – swamping them in the process – the resulting currency strength could likewise overwhelm these relatively small economies. One should not forget that when a big ship sinks it creates a vortex that sucks down any lesser vessels that remain in the vicinity.

In 1985 a conference took place which resulted in the Plaza Accord, so-named after the plush Plaza Hotel in New York. The leading G5 countries at the time, namely America, Britain, Germany, France and Japan, agreed to let the currencies of the latter four countries strengthen, while the dollar devalued. In order to get out of recession and rebalance their economy, the Americans needed to weaken their exchange rate. Theoretically, a softer currency makes a country's goods and services cheaper for foreigners, so exports grow and the economy recovers. When the Louvre Accord was signed two years later in 1987 to halt the process, the dollar had lost some 51 per cent of its value against the yen.

The positive case is now being made that a weaker dollar is good for exports and hence earnings for US companies. However, devaluation has a dampening effect in those very markets that America is trying to export to as foreign countries are hurt by stronger currencies at home. One consequence of similar events during the Great Depression was a round of competitive devaluations which eventually led to trade tariffs (tax on imports) and protectionist behaviour. One might even see a reversal of globalisation which up until recently has helped to smother inflation. For now, it is clear that US companies are struggling to maintain market share[12] and are becoming less competitive.

TOPPLING TALOS

The vacuum-effect of the US property bubble has sucked imports in from the rest of the world. The outpouring of dollars to pay for them has grown in proportion. If it had been any other nation, the lack of equalising exports would have long since devalued the currency. However, the very people who benefit from manufacturing these goods are also mopping up the excess dollars that are flooding the world. By purchasing dollar-denominated US government bonds, this keeps the greenback artificially in demand. In theory the good times will never cease as the money is in a permanent loop, like water in a fountain. The problem from here is one of capacity: there is only so much water, or supply of dollars, that the fountain can hold before it floods. There must also be an end-point where consumers grow weary of spending, just as addicts may become sickened by their own self-indulgence.

As America's oil reserves dwindle and energy prices move ever higher, dollars must once again flow out to pay for the import of these commodities. Much like any other product, if too much currency is sloshing around world markets then the price will fall in the absence of further demand. In the case of currencies, 'price' is the exchange rate or purchasing power. Without demand from incoming investors it will weaken as surely as a severed artery renders its victim lifeless. One scary childhood memory fits the bill perfectly. In the 1963 film version of *Jason and the Argonauts*, the giant bronze statue of Talos comes to life to fend off the crew of the *Argo*. The sailors spot the warrior's weakness and dislodge the nail on his heel, which bleeds the ichor, or essence, from the haunting metal monster. The gushing of his lifeblood renders the giant unconscious, buckling and creaking into an undignified mess.

In 2005, the financial inflows required to refill America's dollar circulation reached a staggering $2 billion[13] a day. It is therefore no wonder that foreigners hold almost half of the US debt through Treasury bonds. So far this flow of funds has been achievable. Even as Asia's appetite for dollar bonds is dwindling, the shortfall is being bridged by petrodollars, or petrol profits,[14] recycled from the Middle East. Historically, money from wealthy nations used to flow to poor countries. Perversely, this process has reversed with the savings of poor nations going to the wealthy. Asians will continue to accumulate America's mass-produced bonds, but only if the US keeps buying Asian goods. Like a drug supplier when you stop buying their merchandise, they have a habit of turning nasty. While this is not currently a perceived threat, it may well be in future if China continues to gain strength in proportion to America's decline. In rather superior tones, Ben Bernanke implied that America was doing Asia a favour[15] by giving it a place to park its glut of savings. This appears to be a convenient excuse for the underlying problem: that debt creation is the easy way out in the short term but destructive in the long run.

The way to look at the flow of funds is through the balance of payments. There are two components to this balancing act, known as the current account and the capital account. The current account shows the difference between what you earn from abroad (exports, services and investments) and what you pay out to foreigners (imports, services and loans). A country running a current account deficit is most likely importing too much and exporting too little. This is the case with America which is destabilising because of the sheer size of the imbalance. We are well beyond levels where ordinary countries would encounter a full-blown financial crises, and the situation is worsening. Running at a blistering 7 per cent at the end of 2005, it is forecast to rise[16] to 10 per cent by 2010. It should be remembered that before the dollar halved as a result of the Plaza Accord, the current account deficit was just 3.5 per cent. A significant but little-publicised milestone was passed in 2005 when the interest paid out to foreign investors exceeded the income coming in from America's assets overseas.

Like any business, a country that produces a surplus may then build up reserves for a rainy day. The money can be used for new investment without having to borrow. Just like going overdrawn, a deficit implies that one is living beyond one's means and that is not sustainable. America must approach its trading partners and borrow money to fill the trade imbalance. If there is a current account deficit ($900 billion for the USA in 2006) then this must be offset by incoming flows through what is called the capital account. This measures the course of foreign money coming in for financial investment. In the past, America had very healthy flow into the capital account. The combination of a dot.com boom and soaring stock market brought in both foreign direct investment (FDI) and share buyers. With two sources of investment-related demand, the dollar strengthened significantly. The position has been reversed such that America has to sell bonds, and lots of them, to make up the shortfall. The country is mortgaging itself to the hilt yet holding the mortgage provider to ransom. For now, foreign central banks are obliged to buy these bonds, otherwise their existing reserves would be hit. For every 1 per cent fall in the dollar, China's reserves lose roughly $10 billion in value.

To overcome the current account deficit, a country can engineer a slowdown through higher interest rates, which reduce the demand for imports. Alternatively, the currency can be devalued, thereby boosting exports and making overseas assets[17] more valuable. However, America is now pinned in the grip of an iron maiden, unable to move either way. Rising rates mean that the interest paid to foreign bond holders will increase which in turn worsens the deficit. They will also push house prices over the edge. Meanwhile the devaluation option is inflationary for import prices and oil. Interest rates must once again rise, thereby worsening the deficit: each move leads to the same checkmate position, or debt trap. It is not just foreigners that are recognising the inherent weakness – US investors are also switching assets overseas in record volumes.

CHINESE LAUNDRY

The phrase 'Chinese laundry' is not meant to be a disparaging remark about traditional Asian businesses in this field. Instead, its aim is to conjure up an image of a washing machine spinning on a continuous cycle, like the flow of dollars around the world. China's domestic position has improved enormously as a result of its currency being pegged to the dollar. As well as providing credibility, it has allowed for its surpluses to be reinvested in America to keep the growth cycle going. It works as follows:

- As a leading low-cost manufacturer, China exports goods around the world
- Trade surpluses have increased their reserves (savings)
- Money is ploughed back into the country through infrastructure projects
- Infrastructure improvements increase efficiency and the standard of living rises
- A new middle class emerges and they become consumers in their own right
- The trickle effect of wealth creation spreads throughout the economy
- Education and reform (not the IMF version) entrench world leadership

As we saw in earlier chapters, the relentless drive to push down US bond yields has fostered a spending spree and indebted America in the process. It has been perpetuated by Asian buying of the dollar and dollar bonds as follows:

- US consumer boom sucks in imports from overseas
- The payment for the imports leaves a glut of dollars
- US government bonds are bought to engender equilibrium
- This keeps bond prices artificially high and yields artificially low
- Lower bond yields equal lower mortgage rates, thus stimulating the housing market and the consumer ... and so the cycle continued in a never-ending spin

In a classic case of unforeseen consequences, America has nurtured its own decline. The hidden outcome of this sequence, where everyone apparently benefits, is that the manufacturer eventually overtakes the borrower, much like America displaced Britain. The country which everyone had assumed was still a sweatshop is instead becoming a sophisticate. Throughout investment banks in the City of London one will often see framed pre-Cultural Revolution Chinese government bonds as a reminder of how big countries can default. The bond certificates are multicoloured and immaculately designed. It would be interesting to fast-forward 50 years when perhaps dealing rooms of Shanghai and Beijing will be covered in worthless bond certificates issued by America. They may reflect and inwardly smile in that inscrutable Asian style, remembering how the US debt bubble funded the rise of the new Chinese Empire.

As part of their cultural heritage, the Chinese like to describe themselves as 'descendants of dragons',[18] the dragon being a symbol of adaptability and change. These qualities are once again emerging after two centuries of domestic strife and foreign oppression. With the end of the Napoleonic Wars, the demand for imported Chinese goods led to silver being sucked out of Europe to pay for them. In order to reverse this flow of precious metals, addictive opium was shipped from India by the British East India Company and sold to the Chinese. In spite of the fact that opium was illegal in both China and Britain, the British demanded that it be traded freely. By 1840 the gunboats were sent in and China was forced to accept the humiliating Treaty of Nanking. This proved to be the first of two so-called Opium Wars, and a further series of settlements were imposed over the next 60 years. Following the 1895 Sino-Japanese War and Boxer Uprising of 1900, foreign powers indulged in a game of geopolitical take-away with yet more concessions wringed from China. In spite of further attempts at modernisation, the last emperor abdicated following the Xinhai Revolution of 1911–12. Suspicion of foreigners did not stop with the end of imperial rule. The Treaty of Versailles handed German interests in the region to Japan and not back to China. The behaviour of the Japanese occupiers during World War II is still an extremely sensitive subject.

Given that the country is famous for the discovery of silk, the production of this ultra-strong material bears some useful comparisons with China's emergence. The voracious silkworm gorges itself incessantly and sheds its skin several times as its body expands. China has likewise grown at an abnormal rate, devouring the world's natural resources in the process. The strong silk that is spun into a protective cocoon is like the accumulation of financial reserves. The dormant phase that follows symbolises the change that China must undergo such that domestic consumption balances out export-driven growth. This is typical of countries that evolve into developed status. If this transformation can be achieved then China will emerge in a self-sustaining cycle, and may one day take on the mantle of reserve currency, with all the benefits this entails.

Any description of China will inevitably contain superlatives of size. It is now the biggest holder of foreign exchange reserves. These accumulated assets are expected to hit the $1 trillion mark[19] in 2006. The main feeder of these funds is the huge trade surplus which came in at $102 billion in 2005. Its GDP grew by 9.9 per cent[20] in 2005 compared with a subdued 1.8 per cent in Britain; overtaking the UK in the process as the fourth largest economy in the world. Typical of many Asian cultures is the strong degree of self-reliance in a country where provision of public services is minimal. This has led to savings rates[21] in the order of 40 per cent. The government would like to encourage a higher degree of personal consumption to unwind these saving pools. The timing of the move from export growth to domestic consumption should prove to be fortuitous as the external situation deteriorates.

While Britain and America make the case that their service economies are the ultimate panacea of development, it is clear that there is a missing link in the so-called value-added chain. As economists at ABN Amro so rightly point out,[22] Anglo-Saxon economies are running serious trade deficits which mean that service industries by themselves are not bridging the gap. Trade deficits go hand-in-hand with overseas debts. These in turn generate further outflows in the form of interest payments in the debt trap described earlier. As Japan and Germany have learned, high-quality manufacturing has to be nurtured to minimise trade deficits.

The low interest rate environment in America spawned a boom in consumer-related activities and real estate. These are domestic concerns which are not exportable but tend to draw in yet more imports. Just as China has to rebalance from exports to domestic consumption, Britain and America must do the opposite. This is hardly likely to happen as outsourcing has discouraged industrial development, which in turn is not conducive to the promotion of science and engineering. The declining interest in these demanding subjects at both school and university is a concern for all our futures.

PEKING PEG

In this section we will cover the controversy that relates to the peg – now loosened – between the currencies of China and America. This link to the US dollar was established to provide an anchor for China's currency, referred to interchangeably as the yuan or renminbi. 'Yuan' means 'round object' while 'renminbi' means 'people's currency'. There are restrictions on the capital account through which investment flows in or out of the country. By controlling these channels it stops speculative money rushing in temporarily then leaving just as quickly at the first sign of trouble. It also prevents domestic deposits going the other way. These restrictions help to protect the currency from exposure to the ravages of financial markets. This is particularly important in a country where the banking system is weak and bad debts abound. More importantly, control of the currency is in government hands and not in those of speculative foreign forces. In many ways, the peg is becoming outdated from a Chinese point of view. Tying a country with growth rates of 10 per cent (China) to one with growth rates of 5 per cent (USA) is bound to create imbalances. It is rather like a midget trying to march in step with a giant. China is under pressure to cut the pace by letting its exchange rate appreciate, thereby curbing growth. However, it is China's recycling of growth-related surpluses that has allowed America to issue debt at will, without the usual inflationary consequences – until recently. The surge in oil and inflation-sensitive gold since 2001 was no coincidence.

Just like post-war Germany and Japan after Bretton Woods,[23] China is maintaining a fixed exchange rate so the economy is overheating. The trade surplus in Asia is of course in direct contrast to the trade deficit in America. It resembles the yin and yang of opposing forces as formulated by philosophers of the early Han Dynasty, some 2000 years ago. To rebalance the imbalance, logic dictates that the renminbi must be allowed to strengthen significantly and without restraint. This would please the protectionists in America who think that a weaker dollar will magically create jobs at home. It would also allow China to cool the domestic boom, reduce pollution and encourage a more sustainable rate of growth across a wider spectrum of the economy. In a cross-linked globalised world, such simplistic solutions are not that straightforward. On the Chinese side, the subsequent cutback in foreign bond purchases would hurt the US dollar. This is very painful when the bulk of its reserves is invested in dollar bonds and would also push up US interest rates. It is estimated that Asian bond purchases have suppressed US yields to roughly 1.5 per cent below where they should be. Should Asian central banks cease their buying programme, the rise in short- and long-term rates would cripple an already weak US housing market along with the export-led Chinese economy.

The pressure from the US Congress to force further strengthening of the renminbi is a classic example of looking for an easy foreign target to cover up faults created closer to home: a case of fiddling with the thermometer rather than curing the patient. The Chinese are only doing what America did to Britain in the nineteenth century. It is called competition and is something that capitalism is meant to encourage. The trade deficit in America is as much down to the overstimulation of its home economy. This is evidenced by the existence of a domestic budget deficit (government spending too high, taxes too low) and a negative savings ratio (consumers have already spent their nest eggs). The phrase 'win the battle, lose the war' springs to mind when dealing with China. Having endured some 170 years of external threats and pressure, it will be interesting to see how it behaves when it comes to have the upper hand. The recent stick-waving by America may be first on China's list of paybacks should relations worsen.

In spite of the unfair pressure, the Chinese have been nothing if not pragmatic. They understand that they are not yet ready to emerge in their own right but must first build up greater critical mass, like the hungry silkworm prior to forming its cocoon. They have played the game to perfection such that on 21 July 2005 they took the first step to ease the currency peg. This was welcomed by the then US Treasury Secretary, John Snow, who had been chief protagonist for a renminbi revaluation. The move appeared to be more symbolic than practical[24] as it was only allowed to appreciate by a mere 2.1 per cent. It was enough to keep the Americans at bay for a brief period but not enough to make any significant difference to the US trade deficit. When labour costs are 1/20th of those in the West, it would take a far stronger currency to make the slightest dent in China's competitiveness. One year later, it had appreciated by just 3.5 per cent.

The push for renminbi revaluation would appear to be misplaced. If China and America were competing in the same areas then it might make sense. However, the Chinese manufacture basic goods while America specialises in high technology. A stronger yuan will not make widget factories or blast furnaces appear in America, so why create such tensions? It seems that the motivation to single out the Chinese is driven more by emotion and politics. The de-pegging in 2005 proved not to be enough for the US Treasury Secretary, who dropped hints that China would be officially labelled a currency manipulator. This system is a hangover from the 1988 Omnibus Trade Act which requires a twice-yearly report on currencies. Originally designed to counter Japanese import penetration, it sought to eliminate unfair advantages through the suppression of foreign currency values.

It has since been amended[25] by the 2005 Fair Currencies Practices Act. This makes the definition of manipulator clearer, as well as widening the scope for satisfying those conditions. When the chance came to issue the tag[26] on 10 May 2006, the US Treasury Department had the good sense to back off. In a week when the dollar was already groggy, an announcement that would have reduced the need for US bond purchases could have sent the so-called greenback sliding in value. Instead, the IMF will be enrolled to put pressure on China to revalue. This will further strengthen the attitude that the IMF is a tool of American policy. When it was set up in the Bretton Woods era, it was supposed to foster stability through fixed exchange rates. Yet here it is trying to unbundle the very thing it was created to encourage.

Senators Lindsey Graham and Charles Schumer[27] have lobbied for populist legislation aimed at imposing tariffs on imported Chinese goods (27.5 per cent across the board) if they do not revalue further. This has since been dropped by the Senators. As protectionist calls from American politicians grow louder, one can only hope that the use of tariffs is not undertaken. The lessons of the Great Depression appear not to have been learned. Like devaluation, the imposition of tariffs pokes a stick in the delicate wheels of international trade and relations. Such behaviour also paves the way for nationalism and military tension. Very few countries are equipped to deal with trade wars where prices would rise and the transformation to self-sufficiency would lead to serious shortages. America's revaluation call is the ultimate act of self-delusion. The Chinese will keep the cycle going for as long as it suits them and decide when to fully detach. By then they will have diversified into gold and real assets to minimise currency losses. They will also use their financial clout to build up strategic reserves in petroleum and mineral products. While China pulls off the masterstroke of the twenty-first century, Washington is stuck in the twentieth with talk of tariffs.

Further pressure has been applied following the World Trade Organisation's (WTO's) call to revalue, coming just before the G7 meeting in April 2006. The Group of Seven leading industrial nations demanded immediate action on flexibility – for which read a stronger renminbi. Interestingly, the statement was not backed by Japan: at least one developed country understands the future political landscape. China's central bank governor Zhao Xiaochuan rebuffed the call,[28] saying that the exchange rate was just one part of macroeconomic policy. Attention was also drawn to the lack of representation for Asian countries outside of Japan, in spite of their leading industrial role.

The scholar and environmentalist Bill McKibben has highlighted some interesting points in his article[29] 'The Great Leap'. He said that a city the size of Houston must be built every month to keep pace with the influx of people from the countryside. Although China has a third of the world's farmers, it has just one 1/14th of its cultivated land. This implies that an army of potential workers is on hand to keep a lid on labour costs. Existing manufacturers are turning out half of the world's DVD players and digital cameras, a third of all laptops and a quarter of all mobile phones, televisions and stereos. As high-tech industrial and science parks proliferate in the new cities, so the workforce is climbing the intellectual ladder. Like a game of grandmother's footsteps, China's progress has caught America unawares and is right on its tail where trade is concerned. A head-to-head contest in high technology may become a reality in the years to come. If a depression ensues in the West, we could even see a 'brain drain' from America to the Orient as skilled, mobile workers move abroad in search of jobs.

There is now a clear recognition that China's future is an industrialised one, albeit with less pollution. In no time at all, it has become the world's second largest market for consumer electronics, behind America[30] and there is no reason why other merchandise should not follow suit. As evidenced by the restrictions on what the Internet search engine Google can display on computers in China, its politicians are not yet ready for full, unfettered exposure to western influence. What's more, foreign companies will subserviently toe the line for a chance to worship at the altar of China's market share.

Any research on that country will soon uncover the quote by Napoleon Bonaparte, 'Let China sleep, for when she awakes, she will shake the world.' This quote was very much a reflection of the time as the country was in decline just as Europe was in the nascent stages of industrialisation. If anything, China has been the dominant culture for all but a few centuries during the previous two millennia. We are fortunate to have been allowed to develop while the dragon was hibernating in its den. That cosy period is now drawing to a close. We seek comfort from the assertion that the Chinese simply replicate our products and intellectual capital. We have even convinced ourselves that they have little innovative spirit. This convenient stereotype may well be rudely shattered when we are reminded that this is a nation whose ancestors were among the greatest inventors and trailblazers in technology, art and design. The arrogant catchphrase by an American economist of 'we think, they sweat' will no doubt come back to haunt him. In a parallel with the rise of Britain and its subsequent displacement by America, perhaps the real world powerhouse will one day be India once China has in turn peaked.

The hangover that follows the good times is upon us. Piece by piece the portents of a downturn are aligning. As Asian support for the dollar dwindles, higher interest rates and bond yields beckon. The weakening dollar will then unleash a surge in commodity prices. This next inflationary ingredient will, paradoxically, make our debts deflationary.

6

BLACKOUT

My father rode a camel. I drive a car. My son flies a jet plane. His son will ride a camel.

Saudi Saying

SEVENTIES SIMILARITIES

A new era may be upon us for the price of commodities, or raw materials, whose previous pinnacle was attained in the late 1970s. For some, those days inspire gaudy visions of bell-bottom trousers and brown bath suites. There are equally unpleasant memories of clutching candles during the blackouts and bad-tempered queues at petrol pumps. Middle East tensions, culminating in the Arab-Israeli War and the Iranian Revolution, were the hallmark of the decade.

There are plenty of parallels to be drawn between 2006 and 1976, both in terms of fashions and financial markets. A search for similarities can yield clues for what may lie ahead. Although natural to focus on experiences during one's own lifetime, we should also remember that cycles have climaxed and crashed over many hundreds of years. Price spikes in commodities are often based on natural weather patterns, population changes and war. Like the arrival of several buses after an insufferable wait, the Murphy's Law factors that crystallise such crises have an uncanny knack of coinciding.

Comparisons with historic cycles, let alone those in living memory, are fraught with discrepancies but are worth noting. Like the Vietnam War, the current conflict in Iraq smacks of an open cheque book policy. The 1970s saw both Britain and America playing fast and loose with deficits and liquidity creation,[1] thereby stimulating a consumer bubble. They also kept interest rates too low for too long to make up for negative effects of the oil shock. There are likewise plenty of dissimilarities: unions were all-powerful and interest rate policy was set with eyes on political popularity rather than inflation. The biggest difference – and one which few investors have truly grasped – is that the lack of supply in the 1970s oil shock was politically driven. This time round a geological shortage is in sight: a very different scenario indeed. Throughout the past four oil crises (1973–74, 1979–80, 1990–91 and 2000) there was always enough oil capacity underground[2] to meet international demand. Although current reserves can meet today's demands for the next 40 years, the problem is that our demand is set to rise beyond recognition thanks to China's emergence and likely consumption in future.

The likes of Capital Economics[3] have made a convincing case that producer profitability will build enough capacity to meet demand and that commodity optimists are simply extrapolating an unusual trend of catch-up. It assumes that commodities are undergoing a cyclical recovery that will soon wear off, or are just a measured rally in response to strong demand from China and America. This may well be true in the short term but we should also consider the case that better extraction techniques and technology are simply using up the known resources more quickly, rather than discovering new supplies of any significance. In stark contrast to office-bound economists, specialists in energy and geology such as Matthew R. Simmons, author of *Twilight in the Desert*, disagree with assumptions that market forces will find a solution.

There comes a point for many commodities where the cost becomes excessive so we naturally seek out a substitute, such as plastic piping instead of copper. In the case of oil, a surge in price is spawning a viable industry for renewable energy. Much like a desert after a flash-flood, the potential for life in an apparently barren environment only becomes clear after the storm. When oil prices were laid low in the late 1990s, there was no incentive to look elsewhere for alternatives so apathy reigned. Now that prices have spiralled we are more willing to accept unconventional options. What was initially deemed as unworkable or impractical suddenly comes to fruition. This is all part of the human conditioning process. Rather like Roger Bannister beating the four-minute mile, once it was shown to be possible then others soon followed suit and surpassed it.

HARD OR SOFT

So what are commodities? They are quite simply the things that we use every day, even when we sit down for breakfast or start the car. These two simple activities could use up wheat, coffee, sugar and oil, to name but a few possible items. They are broadly defined as hard and soft, where hard commodities are the product of mining and soft commodities the product of growing. The soft commodities are agricultural, and are subdivided into the likes of grains (such as wheat and soybean), livestock (cattle, pigs) and food and fibre (cocoa, coffee, orange juice, sugar). The softs are typically renewable. Agricultural prices are dominated by weather conditions and crop disease which are in the lap of the gods. They tend to be less frequently used for investment purposes due to their unpredictable nature.

The hard variety includes industrial metals (aluminium, copper and palladium, for example), precious metals (gold, platinum, silver) and energy (crude oil, heating oil, natural gas). Hard commodities are characterised by their limited source and non-renewable nature. They require significant capital outlay for both initial extraction from the earth and for the subsequent refining thereafter. In theory, the progress of hard commodity prices is more predictable given that their demand – or lack of it – is related to economic activity. Since 2001, this has been the 'hot' area for the market and substantial gains have already been experienced.

Investors own commodities in order to diversify away from 'paper' investments like shares and bonds. They are also bought as a protection against unexpected bouts of inflation. Some price surges can be temporary phenomena, perhaps caused by sudden supply shortages – man-made or otherwise – such as flood, fire and famine. A recent example was seen in 2005 when Hurricane Katrina virtually eliminated the oil refining capabilities in the Gulf of Mexico. Inflation can also be long term or structural and this is the hardest to eliminate. It may be associated with drawn-out military conflicts or periods of widespread debt creation and is a monetary phenomenon. When countries devalue their currencies under such conditions, they may experience prolonged periods of rising prices in spite of an economic collapse. It is in such extreme scenarios that our basic instincts for hoarding come to the fore. We subconsciously seek to accumulate real or tangible assets, such as commodities, that can feed or transport us or be bartered. Gold has been the ultimate bargaining tool for much of recorded history.

Since commodities bottomed out in late 2001, up to the peaks in May 2006, gold has trebled while silver has quadrupled. However, the real action has been in base industrial metals such as copper, which skyrocketed from just above $1,000 to over $8,000 per tonne in the same period. Energy products have likewise been hot, with crude oil prices trebling. The reason for this surge is down to a polar shift in demand that has stemmed from China and other emerging countries. Coinciding with the urgency for such materials, hard commodities are themselves diminishing because there is only a finite or limited supply. The ability to extract them is seriously hampered by the underfunding and lack of investment that accompanied the two-decade commodity slump. What is truly surprising is the performance of commodities when adjusted for inflation. Taken over many decades, stock market investments – once dividends are included – have outpaced inflation to give a so-called 'real' return. This has not been the case for commodities which are way behind their inflation-adjusted secular highs of 1974. If tangibles were to catch-up with inflation then there would indeed be a great upside. The final element in this tale of diminishment is that new discoveries have been few and far between. There has been little impetus for exploration because much of what is readily available has already been discovered. There have been no major oil finds for some 35 years. Future exploration for metals and oil will require serious quantities of capital. A lack of investment in mines and refineries has left them unable to cope with the scale of demand.

To capture the overall move in a market, investors use an index to collect the most important data in one place. Much like the FTSE-100 index represents the biggest UK companies across different industries, commodities have similar indices to represent their performance. The oldest is the CRB or Commodity Research Bureau index which began trading New York in 1986. The split in the index is roughly 60:40 in favour of hard over soft commodities. The main problem with it is that each area of the market is given an equal weighting. This in turn is not a true reflection of financial reality where the energy market is of far greater importance than the likes of livestock. Although the overall commodity indices have rallied well, it is the hard components that have been on a tear. Some of the soft commodities have barely managed a 50 per cent return since the upturn began. No doubt they will have their day as China is now a net importer of grain while American inventories have experienced their second biggest downgrade in history. It is the classic commodity problem of too little supply in the face of rising demand.

Indices have been constructed to follow the progress of these markets including the energy-heavy Goldman Sachs Commodity Index (GSCI) starting in 1992. The later Dow Jones-AIG Commodities Index offers a more diversified content. The commodities guru Jim Rogers created another measure of performance in 1998[4] called the Rogers International Commodity Index. It has outperformed the other major indices since its inception. His timing in creating it was impeccable, being very close to the low point in commodities. It was also the 'new paradigm' era when nothing but technology mattered. As he points out in his book *Hot Commodities*, while other financial institutions were pulling out of the commodity business, he was busy creating an index with which to invest efficiently into the market. This is just one more example of a great contrarian mind going against the herd to catch the beginning of a trend. One message from all the indices comes through loud and clear. There is no getting away from the fact that the high oil and gas content reflects our insatiable energy demand.

There is a very clear relationship between a weaker dollar and rising commodity prices, which has no doubt contributed to the rally. This has two elements within it. First, when the dollar weakens, it is cheaper for foreigners to buy commodities so businesses will purchase raw materials at these points, assuming that demand is still buoyant. Second, the weaker currency is also an expression of elevated import penetration into America. Suppliers must buy materials and build replacement stock to meet future demand. However, these are symptoms of the good times. We should also prepare ourselves for a scenario where the dollar weakens because the US economy is hitting the buffers. This will doubtless hurt Chinese manufacturing and damage demand for commodities. There will be a tug-of-war between the weak dollar pushing prices up and declining demand from Asia, dragging them down. The side that wins will depend on how quickly China generates its own consumer base. Using the 1970s as a guide, currency weakness overcame economic weakness where commodity prices were concerned.

In the Victorian era, the major powers sought to spread their influence and reap the benefits from the colonisation of defenceless countries. As the competition mounted, European powers carved out great tracts of the African continent, whether they needed them or not. This process became known as the 'Scramble for Africa'. Like dogs growling over bones that they did not necessarily want, jealousy and insecurity were inspired by this land-grab. The necessity to service these colonies with a large naval presence led to the arms race and ultimately the waste of World War I. A similar scramble is going on today for influence over the supply and production of all kinds of commodities, especially oil. The overbearing nature of American foreign policy in recent years is giving developing countries all the excuses they need to look elsewhere for allies.

As ever, the consensus-driven nature of our behaviour makes us too aggressive in the good times and too cautious in the bad. Banks call in loans after the economy has bottomed out and companies slash their workforce just prior to a recovery. Commodity producers had likewise scaled down their investment in new capacity when prices started their drawn-out decline in the 1980s. Compounding the problem, emerging countries were desperate for foreign capital in the late 1990s following the Asian and Russian crises. To generate overseas earnings, the likes of Russia were desperate to sell oil at a time when prices were already falling, thereby exacerbating the problem. Much like Lloyd's Names who were selling their fine art into a depressed market, the Russians were flooding the world with their black gold when the price was a mere $10 a barrel. Few oil companies could fathom the logic of investing in further exploration and refining capacity when the value of their product was so low. As ever, the best time to invest or act against convention is in an environment of fear and capitulation, when there are no compelling reasons to do so. With oil trading between $58 and $78 over the course of 2006 there is plenty of drive to undertake infrastructure investments that should have been activated years ago.

Some newspapers are referring to the oil spike as though it were just another price spurt, little understanding that the fundamental differences are seismic. With China and India emerging as new consumers in their own right, their populations want commodities and they want them now. Aspirant people of any culture desire air conditioning and cars so it is no surprise that Asians should share the same ambitions. It was, after all, the mantra of the globalisation crowd who wanted new markets to sell into. However, the emergence of one third of the planet's population from self-imposed hibernation may be too much for our natural resources to bear, rather like an elephant turning up at the waterhole and draining its contents. For now, some 3.5 billion Asians are consuming almost the same amount of oil as just 0.3 billion Americans (around 22 million barrels per day). The world's daily usage is roughly 85 million barrels per day. The combination of Chinese and America demand was responsible for 58 per cent of the increase in 2004 and 43 per cent in 2005. Just a marginal elevation in Asian living standards would cause an unquenchable demand for extra oil. In April 2006, the US Congressional Budget Office[5] said that rising Chinese demand alone could increase prices by $14 per barrel over the next five years. This may well prove to be a naive forecast.

SUPER-CYCLES

There are frustrating times when financial markets appear to exist for the sole purpose of extracting the maximum amount of money from the greatest number of people. Weather and commodity patterns can be equally impish. No sooner has one discovered a recurring cycle with fixed periods than it disappears like a will o' the wisp. The past can only ever provide encoded warning signs with which to mark the general themes of the cycle.

Economists have trawled through data to find these elusive cycles. An early pioneer was the Russian Nikolai Kondratieff,[6] whose 1925 essay entitled 'Long Economic Cycles' concluded that there were cyclical peaks and troughs lasting roughly 50–60 years. Kondratieff analysed a host of factors associated with the economic cycle such as wages, interest rates, raw material prices, foreign trade and bank deposits. Like any ground-breaking research, it is easy to pick apart assumptions of the work many years later. His concentration on wholesale price patterns gave the impression that their trough coincided with a depression, which was not always the case. Kondratieff used seasonal comparisons to describe each phase of the cycle with a spring and summer up-wave and autumn and winter down-wave. From the expansion of spring, economies taper toward a summer phase of stagflation. The latter periods are associated with crisis points known as 'peak wars'. It reminds one of bee colonies that get irritable in the sultry heat, then swarm and separate into two colonies. Each up-wave cycle has coincided with conflict, such as the war of 1812, the American Civil War, the Great War and most recently the Vietnam War. In the second half of the wave, there is an autumnal stage, characterised by debt creation, consumption and benign inflation.

This appears to be the phase that we have just passed through in modern times. A long, cold winter of depression then follows which eventually wipes the debt-slate clean. We may now be on the cusp of just such a season. Canadian financial analyst David Chapman has used the Kondratieff wave principle to map out an updated version of the cycles. Table 1 illustrates the dates, starting from the late eighteenth century, and is based on the US economy. Table 2 is a modification of Table 1 and highlights the number of years involved, to make the trend a little clearer.

Table 1

		Periods	
Spring	Summer	Autumn	Winter
1784–1800	1800–16	1816–35	1835–44
1845–58	1859–64	1864–74	1875–96
1896–07	1907–20	1920–29	1929–49
1949–66	1966–82	1982–2000	2000–20 (?)

Source: <http://www.gold-eagle.com/editorials_02/chapmand062902.html>.

Table 2

		Cycle length (in years)		
Spring	Summer	Autumn	Winter	Total
16	16	19	9	60
13	5	10	21	53
11	13	9	20	53
17	16	18	20 (?)	53 (?)

Source: Author's modification of data in Table 1.

It is interesting to note that the most recent autumnal cycle of 18 years (which brings us into modernity) has been distinctly elongated, compared with equivalent episodes in the 1860s and 1920s. It also appears that the associated symptoms of debt creation are still ongoing, even beyond the 2000 cut-off point indicated. It is no wonder that so many politicians and business people think that booms and busts are a thing of the past. Such arrogance in the face of natural cycles is asking for trouble. Reliance on past patterns should not, however, be depended on to provide perfect turning points. The brilliant Bob Beckman wrote an inspiring book[7] called *The Downwave: Surviving the Second Great Depression*. Its publication in 1983 should have marked the beginning of a downturn based on several classic long-wave cycles coinciding. However, it proved to be the beginning of an era of unusually strong growth. His work is not invalidated – it just needs updating.

Jim Rogers cites some examples from the last century[8] of positive performances from commodities when stock markets were in the doldrums. These were 1906–23, 1933–53 and 1968–82, giving an average rally of some 17 years. The nineteenth century turned out similar phases in 1823–38 (15 years) and from 1848–65 (17 years). These figures may well be down to sheer coincidence and should not be used as a stand-alone reason for selling the house and buying a commodity fund. The severe sell-off in the third quarter of 2006 provided a much-needed lesson in why no market is a one-way bet. Using the past as purely an empirical guide, one could say that we have another ten years of rising raw material prices. Given that the latest commodity rally started in 2001 then it could be many years before inflationary pressures – so far disguised by the 'core' figures – ease. We should also bear in mind that all of these cycles occurred while the West had the upper hand in the world. This may not continue.

While the analysis of periodicity is interesting in its own right, it may well be a case of making a science out of art. There are numerous market cycles for different periods – Kitchin, Juglar and Kuznets – to name but a few. Like some aspects of religion, we can easily become obsessed and overzealous about the specifics of each style: proclaiming them to be the one and only true theory. They all have their merits and drawbacks and we can only hope to cherry-pick the best elements of each. Before proclaiming commodities as the next big thing we should first examine the possible pitfalls. No doubt there will be further spikes and sell-offs for tangible assets along the way. Failing short-term trades that turn into long-term investments are a right of passage for every investment manager. To put the recent rallies since 2001 into some form of longer-term context, we have been through one of the worst bear markets in natural resources since the dawn of the Industrial Revolution, in the two decades from 1980 to 2000. There is a good deal of distrust in this asset class, which is perfectly normal as the longer the last bear market, the harder it is for investors to shrug off their cynicism.

There are three possible negatives for commodities in the near term. First, demand is heavily influenced by Chinese growth. This is driven in turn by the export boom stemming from the US housing bubble. An economy cannot grow at high rates continually, much as stock option holders would want it to. A period of consolidation is required so any pause for breath will no doubt hit commodities. Second, as interest rates rise around the world, it chokes off the cheap source of funding required by speculators, who have no doubt played their part. Finally, we have seen a surge in the number of investors piling into commodity-related hedge funds. Their number has more than doubled, rising from 200 at the end of 2004 to 450 a year later. This may explain why speculative interest in the futures market has trebled[9] since 2004 levels to $130 billion.

Bull markets in any asset often start with some kind of fundamental shift or change which does not necessarily register in the psyche although it may be blatantly obvious with hindsight. Aside from a weaker dollar and supply shortages, commodity demand is inevitably driven by population and economic growth. Real people consume real items: the greater their number, the more is needed. The number of humans has been notching up at an increasing rate. Table 3 shows the population milestones and associated dates.

Table 3

Year	World population	Year	World population
1800	1 billion	1975	4 billion
1922	2 billion	1988	5 billion
1960	3 billion	2000	6 billion

Source: Population Reference Bureau, 'Transition in World Population', March 2004.

In the 13 centuries between the fall of the Roman Empire and the birth of the Industrial Revolution, the rate of population growth was modest. Plagues and pestilence played their part in capping the number of people and diminishing the harvests to support them. The improvement in healthcare and sanitation coupled with the industrialisation of food production – and the infrastructure to transport it – led to a population explosion that is unlikely to be repeated. More people have been born since 1950 than in the past 4 million years.[10] Over the last century, procreation has turned 1.6 billion souls into some 6.1 billion. The world population is expected to continue its rapid rise and level off with some 9 billion people by 2050. Almost the entire growth is expected to come from developing nations. The 'so what' of this human growth story is the relevance of its demand for raw materials. While there is some scope for agricultural output to keep up, the problem lies with the non-renewable items that have to be mined or drilled from the ground at great expense.

ROPEY RESERVES

Rather like the hidden tentacles of the dollar, oil's influence is all-pervasive but rarely registers on the radar because we take it for granted. At the risk of stating the obvious, it is a key component of fuel, fertilisers, paints, plastics, pharmaceuticals and textiles. The gods must have had a mean sense of humour in coming up with a scenario where westerners have become addicted to oil but much of it now lies under unfriendly foreign soil. To affirm its importance to America, one only needs to turn back to America's entry into World War II in 1942. It was the world's leading oil producer from 1860[11] and held some half of the world's known reserves at the time. In 2001 the Bush Administration declared that its policy for the Middle East[12] was to increase oil production while improving security conditions. Bush appears to have failed on both counts, miserably so on the latter. Just as the demand for oil is straining the system, so we see a slippage in supply. There are two exacerbating constraints: the first is the ease of extraction, while the second is the quality of what is left behind. The best has been had and now we have to be more creative, work harder and expend more energy to extract what is left. Next there is the quality issue whereby that which is left is inferior.

The easiest fuels to burn are simple hydrocarbons such as methane (CH_4). The hardest to exploit is bitumen which is made up of a huge amalgam of compounds with long chains of carbon atoms, all racked with impurities. More complicated mixtures require high energy input and specialist catalysts to separate the constituents and break the carbon chains into smaller, or more useful, lengths. This is known as cracking. It is rather like splitting a big log into small pieces of kindling, for ease of burning.

The problem of rising demand and falling supplies is far from being a fresh issue. As early as the 1950s the geologist Dr M. King Hubbert predicted the maximum production levels for each region of the world with uncanny accuracy. There is widespread debate as to whether the world has indeed surpassed its so-called 'peak oil' production. America has already experienced its own version of this problem, having achieved the apex of its output in the early 1970s. The fact remains that no one can really be sure given the inevitable uncertainty of surveying that which is underground, below the sea bed or trapped under an ice cap. In its 'Global Scenarios to 2025' report, Shell predicted that the earth's oil production would not peak until 2025. The most pessimistic forecasts are for it to be reached between now and 2008.[13] The truth probably lies somewhere in between, at some point between 2010 and 2020. The two camps of thought tend to fall between the economists who argue that extraction technology will save the day and geologists who insist that shortages are a permanent feature. The main hope of the optimists is that the recovery rates will improve over time. The highly respected oil analyst Charles Maxwell has put the supply/demand imbalance into context. We are using 31 billion barrels per annum but are only adding a maximum of 10 billion of fresh discoveries to the pot. It does not take a genius to realise that outstripping the new supply like this will eventually end in outright erosion. Demand is rising by some 1.5–2.0 per cent per annum which will further stretch available capacity.

While we become hot and bothered about a 2 per cent annual increase in demand, we should realise that these growth rates are not that exceptional historically. Between 1950 and 1970, consumption rates rose from 10 million to 50 million barrels per day. This equates to a year-on-year increase of 2 million barrels per day, which is not far from what we are now up against. In those 20 years, it was the likes of the USA, Japan and Europe that were buying cars and pushing up oil demand. Now it is the turn of Asia to increase car usage so a surge in demand is only to be expected. This is the reason why the IMF predicted that global demand would grow robustly from 82 million barrels[14] a day in 2004 to 140 million by 2030. The biggest contributing factor will come from China's car ownership, which is expected to rise from a rate of 1.6 per cent at present to 27 per cent by 2030. This equates to some 390 million new vehicles and will contribute to a quarter of the expected increase in oil demand worldwide. In America, there are around 275 million cars for a population of roughly 300 million. It is almost beyond comprehension to think of China matching this penetration of vehicle ownership. The mind also boggles at the likely requirement for car-related commodities and the raw materials necessary for road-building and other infrastructure projects. Roughly 40 per cent of the world's energy consumption is based on petroleum usage. Of this, some two thirds is used up on transportation alone. Transport has literally been the biggest driver of oil demand over the last five years. In spite of the constant escalation in petrol prices, nothing seems to deter drivers. Perhaps the transportation of increasing volumes of mass-produced goods is also playing a part. It is estimated that overall world energy demand could increase by a staggering 50 per cent by 2030.[15]

The strength in prices has not as yet had as grave an impact as that seen in the 1970s. This is partly because the rise has been more drawn-out and is a symptom of strong growth rather than politically driven supply cuts. The efficiency of its utilisation has also greatly improved as the developed world can produce the same level of economic output with just half the amount of oil, compared with three decades ago. Oil producers, whose revenues benefit from a higher price, are partially recycling petrodollar profits back into the US bond market. However, there are deep-seated fears of having their assets frozen should tensions escalate between America and the Middle East. Arabs therefore feel safer investing their wealth in friendlier markets, such as in Europe. A good deal of their petrodollar profits were invested close to home, thereby sending Persian property and stock markets into rapture in 2005. The region's equities have since slumped.

As oil reserves dwindle in the West, we now find that the remaining capacity is becoming more and more concentrated in the Persian Gulf. The sources outside of the MENA (Middle East and North Africa) are mature and in decline, consisting of onshore US, the Gulf of Mexico and the North Sea. Unlike western countries, Arab nations are looking to consolidate their wealth for the benefit of the next generation. They wish to leave a legacy without squandering their most valuable natural resource and do not want the West to bleed them dry, leaving them to fend for themselves once the foreigners have had their fill. This may be the reason why some are so cagey about publishing their reserves. As Jim Rogers points out,[16] Saudi Arabia's state oil company, Aramco, has not had its reserves independently audited since 1979, when the figure came to 245 billion barrels. In 1988, some nine years down the line, it stated it was 260 billion. It has stuck to this figure ever since, despite pumping out 63 billion barrels in the last 17 years.

Oil production is running close to the maximum output. This means that the balance between supply and demand is very tight and can easily cause a crisis if the supply element is disrupted, as Hurricane Katrina made all too clear in 2005. The major bottleneck in the process is the amount of refining capacity. Refineries are where the components of crude oil are separated through heat and chemical treatment into many useful forms, one of which is gasoline. They have been running at rates of up to 96 per cent of their production capacity in 2005, although they have since fallen back to a more sustainable 84 per cent.

For any machine or process, running above 90 per cent capacity is tough to maintain, with all the inherent wear and tear. The reason for the lack of capacity again stems back to the fact that no new refineries have been built in America for some 30 years. The mild temperatures in 2006 have allowed US crude stockpiles to accumulate, which has helped to ease this pressure.

Economists argue that higher prices spur innovation, encouraging a willingness to explore all options in previously marginal areas. This idea has a degree of merit. We now see potential in the likes of the Caspian Sea, West Africa, Brazil and Canada. A note of caution should be added. None of these discoveries are anything like the scale of the finds in the North Sea. The so-called 'oil sands' in Alberta, Canada, contain an estimated 2.5 trillion barrels of bitumen. As well as the chemical impurities discussed earlier, there are physical contaminants such as sand and water to contend with on initial recovery. New sources also require significant expenditure. Shell Canada will be increasing investment in the Canadian oil sands[17] from some $4 billion to $7.3 billion. This heightened investment will yield a mere 100,000 extra barrels per day. This further supply provides little more than 0.1 per cent of the world's daily requirement.

If, as expected, this demand is set to increase by around 2 per cent per annum, then in the first year alone an extra 1.7 million barrels per day must be generated. This is still quite a conservative figure given that the growth in 2004 was 2.7 million barrels per day (although that was above trend). Even the roughest calculations will show that the extra investment required to meet demand will be astronomic. The International Energy Authority[18] has estimated that governments and companies will need to invest some $17 trillion up to 2030 to generate enough capacity to meet all future energy demand, not just from oil. This would inevitably involve more foreign investment in a climate of worsening security and possible government intervention through nationalisation or higher taxes. Should we return to a period of isolationism, multinational companies could run the risk of having their assets confiscated, having made substantial investments. Prices will need to rise to justify such expenditure and risk, along with further refining costs to maintain the quality.

Russia has been something of a tale of woe in terms of oil output. Having been a world leader in 1988, output nose-dived in the 1990s with the break-up of the Soviet Union. Production slumped from its peak of 12.5 million barrels per day to just 6 million in Russia in the early 1990s.[19] It now yields in the region of 9 million barrels per day. The high profile blowout of the oil industry did little to help the cause. This followed the government demand for $28 billion in back taxes from Yukos, the flagship Russian oil company. At a time when emerging markets were all the rage for investors, 2004 saw a tumble in the Russian stock market such that capital outflows from the country amounted to almost $8 billion. President Vladimir Putin's grip of the industry has continued to tighten. Compounding this, the producers are only able to export around 40 per cent of their output through the pipelines of Transneft, the state-owned monopoly. This means that the balance has to be transported inefficiently and expensively by rail. Although output continues to rise at close to 4 per cent per annum, the rate is just half of that seen over the last five years. Away from oil, Russia is a major player in the natural gas market, and Russia, Qatar and Iran together hold over half of the world's proven gas reserves.

Following the 1970s oil shock, the USA spent some $20 billion on building its own strategic reserve to act as a cushion in the event of an emergency. Some 700 million barrels of oil are stored in salt caverns on the Texas and Louisiana coasts. It has only been tapped in recent times following hurricane-related supply shortages – Ivan in 2004 and Katrina in 2005. In the very short term, the reserves will be of little use[20] because of the limited scope for them to be mixed with ethanol. Since 2005 there has been a shift away from the application of the polluting additive MTBE in petrol (methyl tertiary butyl ether) toward ethanol as a cleaner replacement. Bottlenecks are building because the two must be stored separately and not as a blend as ethanol attracts water and contaminates the mix. Like oil refining, ethanol production is already running at full capacity.

As well as being the second biggest consumers of oil, the Chinese are also looking to build up their own strategic reserves. They have stated that they would like to build enough to cover their needs for 90–120 days. This is equivalent to 800 million barrels or roughly ten days of worldwide production. Given the current capacity constraints, this is indeed an aggressive amount to accumulate and may well artificially prevent the price from dipping significantly. For now, Asian oil use is proving to be far less efficient than that in the West, which will exacerbate demand in the short term.

The US government has not been slow to recognise the inherent risk to the country's energy security in being dependent on the Gulf States for homeland requirements. In 2005 Congress passed the Energy Policy Act which introduced significant changes for the production and distribution of energy domestically. The nuclear industry was a big winner with subsidies for research and loan guarantees to cover some of the building costs for new nuclear plants. Exemptions abound for hydroelectric companies who had previously been severely restricted by environmentalists. Subsidies and tax incentives are also on offer for both traditional and alternative energy sources. The implication is clear that America is serious about self-sufficiency in energy production; no matter the objections. This may be a recurrent theme for other countries in the years to come.

As ever, the stock market provides investment clues for those who are prepared to look. When technology stocks peaked in 2000 they dominated a disproportionate share of the market indices. When oil prices were at their lowest ebb in 1998, energy stocks made up just 6 per cent of America's S&P 500 stock market index. By 2006, their proportion had risen to some 10 per cent of the market. This is still modest compared with the peak level of 1980 at 27 per cent of the index. Even if the sector were to expand halfway to the record then this would imply a good 80 per cent revaluation of these equities.

Taking delivery of raw materials – particularly perishable ones – serves little purpose unless one is a food manufacturer.

Investors therefore prefer to participate artificially through financial instruments called futures. They have their own quirks as the price for future delivery may in some cases be higher than the spot, or current price, of the item (known as a contango) perhaps due to increasing consumer demand. Futures may also be lower (backwardation), because producers are prepared to discount the price in return for certainty of demand. During the bear market, sellers frequently outnumbered the buyers so prices for future delivery were often depressed. In such cases the discount, or so-called roll yield, allows one to hold the contract such that in a matter of months, the low future price rises up to the higher current price. It is rather like standing at the top of an escalator and waiting for someone to come to you. For commodity traders it has been a major part of performance in the past, far outstripping the returns on the physical commodities themselves. As more funds and buyers come to the market, such opportunities are diminishing. Trading in these markets is best left to specialist hedge funds or commodity trading advisers (CTAs). Such investments require large sums of money and are beyond the reach of most investors, although some offer lower entry levels of around $10,000. One should only be placing a small percentage of one's assets in such funds so a substantial portfolio is required before considering such investments. Exchange Traded Funds (ETFs) may also be bought for direct commodity investment.

The closest that most retail investors come to general commodity exposure, away from precious metals, is through the purchase of collective investment funds that hold oil or mining shares. Although the shares of such companies do not have a perfect correlation with the movement of the underlying commodity, they are not a bad proxy. One useful point to note about oil stocks is that they pay good dividends as a proportion of their price (known as the dividend yield). Whatever happens to other companies in the market, one can feel comfortable that oil producers will have the income to generate good dividends for many years to come (assuming their assets are not nationalised overseas). The long-term trends for oil prices do not yet appear to be fully discounted in this sector of the stock market. The forward-looking version of the price-to-earnings (P/E) ratio (see Chapter 8) is close to a ten-year low, making the sector appear attractive. Unlike other companies which have had an earnings bonanza based on debt-fuelled consumer purchases, oil is real and valuable in its own right.

Commodity investments have historically provided a good form of diversification in an investment portfolio. Unlike shares or bonds that are valued on subjective views of interest rates or earnings in the future, commodities are priced on the here and now. They are depressed when an economy is emerging from recession because demand is low and large stocks of inventory have built up which will take time to be depleted. In the second stage of the growth cycle commodities rally because demand overtakes supply and the two fall out of sync. The reason why commodities have surged from a very early stage in 2001 is that shortages were soon apparent[21] due to acute underinvestment in the industry. For wealthier investors, private banks offer structured products that track specific themes such as soft commodities, alternative energy and nuclear-related investments.

In the past, commodities have been subject to the trend of reversion to mean. Excess demand has eventually been met with greater capacity, leading to sufficient supply, and prices have fallen back. Unlike previous cycles, the looming problem for hard commodities is a dwindling supply coupled with shortfalls in modern infrastructure. Prices are unlikely to revert to the levels seen in 1998, especially for oil. Away from the acute crunch caused by the emergence of Asia we must also prepare for the devaluation of the dollar. Even without developing-country demand, the dollar's collapse will create severe price shocks in many commodities given the inverse relationship between the two.

While the West has partied, developing countries have parleyed. Those economies that have not secured future commodity supplies will be utterly exposed to supply shocks. It could be the beginning of the end for those whose lifestyles of plenty have been funded by a combination of cheap goods and readily available supplies of credit. As inflation is met with higher interest rates, the cost of servicing our obligations will squeeze our ability to spend beyond our means. While surging prices may one day revert to mean – because a buyers' strike could eventually lead to demand destruction – the accompanying economic downturn cannot be ignored. Price shocks destroy consumer confidence, especially when disposable income is already being gouged by higher interest rates. Such confidence is hard to win back as nervousness becomes the norm. We have all the reagents in place for a chemical reaction to commence – and an abundant choice of catalysts. The debt cycle will then be broken as the psychology switches to saving. Next we will look at a temporary antidote that will carry us through the first stages of the coming slump, allowing for rational thinking while others flounder.

7
ANTIDOTE

Governments lie; bankers lie; even auditors sometimes lie: gold tells the truth.
Lord Rees-Mogg

Money is a classic example of an everyday item taken for granted. Few people understand its mechanics or origins, or even how it came to exist in its current form. Jack Weatherford's *The History of Money* explains this masterfully and in more detail than this chapter can allow. We will instead concentrate on the ancient and modern aspects of gold. Up until the last century, coins were worth something in their own right thanks to their precious metal content, whereas today they simply have a token value. While the use of precious metals in backing western currencies has long since ceased, the qualities that made it so functional are still deeply ingrained in the human psyche. Despised for two decades by many in the investment community, gold is making a serious comeback.

It is no coincidence that it has been a symbol of wealth for thousands of years and not just as a decorative item. The combination of durability, purity and portability has been an overriding factor for its monetary use, as has its physical qualities of malleability and ductility that allow for easy division. Its relevance in the modern financial world is more significant than ever, given its resistance to mass production. Unlike other commodities, it is not subject to the substitution effect when prices get too high.

COIN CLIPPING AND CASTRATION

John Steinbeck, author of the Depression-era novel *The Grapes of Wrath*, once wrote 'the study of history, while it does not endow with prophecy, may indicate lines of probability'. The distillation of history's lessons can indeed save many years of toil and disappointment. Great generals down the ages have appreciated this, by studying the methods of military strategists from the ancient world. Just as Napoleon Bonaparte was fascinated by Julius Caesar, so Caesar was obsessed by Alexander the Great before him. Awkward new emperors frequently adopt the architecture from a previous Golden Age: the Normans mimicked the Romans while the Romans copied the Greeks. A short walk past gentlemen's clubs in London's Pall Mall will show how the British Empire used architectural themes from both. In modern times, the Manhattan skyline is replicated throughout Asia as a statement of intent: that theirs is the new money-making metropolis.

There are many useful lessons from the history of the Roman Empire which used gold and silver coins as part of its currency. Following a build-up of deficits by a series of lavish emperors, Nero used the excuse of the Great Fire of Rome to reduce the gold and silver content of coins, thereby creating a greater number of them, starting with the same amount of precious metal. By the time the empire folded, its percentage inclusion was close to nought. It took the Romans several centuries to achieve the dubious honour of total devaluation – the fast-moving Americans are doing their best to beat them.

After Rome's decline and departure from Britain, the country survived a prolonged period without an organised national currency although foreign coins were widely used. This was partly a reflection of the decentralised culture of the Saxon invaders which depended more on local trade and coinage rather than national. As England emerged from the Dark Ages it attracted the unwanted attention of marauding Vikings and then one of their descendants, William the Conqueror. It was clear from architecture of the period that the Normans had grand designs on conquest. The revival of harsh stone structures and classic arches in northern France was a clear throwback to the Roman era. The Normans' imposing castles and cathedrals were soon to be found throughout England after the invasion of 1066. Just as unflinching Roman roads scarred their trail over the Celtic land and culture, so the Normans stamped their authority on the defeated Saxon foe with their constructions. One of the earliest examples is the Tower of London, which is of course still standing today.

When Henry I reached the throne in the early twelfth century, the value of the English currency was fading.[1] The Mints of England that manufactured and stamped the coinage were substituting the silver content with base metals like tin. This is the origin of the term 'debasement' to describe a devaluing currency. Apart from precious metal substitution, coins were tampered with by clipping off the edges. By collecting scraps of silver, one could effectively conjure up coins from nothing. In common with similar episodes when a currency is debased, a period of inflation – or rising prices – sets in. In order to receive the same quantity of silver in exchange for one's goods, a greater number of these clipped coins would be required, so higher prices had to be charged.

By 1124 Henry I had had enough of this abuse and summoned the various Mints to Winchester (then the capital of England) in what was called the 'Assize of Moneyers'. Two thirds of them were found guilty of debasing the currency and they either had their right hand cut off or were castrated: it was unlikely that they were given a choice between the two options. The law and logic of the day dictated that they were effectively stealing, so the removal of a hand was called for. Likewise, clipping the edges off coins was defacing the image of the King, so castration resulted. Perhaps castration – which of course prevents procreation – was an apt punishment. Debasing currency is the same as stealing wealth from the next generation, much like we do with debt today. The harshness of these penalties did not completely prevent further abuse. All coins were later recalled and replaced by the Short Cross penny, lasting some 70 years.

Debasement has frequently been a deliberate policy of kings and emperors to expand the monetary base. However, in the twelfth century a combination of coin makers' greed and shortage of precious metals was at fault. The Crusades had cost a fortune while the ransom for the 'never-present' Richard the Lionheart had stripped the coffers bare at the Treasury. Although his younger brother King John was legendary for his unpopularity, we should try to take into account the appalling financial legacy that he was left with. In the space of a generation, John had lost much of the family land which at one point stretched from the north of Scotland to the South of France. It was created by the union of the ultimate power couple of the era: his parents Eleanor of Aquitaine and the Plantagenet King Henry II. Little wonder that he was seen as the black sheep of the family who sported the disparaging nickname of Jean Sans Terre ('Johnny No Lands' in modern parlance). His loss of Normandy eight centuries ago crystallised the decision of the Channel Islands to give their loyalty to the English Crown, rather than the French.

The rationale for this history tour is that the same elements of greed, war and religion emerge time and again. The reduction of precious metals in coins is equivalent to the dilution of a currency today, as debt creation reduces its worth or purchasing power. In wartime, governments lose their financial discipline to win at any cost, which ends up costing everything. Yet another conflict in the Middle East reminds us that a modern debasement is brewing, this time for the US dollar. Surveying today's scene it is clear that our behaviour bears a striking resemblance with the Crusades era. Just as the Pope called Christendom to arms to fight the Infidel under the banner of the cross, so we now see the American President's call to fight worldwide terrorism, conveniently concentrated in the oil region. Religious undertones are abundant in public pronouncements, whose traditionalist appeal tipped the electoral scales in his favour at the last election.

HOLD GOLD OR FOLD

In the absence of the gold standard, there is no way to protect savings from confiscation through inflation. There is no safe store of value. If there were, the government would have to make its holding illegal, as was done in the case of gold. The financial policy of the welfare state requires that there be no way for the owners of wealth to protect themselves ... Deficit spending is simply a scheme for the confiscation of wealth. (*Alan Greenspan*, 1966)

From the concluding paragraphs of Greenspan's paper,[2] which he wrote 40 years ago, one sees that he did at one time have a soft spot for gold. The confiscation he refers to relates to events at the height of the Great Depression in 1933, when Franklin D. Roosevelt became President. One of his first acts was to initiate the Emergency Banking Act whereby the public had to exchange their gold for dollar cash. In a string of 'Executive Orders', US citizens found that they were no longer permitted to own bullion or gold certificates, nor could they send gold abroad. Monetary forms of the metal for values over and above $100 were confiscated. Anyone found in possession faced a maximum term of ten years in jail or a $10,000 fine. Collector coins and art were excluded, as were industrial-related holdings. These were defined as commodity, not monetary, holdings. If the economy was to be inflated artificially to overcome the Depression, then no US citizen, rich or poor, could be allowed to preserve savings by hoarding precious metals. Having removed the financial lifejacket, the dollar was then scuttled, devaluing significantly against gold in January 1934. Having traded-in one's gold for $20.67, it would then theoretically have cost $35 to buy it back:[3] hardly the deal of the decade for American citizens. In spite of the Depression, gold mining shares surged in price while property values and stock markets wasted away.

Little has changed in that the proliferation of debt, and the inflation that follows, transfers wealth from the frugal to the profligate. Apart from the injustice, it is also damaging to the economy as capital concentrates in the least productive areas, such as the property market. The rules on ownership of gold coins and bullion remained on the books for some 40 years until 1974. The only other regimes where gold ownership restrictions were in place were Marxist states. Any modern form of confiscation would appear to be unlikely given that the US Mint itself is an active seller of gold coins. It would also be unnecessary given that there is no longer a gold standard and because so few have any meaningful investment in precious metals. In any case, the majority of the public have little idea about gold's protective qualities. The wealthiest Americans have already learned their lesson and hold metal accounts with private banks overseas, just in case it happens again.

The right to protect one's wealth from inflation was well understood by the Founding Fathers who enshrined it in the American Constitution, which took effect in 1789. They believed that their currency should have real value behind it in the form of precious metals. This hard-learned lesson was seared on their memories by the likes of the Mississippi Bubble in the 1720s, where the French were bankrupted during their first dalliance with paper money. There were more salutary lessons from their own era also, when once again the French proved to be the whipping boys of finance. Their profligate policies, coupled with the assistance given to America in the War of Independence, proved to be their undoing. The build-up of massive debts resulted in a tax burden that fell most heavily on the poorest members of society. The end result of this stalemate is well known: abject poverty leading to revolution in 1789 – the same year as the birth of America's Constitution. The French clergy and aristocracy stood aloof from these taxes so it was not surprising that the ensuing revolutionary wrath fell directly on their heads (or necks in this case). A currency backed by gold and an absence of deficits was therefore a big issue in the formation of the United States.

Running deficits at the height of one's imperial power has not always been problematic. Britain's debt levels during the Napoleonic Wars were truly crushing, relative to the size of its economy. In spite of this burden, long-term borrowing rates during the period remained below 5 per cent[4] and exchange rates returned to pre-war levels soon after the Battle of Waterloo. It was just after this era that both Britain and America adopted formal gold standards which set a stable value of a currency relative to the price of gold and sometimes silver. The downside of this action was a bout of poverty and scarcity as banks were forced to call in wartime loans. The problem for a superpower currency becomes apparent when imperial power wanes and the weight of debt can no longer be carried. The last time we witnessed such a decline was for sterling after 1945 when the sun had truly set on the British Empire.

Although financial market professionals view American central bankers as demi-gods, they are in fact only human. Just as our musical tastes and fashion sense are heavily influenced by what was prevalent in our youth, central bankers are likewise shaped by the economics they grew up with. Many are in their autumn years and were brought up with stories of their parents' suffering during the Great Depression. They learned that adherence to the gold standard brought on several episodes of deflationary hardship in both the eighteenth and nineteenth centuries. Shortages of money were occasionally alleviated by gold discoveries in the likes of the Klondike. In effect, the extra supply of the precious metal allowed for an increase in the supply of money in circulation, which in turn brought the economy back to life. While there were other interim problems such as the 1920 commodity crash after World War I, the most severe bout of deflation hit home in the 1930s: this time there were no big gold strikes to offset the burst stock market bubble and subsequent credit crunch.

While it would be convenient to say that the final vestige of the gold standard was killed off solely by the demands of the Vietnam War, it had already been fiddled with continually since the establishment of the Federal Reserve in 1913. Prior to the Great War, the gold standard had acted as a braking mechanism in the economy. When too many loans were granted and banks were up to the hilt with what they could lend against their gold reserves, money was scarce (or expensive) so interest rates would climb. This acted to choke off a boom before it could start. Unfortunately, the idea came to pass that if banks could grant credit continuously then interest rates would not need to rise and the business cycle could continue ad infinitum. This was a lesson from the John Law (mastermind of the Mississippi Bubble) book of economics. It still appears to be the unspoken wisdom today that excess debt can be countered with yet more, without any consequence.

Since the early 1980s most mainstream central banks have thrown their resources into fighting inflation, taking their lead initially from Greenspan's predecessor, Paul Volcker. Between 2001 and

2003 the war moved to the other camp of fighting deflation. Paradoxically, by keeping interest rates too low for too long, well into 2004, deflation has become a genuine threat thanks to the resulting debt bubble. Those who believe that a little inflation through devaluation does no harm should think again. In the face of punitive Allied reparation demands after World War I, the German Weimar Republic devalued its currency while attempting to pay off unrealistic reparations or debt impositions. The spectre of demoralised workers taking their pay home in wheelbarrows overflowing with cash is a stark reminder of the extremes of inflation. It was eventually cheaper to burn money than use it to buy fuel, which is now the case in Zimbabwe. The later consequences of this instability are of course scarred across the world's history books as Nazism flourished. The Latin American debt and inflation crises of the 1980s likewise left that region impoverished.[5] Workers would rush to convert their weekly mound of paper pay – before it devalued further – into something tangible or edible that could then be bartered or consumed.

In the 35 years since the gold exchange standard was abandoned, central banks have been free to control their economies through monetary policy, uninhibited by the constraints of holding real assets to back paper money. Some dismiss the rise in bullion as it is seen as a vote of no confidence in the currency they print and hence a bad reflection of their abilities. However, like the German Bundesbank, they seem strangely reluctant to dispose of it. One should remember that bank notes are simply an IOU, albeit on fancy bits of paper that promise to pay the bearer yet more of the same.

Gold has stood the test of time as a keeper of value for thousands of years, subject to the cyclical peaks and troughs. Many investors still sneer at it the same way they dismissed bargain-basement shares in 1982. Some have noticed that since 2002, the classic weak-dollar, stronger-gold price relationship has come back to life and since then mining stocks have performed spectacularly. While many complain that physical gold does not provide an income or yield, a few years earlier they appeared willing to buy technology shares with no dividends and little hope of making a profit. The topic has been off the investment radar for two decades and has only in recent years been taken up by the investment industry.

Before the stock market buckled in 2000, we felt reassured that shares would churn out returns above inflation for ever and a day. Our mounting pension fund deficits have now made us more cynical of this outcome. Next it was the turn of property to provide protection for our purchasing power. The first two chapters should by now have dispelled that comfortable notion. Given the growth of debts generally, it is reassuring to note that gold is an asset which is not someone else's liability. It does not depend on anyone else's promises and, as we saw in the quote from Lord Rees-Mogg, its price tells the truth about inflation. If nothing else, it is a great hedge against future inflationary risks and is a key ingredient to one's investment portfolio, albeit as a small percentage. Those who are positive on gold are contemptuously labelled as 'gold bugs'. Long-term history shows that gold has been anything but speculative. 'Sage' middle-aged investors have been mentally tarnished by the memory that the metal price quadrupled in the two years up to 1980 and subsequently slumped. They are therefore stuck with this one-off spike in their minds. For some reason it is all right for oil prices to rise from $10 to $70 in recent years, but when gold rallies from $250 to $650 it creates enormous emotional conflict.

Many professional investors seem threatened by this contrarian approach as it is seen to be disloyal to shares and bonds: the mainstay of investors' portfolios. It causes them to question their own logic and creates discomfort where debt-based paper assets are concerned. Human beings have an ingrained herding instinct when it comes to conformity in group decision-making. They will even indulge in self-censorship to suppress alternative thought. This is a well-documented phenomenon[6] – possibly a hangover from our evolution – where groups look for unanimity and overlook risks in the process. While some elements may provide benefits for cooperative teamwork, its remnants can be highly detrimental for investors.

Great leaders with contrarian views are often vilified before their time has come and are regarded as mavericks in the intervening period. Such figureheads may spend many years out of favour, but their ideas are welcomed and implemented when the time and mood are ripe. So it is true of gold which languished for so long. By 2001 it appeared comatose at just $250 per troy ounce – some two thirds off its peak value. It was at this point that 'prudent' Chancellor Gordon Brown sold half of Britain's gold reserves[7] (395 tonnes). The ill-gotten gains were used to prop up the newly launched euro which promptly sagged. Since that time gold has come close to trebling in value. He has again spoken of selling gold to cancel Third World debt. While the sentiment is laudable, with his investment timing he would be better off leaving the debt in place and giving them the gold instead. In a few years they could walk away with a tidy profit – and more – to wipe the slate clean.

DEALERS AND USERS

The whole crux of the gold story and the reason why its outlook is so promising comes from the ongoing imbalance between too much demand and too little supply. This is a common theme for many commodities already discussed. According to the World Gold Council, demand for physical gold was up by a hefty 21 per cent in the first half of 2005 compared with the year before. A year later, rising prices had curtailed the appetite of jewellery manufacturers but this was brushed aside by investors clamouring for exposure,[8] which led to the price reaching a 26-year high, at $730. Investor appetite is frequently in marked contrast with industrial demand where precious metals are concerned. When the gold price rises, investors' interests are aroused but jewellery manufacturers begin to back off, and vice versa.

On the demand side, a total of 4,000 tonnes per annum is required. This stems from industrial applications, jewellery manufacturers and of course investors. The current supply from mines is a good deal less than demand at just 2,500 tonnes per annum. The 1,500-tonne shortfall has to be made up from central bank sales and recycling. In the financial futures markets, the degree of trading is very large and liquid. Given that the deals are designed for hedging risk or for speculation, the requirement of a physical delivery of gold is not a necessity. To put these figures into context, all the gold ever mined[9] amounts to roughly 155,500 tonnes.

Gold mines are beset with problems in terms of new finds, production yields, skill shortages and equipment deficiencies, particularly in South Africa. One example of the endemic shortages can be seen with the scarcity of enormous tyres required for plant at open cast mining sites. Existing ore bodies are in decline and new discoveries are few and far between. The last world-class find was in 1994. In a similar parallel to oil reserves, the quality of the remaining ore is inferior to what has previously been available. In the likes of South Africa, a combination or rising energy and labour costs, and a strong rand, have pushed up fixed costs and hence hurdle rates for making a profit. In line with other energy-driven businesses, production costs have surged[10] from $280 an ounce in 2003 to roughly $380 in 2005. Prices above $525 are required to justify new investment, which even then requires a good ten years before hard cash turns into burnished bullion.

Environmental considerations are an increasingly important aspect in obtaining permits. Another concern for mines is the difficulty in maintaining their output levels, let alone increasing them. There is the temptation to promise more than can be delivered to please shareholders or to preserve what is there in order to maintain the life of the mine. All of these factors make the gold supply inelastic which means that a rise in demand is very hard to counter with fresh supply, so the price surges. It also works the other way when demand falls, so this can make the price volatile. Weak investors are often panicked out of a good position by such moves, so it pays to hold some of one's gold positions in tangible form, which is psychologically harder (and more expensive) to sell.

Another source of supply that is drying up is that of forward selling. When the gold price was declining, mines could maintain a lifeline by selling their produce forward in time at a pre-set price. In this way, they were able to survive some very tough years by locking-in a good price. Now that the price has swung up, these forward contracts have turned from an asset into a liability. Central bank sales are also a significant source of supply although it appears that there is a growing reluctance by some, such as the German Bundesbank, to offload gold. The USA and Europe own roughly two thirds of central bank bullion. While this may sound heartening, the total financial reserves of developed countries are completely dwarfed by those held in Japan and Asia. The latter holds some $2,563 billion while the G6 western nations can only muster a fraction of this with $424 billion. Even without Japan in the equation, Asian countries hold four times more reserves[11] than we in the West. While the likes of Russia and India hold 3.6 per cent of their reserves in gold, China holds just 1.3 per cent. An official at the Beijing Gold Economy Development Research Centre said in May 2006 that China should raise its proportion of gold reserves[12] to between 3 per cent and 5 per cent. This would swallow nine months' worth of production or 1,900 tonnes. Given the outlook for the dollar and increasing antagonism towards America, this option is becoming ever more likely. Russia plans to double its holding, while Japan is considering an increase to 10 per cent. This action alone would use in excess of an entire year's worth of production. In terms of supply shortages, the central banks have historically been a vital source of supply for the market as their worldwide holdings are in the region of 31,000 tonnes. They are, however, bound by the Washington Accord[13] which limits sales to 500 tonnes per annum.

Moving on to the demand side of the equation, the principal need for gold stems from jewellery production which makes up some 75 per cent of the market. India is by far the biggest user and accounts for over a quarter of that total. The reason for seasonality in the gold price is due to the Indian wedding season. Being both valuable and substantial, the bride's present is a kind of insurance policy. Although diamonds are also proving to be popular, gold will likely continue to dominate this area of Indian culture, where women are increasing their personal wealth and independence. The Chinese government has been encouraging public ownership of the metal, although the motivation may be one of bringing under-the-mattress money into a taxable arena.

INSURANCE OF INVESTMENT

While it would be easy to become downhearted at not participating in the strong performance of gold over the last five years, this would be missing the point. Precious metals are not an all-or-nothing choice between shares or cash or bonds but form part of an overall jigsaw. Neither should they be anxiously bought and sold like a stock. Taking profits in the early stage of any bull market is one of the worst and most frustrating errors one can make. In the forthcoming environment of currency devaluation and inflation, gold could be one of the few anchors for one's wealth, although every asset will initially suffer in a crash (bar bonds). While financial and property assets may be battered by inflation-induced interest rate rises, the precious metals should offset some of these losses once the initial sell-off has occurred. Like the settling of muddy water, it will take time before one can differentiate the good from the bad in markets. The next downturn will likely be one where losing the least could be the best outcome.

To avoid being drawn into the speculative side of investment, one must view gold as an insurance policy. If one's property and investment portfolio continue to surge then that will be great for investors. Gold may do little in such circumstances, but in any case, only a small part of one's assets will be lying fallow. Like insurance, it is there to reassure and to reduce risk. Making a claim on the policy is the least-desired outcome, but if called upon, that policy will be invaluable. There is much debate over how much is enough and, like all investment or insurance choices, it comes down to personal taste. The litmus test for precious metal holdings is whether one loses sleep over them. If that is the case then you hold too much. The object of the exercise is to buy peace of mind. Fretting over the daily price of a piece of metal is not conducive to that end. After all, you don't value your property every week or month and the same should apply to gold.

Having made a positive case for holding these items, the practical and financial aspect of doing so is not that straightforward. As well as gold, precious metals also include silver and platinum. Many investors buy the shares of mining companies to gain access to the appreciation of these metals. For diversification purposes it is simpler to buy a specialist investment fund that holds dozens of such companies in a well-managed portfolio. There are several available which can be found by looking up gold funds on the Internet. For those who wish to go direct and buy the underlying shares then James Turk and John Robino's *The Coming Collapse of the Dollar and How to Profit From It,* gives an excellent guide. The shares of mining companies are more volatile than the precious metals themselves. Once the production costs are overcome in a mining operation then any rise in price will feed directly through to profits. This gives rise to a geared effect whereby the price of mining shares in a gold bull market will rise more substantially than the metals they are extracting. Over the last 15 years, for every 1 per cent rise in the metal, one should have enjoyed a 1.7 per cent rise in the shares, although the gearing effect will vary by company. As with any leveraged process, its operation works on the downside as well. If metal prices fall, then fixed costs will eat up a larger proportion of the profits. The share price will therefore fall faster.

As well as providing a more spicy performance, gold shares also show negative correlation[14] with mainstream equities over the long term. If the overall stock market is performing badly then there is a good chance that the gold shares will do well and help offset losses elsewhere. However, it should be noted that this relationship has reversed in recent years. As the spring 2006 sell-off showed, unrelated assets can fall in tandem in the short term and gold was no exception. One very encouraging aspect of the move in the gold price in 2005–06 is the manner in which it has broken away from the dollar. In the past, gold acted much like any other commodity where a weaker dollar leads to higher prices in the likes of oil and industrial metals. From a foreign investor's point of view this is not helpful because what you gain on the one hand from the asset, you may lose on the other through currency losses. However, gold has been surging while the dollar has done little, implying that the trend has now turned bullish for the metal in its own right. It remains excellent value when adjusted for inflation.

The major problem when buying quantities of physical gold comes with where to keep it. Without a safe or strong-room, storage at home would be unwise, especially in Britain and America. Some banks will provide what is called safe custody, but they will of course charge an annual fee for the privilege. There are private banks that can provide safe deposit boxes in which to safely place valuables. These are known as allocated holdings. One can also have access to communal storage of gold coins and bars of differing sizes in secure vaults (unallocated). There is in theory a greater risk for unallocated assets because one is then dependent on the credit quality of the bank should the worst happen. As ever, the custodians of one's assets should be thoroughly vetted in terms of knowing and understanding their risk and credit rating.

It is more common for investors to instead open what is called a metal account. Rather than taking physical possession of bars, which may have VAT (value added tax) implications and storage costs, one can acquire legal possession in the form of a transaction on the books. It is likewise common to buy silver and platinum in this artificial manner. Coins are frequently held as a form of bullion, the most common being South African krugerrands. While it is tempting to buy precious metals in the form of jewellery, one should always remember that like any high street item, a significant profit margin is built in for the retailer. There is also a high degree of subjectivity in the value.

Coins and bars can also be bought from private banks or specialist gold dealers. In the UK, bullion brokers such as Baird & Co. can make transactions in retail size and make money on the difference between the buying and selling price, known as the bid-offer spread. Simply by typing in 'krugerrands' in an Internet search engine, one will find a variety of dealers in both the UK and the USA. Like all online purchases, *caveat emptor* ('buyer beware') should never be forgotten. Each country has its national coins, such as Gold Eagles for America or the Maple Leaf coin for Canada. Coins may also be bought from the Royal Mint.[15]

While derivatives are a step too far for most investors, banks are increasingly producing structured products to invest in precious metals for set periods of time, with capital guarantees in some cases. Other innovative products have also been launched in the last few years that can be bought and sold like a normal share. In America these are known as ETFs (Exchange Traded Funds). The gold version (GLD) has been so successful that it has accounted for an extra demand of some $9 billion[16] in just 18 months of existence. The recent launch of a silver version by Barclays Global Investors (iShares Silver Trust) has sent this metal into overdrive also. Another investment vehicle called Gold Bullion Securities is traded on the London Stock Exchange as an initiative of the World Gold Council. The benefit of these funds is that the dealing costs are small – in the region of 0.5 per cent – compared with coins and bullion where there could be a premium of around 5 per cent.

Many investors ask about price targets which may be missing the point: gold should really be for insurance rather than investment. Commodities are where the real action is for the more active investor. If gold can better its old highs of $850 then this may well be jumped on by many traders as confirmation that an even bigger move is in store. It is important to understand the grounds for their positive sentiment. Bull markets tend to come in four distinct phases.[17] After a long-term slump, the first stirrings of a rally go unnoticed as the asset is viewed with cynicism: only the most contrarian of thinkers is involved. The second and third phases are the main accumulation periods for professional investors. Finally, the public are drawn into the fourth climactic period where exuberance abounds. By this time the smart money has made an exit, most probably being ridiculed for making such a 'dumb' move when the bull market is so obvious.

Gold appears to be emerging from the stealth of the first phase. As the bull market progresses, one's mind must be open as to the possibilities of where the metal may go. One should avoid the temptation to sell early as this may be the move of a lifetime and it may be offsetting bigger losses elsewhere, such as on one's house.

Should gold start to act like Internet stocks in the late 1990s, then there could be a case for top-slicing or halving positions. This allows one to take some money off the table but still be involved. It avoids the wrench of emotion as to whether to sell all or leave all at risk. Gold investors should permit themselves the same luxury once prices become unbelievable. By this stage it will be in bubble mode, where the size and time of expansion is usually greater than expected. The insurance aspect will already have done its job, so selling a good percentage will be prudent at this maturing point of the cycle.

According to South Africa's Investec Asset Management, the proportion of gold-related shares in the world's stock markets is just 0.5 per cent of the overall value (worth $200 billion compared with a total of $37 trillion)[18] of total financial assets. In times of financial stress, this level can rise to 20 per cent plus, as seen in 1934. As common stocks collapsed, those that derived their earnings from gold expanded. It is a common theme of the super-cycle referred to in the previous chapter where financial assets perform poorly when real assets are rallying. This counters the argument of many gold bears who think that gold performs badly during deflation. This was clearly not the case in the Great Depression when mining stocks flourished.[19] The prospect of a repeated rebalancing process has mind-boggling implications for the gold shares. Another attractive aspect highlighted by Investec Asset Management is that the gold industry is consolidating. While the top ten gold producers control some 37 per cent of the market, this is relatively low compared with other metal producers – copper, 54 per cent; platinum, 98 per cent. This implies that there will be a considerable number of mine mergers, which is positive for investors.

As the dollar decays and the political picture clouds, there will be plenty of fundamental reasons to own gold. It is a key part of the preparation phase – as important as securing water supplies before a siege situation. It is time to move on to the stock market as the bell-wether of the economy. Its crash will be the ultimate signal of a greater downturn to come, which in turn will alter the very way we lead our lives – surprisingly, for the better.

Part III

DETOX AND REHAB
Depression and Drudgery

8

COLD TURKEY

Most people get interested in stocks when everyone else is. The time to get interested is when no one else is. You can't buy what is popular and do well.
Warren Buffet

Cold turkey is a well-known condition that affects addicts when they come off an addictive drug after prolonged abuse. Its sudden abandonment after years of overstimulation causes physical side-effects such as cramps, shaking and even hallucinations. This chapter deals with the wretched withdrawal effects that follow the end of easy money, concentrating mainly on financial markets. The misuse and excess application of debt and leverage has brought about new highs in many asset prices. On the consumer front it is manifested in the cost of housing, day-to-day services and luxuries. In financial markets it is expressed through the rally in risky assets and the demand for any investment vehicle that produces a high level of income – no matter how obscure. During the 1990s technology bubble there was a severe dichotomy in stock markets where dot.coms and derivations thereof were all the rage. While traditional, or 'old economy', shares were unloved and wallowed in the mire, they still had good valuations and dividend yields that could attract a contrary thinker. This is no longer the case in today's markets. Gearing has not only increased the correlation and behaviour of many assets but has also made the majority of sectors converge in value terms[1] – at the expensive end of the spectrum. As the May 2006 sell-off made all-too-clear, in such conditions of endemic overvaluation, there is nowhere to hide; even in those areas where pockets of sanity exist.

CASSANDRA COMPLEX

In Greek folklore, Cassandra was a mortal woman who received the gift of prophecy from the love-struck god Apollo. On finding that his advances were not reciprocated he exacted his revenge. Although Cassandra could still foretell the future, Apollo made sure that no one would believe her prophecies. Her warning to the Trojans to refuse the Greek gift of a wooden horse therefore went unheeded. There have been times when one has great sympathy for her dilemma. There is often the danger of sounding like a crank when warning of a crash in markets: they are in any case rare events that require an unusual confluence of factors. If the same message is churned out for years on end then markets may eventually prove one right. While some enjoy the attention of spreading a fearful message, others like to be different just for the sake of it. There are also those who are permanently negative and see the bad in everything, which is just as bad as the permanently bullish broker: both conditions are signs of pig-headedness. When discussing the risk of a downturn with investment advisers, the response is surprising, with either sympathetic agreement, vehement denunciation or patronising denial. Weak markets are a threat to bonuses and job security: anyone rocking the boat is regarded as a traitor or madman

Having been through a vicious bear market from 2000 to 2002, one would have thought that the investment community would have learned that buying on dips is pretty risky, particularly after a four-year rally. The well-known aphorism of 'catch a falling knife' vividly describes the danger of this approach. However, there is still a consensus view that a 10 per cent fall in an index makes investments 10 per cent cheaper, in spite of changed fundamentals. Markets do not conveniently follow the codes instilled in us from childhood. Advice such as 'don't be greedy' and 'stick with it through thick and thin' are the exact opposite of how investments should be approached. When stocks turn bad, one should be a coward and sell. When they are behaving, don't take profits, just let them run. Investment folk trade in the art of selling hope and clients prefer to be pacified than terrified. Their argument runs that if you sell your shares and stay in cash there is no hope of getting the money back. The emotion of missing out on something is too painful for the majority of investors to bear. They are even willing to lose money waiting for an elusive rebound. This is why so few sold as markets withered in 2000. It is also why gamblers double their bets when they should walk away with what they have left. Cash is king in a bear market and allows for emotional detachment to buy when others have thrown in the towel.

There are thousands of highly intelligent people operating in financial markets and this is reflected in their pay. However, many analysts appear unable to apply the rules of valuing a company to that of an economy as a whole. We see time and again that aggressive expansion and excess debt can eventually break a company and the same is true at the national level. While there is a widely held view that countries cannot go bust, there are many in Latin America who would disagree. If analysts were to view America dispassionately then they would say that the country's balance sheet looks bankrupt. The weakness is hidden by active economic growth, which is equivalent to high turnover figures that yield little by way of profit. As rates move ever higher, interest payments to support deficits will swallow up the economy as surely as a python with its prey. Both companies and financial analysts need to come to terms with the strong likelihood that this once-in-a-lifetime flood of liquidity from low interest rates is coming to a close. The impact of a scarcity of funds will be dire for the stock market, which has been priced for perfection. Market participants likewise feel a false sense of security by endlessly extrapolating the recent low inflation, strong economic growth and positive corporate earnings. This has been labelled the 'Goldilocks' economy, where the economic conditions are 'just right' for markets to prosper. Like the little girl drawn into a state of slumber when her hunger was sated, markets have been lulled into complacency, unprepared for the return of the begrudging bears.

GETTING HIGH

Every market cycle throws up a new fashion in valuation methods: sometimes plain, sometimes fancy. Many books are dedicated to the subject but the bible of valuation was written over 50 years ago (*The Intelligent Investor* by Benjamin Graham[2]). As we are sticking to basics then we will first concentrate on the hard-core fundamentals that drive markets. Empirical observations of patterns and cyclical behaviour will be considered later. In the old days, companies were bought for the size and sustainability of the dividend they could pay. This is the annual or semi-annual distribution of the company's earnings to shareholders. Some of the profits would be retained for further investment in the business while a proportion would be paid out. They were a reward to investors for the risk they had taken. The safer the company, the more cash it had to cover the payment (known as dividend cover). Nowadays, dividends are less fashionable but they may well become the craze in years to come when capital growth is hard to come by. Our job now is to look at the valuation of the stock market to see if it is overpriced and at risk of a decline. Like every topic researched in this book, one can find extremes on either side of an argument. An experienced investment manager, like a good barrister, should be able to make the case for both. Where markets are concerned, winning the philosophical debate does not make you right: the ultimate judge is the profit or loss on a portfolio.

The price of securities is determined by the manner in which earnings and cashflow are expected to evolve, combined with the future direction of interest rates. One of the simplest ways of looking at the value of individual shares or whole stock markets is through the price to earnings ratio or so-called P/E ratio. We saw previously how rising house prices can be supported by personal wage growth coupled with low interest rates. Similarly, the driving force for equities is the outlook for company earnings coupled with the interest rate backdrop. Buying a share, or equity, is a way of gaining access to this future income stream. Unlike bonds, where the income is fixed and the price reverts back from whence it came, shares can experience a growth in their income which in turn makes the price, and capital value, grow. If the good news and expectations are already known then there is little chance of finding a bargain, as this will be embedded in the price already.

If the gloom and doom is overdone then perhaps it offers value. Another way of looking at a valuation is to say that a P/E ratio of 10:1 means that you could recoup the purchase price of that business after owning it for ten years. The faster the earnings grow, the quicker one is rewarded for the risk undertaken.

The other factor away from earnings is that of short-term interest rates and long-term bond yields. The higher they are, the more a company must pay to borrow, which will eat into profits. When rates and yields are elevated, investors need to be convinced that earnings prospects are substantial enough to justify the extra risk. Interest rates act as a form of pressure bearing down on share prices. When they are high, they become a dead weight and share prices may be cowed. This is known as P/E compression. Even when successful companies grow their earnings, they can still be held back by this smothering force. With a static share price and rising earnings the stock looks better value because the P/E ratio is lower. In mathematical terms the denominator (the bottom number) increases faster than the numerator (the top number), thereby giving a diminished ratio as a result. While a low P/E ratio is a sign of good value, care must be taken to make sure that it is low compared with its historical levels. Each sector of the market has different P/E characteristics that reflect their business, such that slow growth utility companies will tend to have lower ratios. One has to ensure that apples are compared with apples.

In the late 1990s shares underwent a process where prices rose much faster than the underlying earnings. This was known as P/E expansion, but in this case it was due to wildly optimistic earnings expectations rather than low interest rates. More recently, falling rates like those seen in 2001–04 provided buoyancy for the stock market as though unshackled from a dead weight. The combination of low rates coupled with a spending spree has allowed shares to rally substantially from their lows in October 2002.

When looking at P/E ratios, it is common practice and common sense to use next year's earnings forecasts. The market is forward-looking so this is entirely logical. However, there is a danger of self-fulfilment. The ratios may look cheap but only because analysts are bullish about the earnings outlook. A circular argument then ensues whereby bullish advisers tell clients to buy because of value but the value is only created by positive earnings estimates. The ratios are conjecture and not a statement of fact. Such forecasts are often subject to consensus opinion so it is no wonder that analysts expectations follow,[3] not lead, the cycle. To value a share one has to assume a discount rate which is used to calculate the price we pay today (the present value), for its future potential growth. Two methods are popular: weighing up a company's earnings prospects (DCF, or discounted cashflow) or applying the same idea to dividend growth (DDM, or dividend discount model). This was eloquently portrayed during the 1930s in *The Theory of Investment Value* by John Burr Williams. It was an attempt to bring some degree of orderly analysis to what had become a rogues market in the Roaring Twenties. Analysts may also assess companies through the sum of their component parts. Another measure, known as Tobin's *q* ratio, is showing extremes of price compared with underlying values, as it did in 2000 at the previous stock market peak. This is where the stock market capitalisation (share price multiplied by the number of shares) far outstrips the replacement cost of a company's capital.[4] Perhaps the reader can now understand that valuing a company is subjective stuff at best and full of easily manipulated assumptions which can vary with the mood of the day.

The use of debt has created abnormal levels of spending which are now assumed to be the norm. Many forecasters appear to overestimate the sustainability of the earnings element[5] where valuations are concerned. We have a combination of peak earnings and peak profit margins at a time when both are unlikely to continue. We may also be underestimating the upward trend of interest rates. Having become accustomed to living with low borrowing costs and bond yields, it is very difficult for us to imagine them being substantially higher. From 1953 to 1982 the ten-year US government bond yield ratcheted up from just 3 per cent to 15 per cent. Not surprisingly, it was during the latter half of this period that the stock market became utterly range-bound. Since 1982 we have been reaping the benefits of falling yields, which in 2004 fell to levels not seen in half a century.[6] The low point coincided with Greenspan's warnings of deflation. It is no coincidence that this period of falling yields coincided with the longest-ever bull market in shares. At the same time, corporate profits as a proportion of GDP have doubled[7] over 25 years. This means that corporate earnings (which result from consumer spending) have risen faster than their costs (the wages they pay to those same consumers). In other words, the public has been purchasing goods at a faster rate than the wages they have earned from those same companies.

The only way to account for this anomaly is through the decline of household savings, which are at levels comparable to those seen during the cash-hungry Great Depression. Profit margins and earnings are already at record highs and it takes a leap of faith to extrapolate them up from here, especially when every cost is rising. We have experienced the most prolonged era of economic expansion, not on the back of organic growth, but because interest rate declines resulted in debt creation coupled with a savings reduction. What we thought was permanent prosperity will result in omnipresent poverty when such conditions reverse.

We already know that US bond yields are significantly lower than they should be courtesy of Asian purchases. Any market which is artificially supported this way runs a much greater risk of trouble. Rising interest rates and higher inflation are setting the scene for an upward propulsion of bond yields. Apart from losing money for low-risk investors who buy government bonds for safety, it will also pull the rug from underneath the equity market. Even if earnings continue to surprise, prices can still be significantly depressed[8] as higher interest rates drain liquidity out of the market. The sustainability of company earnings, driven by consumer debt, is likewise questionable. The factors that elevated the stock market to the penthouse may soon send them back to the basement. We could end up with spectacularly lower share prices in future.

Bullish investment advisers always have a handy selection of reasons why shares are good value or the market will continue to rally. They are currently pointing to corporate spending and takeover activities as positives for the market. These are known as late-cycle phenomena. Companies only feel able to launch takeover bids when their own balance sheets are strong. This usually coincides with a peak in the cycle when the target company's share price has also appreciated. The other positive case proposed is that investor funds are flowing into markets. For the first time ever, more money went into foreign funds[9] than into domestic shares. In the year to February 2006, US investors pushed a total of $107 billion into overseas markets with an eye-popping $23.5 billion in January alone. Needless to say, emerging markets fell sharply just four months later. Hot money chases hot markets such that when prices peak, new investor inflows follow right behind. Even after the NASDAQ technology index had begun to fall in 2000, funds were still pouring in at record levels. This goes to show that buying alone cannot support a falling market, just as running with the lemmings will not defy gravity. Between May and July 2006, $20 billion was withdrawn from the US stock market, giving the biggest exit of funds since the end of the 2002 bear market. Brown Brothers Harriman has pointed out that a lack of fresh funds and rotation around different sectors are signs of a market topping-out. Although some indices such as the Dow Jones have broken new highs, the participation is not widespread or convincing as only the largest companies are involved. This is masking more generalised weakness, rather like the end of a race where the winners have just passed the post but the majority of the stragglers are spread across the rear of the course. It is an indication of insufficient liquidity in the market.

Genuine long-term investment, as opposed to speculation, is based on values and yields. Where dividend yields are historically low, such as now, it means that share prices are overextended. It is much the same for bonds. Even during the climactic sell-off in 2002, the US markets never offered yields or valuations anything like those seen at previous bottoms such as 1932, 1942, 1949, 1974 and 1982. Instead they maintained P/E ratios in excess of 20 with dividend yields of little more than 2 per cent. These ratios are characteristic of bull market peaks, not troughs. The other positive case is made that P/Es based on last year's earnings have oscillated around an average level of 14 since the early 1960s. Given that the figure stands at 16 in 2006 then the deviation would appear to be acceptable. However, it would be wise to recall that bond yields and interest rates are still very low and earnings are at record levels thanks to the one-off consumer binge. With the slump in the housing market, such conditions appear to be untenable. The 1990s equity bubble was easier to identify as there was a spike in prices. The stock market surge since 2002 is an earnings bubble which is much harder to identify because the very thing that determines value (earnings) is also the very thing that has spiked up unsustainably.

We should also remember that dividends have made up around 40 per cent of total returns from stock markets since 1900. It is only in the last decade that capital appreciation has outstripped dividends. This was in part due to the reduction in dividend payments in the boom years. As share prices dive, dividends will once again provide a greater slice of future reward. One day we may even return to the pre-1960s environment where dividend yields were in excess of interest rates. In those days shares were rather like bonds in that they were bought for their income generation rather than for capital gains. In 2003, George W. Bush cut dividend taxes from 35 per cent to 15 per cent to boost equity markets, but there are now calls by the Democrats for them to be raised again. Governments display an astonishing ability to increase taxes in areas that have just peaked. Britain's Chancellor Gordon Brown raided UK pension funds by taxing previously tax-free dividends. As we know from the P/E ratio analysis, anything that hits the future flow of earnings (or income in this case) will have a whiplash effect on prices today, thanks to the discounting mechanism. It is no wonder that Britain's FTSE-100 share index has failed to advance in eight years, thereby further worsening pension fund deficits. It is just another example of front-loading expenditure today which has to be paid for tomorrow.

There have been four clear phases for America's Dow Jones index in the previous century, involving decades of trendless performance followed by major bull markets. During 1922–42 there were plenty of gyrations, including the 1929 Wall Street crash, but the Dow Jones index began at 100 and ended at 100. During 1942–66 there was a ten-fold rally such that the index rose from 100 to 1,000. During 1966–82 a range-bound market was once again in evidence with years of ebb and flow between 600 and 1,000. As inflation was on the rampage over this period, such static market performance effectively dissipated investors' savings. The market then rose ten-fold once again and broke the 10,000 barrier in 1999, later peaking just shy of 12,000. As a possible portent of things to come, in 2005 the index experienced its most range-bound performance in 100 years. It was no wonder that volatility measures had fallen to such low levels.

There is a common belief that equities provide a protection against a rise in the cost of living. While they surge in conditions of low inflation, they perform terribly when it is rising. Over very long time-periods, the good performance masks the bad to give a reasonable 'real' return on average. Over the last half-century, every five-year period where equities beat cash deposits has been marked by a phase of declining inflation. The process is reversing as interest rates tighten to counter rising price pressures. Data from the National Bureau of Statistics show how yield curve inversion is frequently followed by a recession (see Table 4). There is no definitive pattern where the timing is concerned. Likewise, the minor inversions of 1966 and 1998[10] saw no negative follow-through. Just as a reminder of what inversion involves, it is where short-term interest rates are higher than long-term bond yields. Using the water analogy from Chapter 3, as the bottle is lowered from one's lips the liquid tips away down the incline. The rise in interest rates similarly draws liquidity out of the markets which in turn takes away yet another support for share prices.

Table 4

Start of inversion	Start of recession	Start of inversion	Start of recession
February 1973	November 1973	January 1982	January 1982
September 1978	January 1980	February 1989	July 1990
September 1980	July 1981	May 2000	March 2001

When risk aversion returns, investors will flock to government bonds while high-risk (high yield) bonds will be ditched. Borrowing for companies, especially indebted ones, becomes more expensive as these yield differentials expand. A slowdown in the US economy is not always a negative for the stock market. Lower earnings can be offset by falling interest rates, thereby allowing the P/E ratio to remain constant or even rise. Like the property market, share valuations need to be supported by a surge in consumers' earnings coupled with lower interest rates and bond yields. Given the combination of a falling housing market, lower potential demand for US bonds and rising inflation then a bull market is unlikely from here. Like the two examples of flat markets in the previous century, perhaps the best one can hope for is another ten years of trendless performance. We have examined the quantitative elements of the stock and bond market where a bear market appears overdue. This is the beginning of a process where a bear market correction evolves into a crash. We now need help with the timing, or technical side.

TOOLS OF THE TRADE

While academics and economists favour the fundamental picture based on evidence and reason, battle-scarred traders tend to veer toward charts and patterns showing historical price movements. Given the constancy of human nature, these soft clues can be just as important as hard facts. As with religion, each side of the divide is typically unheeding and unyielding: embroiled in the minutiae of their argument, like Catholics and Protestants fighting over Transubstantiation centuries ago (whether Communion wine was a symbolic or real sample of Jesus' blood). In the same way that some may criticise this book for being too simplistic, it is the basic rules and the big picture that will rule the day. One often hears the phrase 'you cannot see the wood for the trees'. This is especially true of the volume of research that drowns out the otherwise obvious message of markets.

No technique works all the time and total loyalty to one style can easily lead to disappointing performance or many years in the wilderness. Markets evolve and flip unexpectedly between high- and low-risk approaches based on the fashions of the time. Great investors return to the theme of avoiding emotional attachment[11] where stocks or styles are concerned. As ever, we try to blame someone else to take the heat off our poor judgement when decisions go wrong. Successful investing is about being humble, while identifying then beating one's own bad habits. All the market does is put a magnifying glass up to your weaknesses and exposes them for all to see in one's performance figures. As Miguel De Cervantes, author of *Don Quixote*, once said, 'our greatest foes, and whom we must chiefly combat, are within'.

While one should never personify markets in an attempt to concentrate one's ire, they do bear some resemblance to the impish character Puck in Shakespeare's *A Midsummer Night's Dream*. Causing chaos for the sheer sake of mischief-making, markets seem to exist for the sole purpose of bamboozling one and all. It is fascinating to see just how often they throw a sucker punch or put up a smokescreen to hide the real action. For example, markets have at last begun to factor-in inflation, with the usual positive spin that its appearance is simply a by-product of strong growth. However, it is excessive borrowing that has spawned its revival. Paradoxically, the combined effect of debt addiction, and the inflation that inevitably follows, will lead to debt revulsion and deflation. This is a core premise on which this book is based.

We can now turn to the technical side of markets to see if fragility is evident from this angle also. Technical analysis is associated with the study of chart patterns and market sentiment. It helps us to understand when the price of any asset may be out of kilter, being overbought or oversold. Similar trends observed in the past can then provide an indication for the next movement. Many measures are short term in nature and can be helpful in timing entry or exit points. Others, such as Elliot Wave Theory which was developed in the 1920s, can map cycles over many years. Technical analysis attempts to show when prices are overstretched, especially when they have moved well beyond the normal deviation ranges of the past. They illuminate significant trend changes when, for example, a price falls through its 200-day moving average. The progress can then be cross-checked with the volume of shares or futures contracts traded at the same time. This gauges the participation that can be seen as the fuel for a particular move. If a share rallies but there is little volume then it is a good indication that the rise will peter out and perhaps reverse.

Technical analysis is often derided as witchcraft by the fundamentalists. Even if one does not believe in the theory, it can help to explain why share prices rise and break out or fall and break down in the absence of other news. They could even be a self-fulfilling trend because so many traders act on the signals they give. If nothing else, one can at least hold back from making a purchase if other investors are about to offload it in spades. While short-term moves are of interest to the professional investor, we are more concerned with the sentiment angle and emerging long-term patterns. If both the fundamental and technical cases are bad then it does not make sense to be drawn into the market. More importantly, the stock market is a measuring device or discounting mechanism whose implosion acts as a warning of worse to come. You simply do not get a crash without a severe follow-through in the real world. The slump in US property-related shares in the summer of 2005 (well before a decline in the real market) was a very good example of the predictive powers of share prices or combined wisdom of crowds (which is different from the herding instinct).

By including this technical topic there is a danger of being ridiculed by those who vehemently deny its existence. This book is not written for those with closed minds on either side of the debate, for they will not change their views. This subject is for those who are open-minded or are reading about it for the first time. The conclusions of technical analysis are not always correct but that does not necessarily invalidate them. If one remembers that the use of patterns is simply another tool rather than the be-all and end-all of investing then that is a useful addition to the investor's armoury. It is helpful to think of empirical patterns in the same way that proverbial sayings apply to the weather. These maxims have come about through the culmination of years of experience. While meteorologists can provide an accurate long-range forecast, a farmer may be just as good a judge of the weather in the short term. There is no harm in asking both for an opinion.

Chart patterns or cycles are ultimately a reflection of fear and greed or even total disinterest. In 2006 the world economy appeared rosy on the surface with synchronised growth all around. However, the first cracks appeared in May. For those who had studied patterns it was obvious that the bull market was very mature and ripe for a sell-off. It was an unusual period because there had not been a fall of greater than 10 per cent throughout the upturn. Using the USA as an example, between 1934 and 2000 there have been 17 bull market cycles.[12] The median percentage change for the rallies was 73 per cent and the length of their existence came to a median period of 32 months. For the latest rally from the lows of October 2002 to April 2006, the bull market run had lasted some 42 months. The gains for the period were close to 70 per cent. We therefore had a cycle that matched the usual returns but was well in excess of the usual time spent in bullish mode. By the beginning of May, smart investors were aggressively selling equities before the steep slide later that month.

Although it is rather esoteric, the next sequence to highlight is that of the four-year stock market cycle. Since 1934[13] there have been 18 four-year cycles. Some 13 of them have delivered a major sell-off on cue. Even when there had not been a direct hit in year 4, the low point had occurred within plus or minus nine months. The troughs crop up most frequently in September and October. Bizarrely enough, geomagnetic storms peak in April and October and there is a possibility that they influence markets,[14] given that there appears to be a relationship between such events and depression in human beings. It is interesting to find that the climax of long-term solar storm cycles often coincide with stock market slumps: the next peak is due at the end of this decade. As ever, these patterns should not be viewed in isolation as conclusive proof. Like previous examples, such trends can easily disappear in order to confound the maximum number of investors, as markets are wont to do. As the Wall Street adage goes, 'when you think you have found the key to markets, they go and change the lock'.

We can retrace our steps in the recent four-year bull market to pin-point where we now stand. We have already experienced the liquidity-driven phase where interest rates have been reduced to fight off recession. This allows P/E ratios to expand such that shares prices reflect the positive earnings to come which are not yet manifestly visible. A mid-cycle correction is then typically experienced as interest rates begin to rise. This equates to the comparatively mild decline of 8 per cent witnessed in US markets in mid-2004. Next comes the earnings-driven phase. As companies prosper, their earnings surprise investors on the upside. Corporate spending and takeover activity are also common. There is a more speculative atmosphere as investors become complacent toward risk. All of the above markers have now been satisfied and it appears that the recent bull market is over.

The growing appetite for speculation pushed hot money overseas and into higher yielding assets. With the pedestrian performance of US stocks in 2005 it was little wonder that so many investors were lulled into a false sense of security and adventure. A way of quantifying volatility can be seen with the VIX index,[15] otherwise known as the Chicago Board of Options Exchange volatility index. This measures the urgency of investors to protect themselves from falling markets. By purchasing what are called put options, these instruments go up in value as markets fall. They can therefore offset the loss on an investment portfolio. It is a form of insurance and like household insurance it requires that you pay a premium in return for protection. When investors are carefree the index is subdued such that in 2005 it was meandering around its lows of 10–12 on the scale. During the big declines of 2002 it traded above 30 and during the 1998 Russian crisis it pushed up to a record of 45. Following the snap sell-off in May 2006 the index surged back up from 12 to 20 in short order, but by the end of the year had slumped back down to a record low. Other portents appeared in the same month when there were a record number of buying climaxes. These occur when a stock achieves a new high but ends up being lower in the same week. It is a sign of what is called distribution, where institutions offload shares at market peaks to gullible investors.

The biggest influence on any stock market decline will undoubtedly be derivative activity. As we know from Chapter 4, the size and scope of hedge funds has ballooned. When markets fall and become more volatile, some funds become forced sellers. This has become apparent in late European trading[16] when financial institutions have to balance their books. It was noticeable that futures trading surged to record volumes as the May sell-off began. When a crash unfolds, selling begets selling, especially in the obscure and illiquid markets that some of these funds trade in. Should it transpire late in the day then the pressure to offload will burst overnight, with sell-offs following the sun as markets open around the globe the next day. One final technical point to note is the way that global equities appear to have formed a 'double top'. When shares reach a pinnacle in a bull market then sell off, they leave a high water mark of where they once were. If they try but fail to break through this point in the next bull market then this is known as a double top and can be very negative. Like a drowning man trying to re-enter a lifeboat without assistance, after a few energy-sapping attempts to emerge from the water, he drops back into the depths from exhaustion. At the time of writing, the Morgan Stanley World Index of equities[17] has reached its old highs last seen in 2000 and it remains to be seen if a break-out is achievable from here.

Stock market crashes frequently occur in a news vacuum.[18] This happened in 1929 as well as 1987. One day the accumulated negatives, known about for months in advance, become too much to tolerate.[19] One precursor worthy of note is that crashes are often preceded by periods of market instability and uncertainty. It is rather like the tingling sensation one gets on the lips before a cold sore or the toxic woe that pervades just before the 'flu strikes. The surge in volatility in spring 2006 may be the first of many, having experienced unprecedented levels of complacency before and after. Prior to this, markets performed a good impression of the Indian rope trick, capable of climbing vertically with little support. This illusion is over and before long the scales will fall from our eyes.

CRASH TO CRUNCH

Bear markets are fascinating to watch when one is emotionally detached or sitting smugly in cash. The poor souls who just days before have been pushing the latest fad find themselves staring at their screens in disbelief. Their egos are bruised and they start to receive calls from anxious clients with cries of 'What do we do now?' We know that the answer should be sell, sell and sell again. However, this would require the adviser to admit mistakes and be humble; not an abundant characteristic in the investment business.

When crashes unfold, prices plunge through their so-called support levels which would otherwise act as a ledge to cling to on a cliff face. Wise investors may have taken precautions with stop losses (automated selling instructions at lower prices), but even these can be discarded if there is a 'quick' market which falls too swiftly for the order to be executed. It is not in the interest of the stock exchange to allow shares to fall in such an unrelenting manner, so there are braking mechanisms in place to prevent this. They can prevent computerised selling and even call a halt to the trading session while the dust settles. In the aftermath of 9/11 the US market even closed for several days. In any case this is simply delaying the inevitable, but at least the fall is more orderly.

Just as investors relax on the way up, so they tense up on the way down. As bull turns to bear, investors sell risky assets for any price, buying safe assets at any cost. This is known as a flight to quality. Normally, the US dollar and US Treasury bonds are the first haven of choice. In a typical smokescreen effect, as panic sets in and loans are cleared the dollar will benefit (the so-called short covering effect discussed previously). However, if dollar devaluation and US bonds are the problem in the pipeline then both these options will lead investors into a trap – a form of double ambush as they stagger from one killing zone to another. As ever, one should be prepared for several scenarios and quickly select the predetermined exit strategy of choice as events unfold. The most important preparation is to be heavily in cash in the first place. This is a much easier option now that deposit rates have risen. If caught out without a plan, then panic selling of risk followed by snatch buying of safety will double the workload when you have the least time to react.

Time and again, crashing markets go into a tailspin that feeds on itself. Away from hedge funds and derivative activity, this often comes from two sources. First, insurance companies become forced sellers as the market freefalls. They have to match liabilities such that the more equities decline, the more they must sell to cut back on their risk. The other source of selling comes from the banking sector. Many clients and institutions borrow money using their investments as security for a loan. The credit offered may well be in the region of 60 per cent of the value of a share portfolio. This gives the bank a cushion such that it would take a significant fall for the remaining share value to equal the size of the loan. The last thing a bank wants is to hold an asset worth less than the loan itself as it could easily turn into a bad debt. They therefore use a formula to sell increasing portions of the share as it falls, turning their security into liquid cash to protect the bank's position. Like many examples of Murphy's Law, one bad thing leads to another. A buyer's strike then ensues whereby no one is prepared to risk their money while a surfeit of sellers attempts to reduce their exposure. Every element that built a bull market is reversed to create a bear market. There is frequently an overshoot leading to good value, but there is little interest in buying while panic is widespread. The knock-on effect is not imaginary but very real as banks call a halt on new lending. Borrowing costs increase for companies and raising money becomes a battle.

A combination of high risk and high rates keeps both consumers and corporations in cash accumulation mode. As we saw in Japan, markets can fall for years at a time and the uncertainty leads to a high savings imperative, in spite of interest rates being slashed. The bad publicity spills over from Wall Street to Main Street and a consumer slump ensues. This is when the truth of a debt-based economy is exposed for what it truly is: a process of relentless and artificial growth for the sake of banks and business leaders.

Forecasting where markets will bottom out is incredibly difficult. In orderly declines, markets have stabilised for a time at various staging posts. These are known as Fibonacci levels which are based on naturally occurring number sequences that apply to both growth and decay. It is unlikely that any purchase of shares made within a short time of a crash will work out. Given that the market is discounting economic woe ahead then it makes little sense to rush in and be a hero. Any investing should be left until the turmoil and misery is at its height but that may be some years away. We are also making the assumption that western economies will follow the classic sine wave pattern and one day rebound. This has always been the case over the last two centuries. This time round there may be no bounce-back which is the reason for the book's title, *The Final Crash*.

Having been through the longest-ever expansion, there is much debt and speculative excess to unwind. The difference this time is that developing countries are emerging to compete with the West. Asia has the financial reserves to cushion them while we are left with huge debts, an ageing population and looming liabilities. There is no god-given right why we should maintain the lifestyle we enjoy today and expect the rest of the world to wallow in the mire. It has to be earned in what will be the toughest economic environment for centuries. A rebalancing from developed to developing is long overdue. The one thing that cannot be determined with any certainty is when or how the crisis will commence. Like climbers attached to an unsecured rope, any one slip could pull the rest down in any order. It could be the $17 trillion credit derivatives market or the stock market or the dollar or the bond market. This is not the time to be smart in guessing the sequence and timing of the tumble. Preparation work must be undertaken now to reduce risk, liquidate assets and prepare for the meltdown. With investments, there are times when it is best to do nothing: either letting stocks off the leash in a bull market or cowering in cash during a bear market. Instead, we seem incapable of leaving well alone but love to tinker and fine tune. From a cynical point of view, banks and brokers need invested assets and trading activity to generate commissions, not cash and contemplation. Perhaps this is why one can appreciate George Bernard Shaw's quote, 'Every person who has mastered a profession is a sceptic concerning it.'

A collective feeling of doom and despondency will become palpable with the realisation that past assumptions are no longer valid. When markets slump, investment advisers will feel utterly shocked, as though betrayed by a best friend that had supported and nurtured them during their entire career. No doubt there will be public and private sector attempts at intervention and manipulation which will prove to be skin-deep makeovers, with little substance or sustainability. Perhaps we will finally learn – too late – that intervention has already made matters worse and that we should accept our fate. Once crashing markets perform their job as oracles of austerity, the follow-through into the outside world will be unleashed.

9

2020 VISION

It is a mistake to look too far ahead. Only one link of the chain of destiny can be handled at a time.

Winston Churchill

While Churchill's words are wise, they are also surprising: after all, his was the lone voice that gave advance warning of Nazi Germany's rearmament. It reflects our natural tendency to be coy where predictions are concerned. The annals of the investment business are littered with the doomed prophecies of the great, the good and even the gormless. Like shipwrecks off the Skeleton Coast, the demise of others leads us to fear – and steer clear of – extreme forecasts. It further serves to reinforce our herding instinct, especially where investment strategy is concerned. No one gets sacked for making bad decisions in good company, but you will be sued for being brave and wrong. As the Depression-era economist John Maynard Keynes once wrote, 'worldly wisdom teaches us that it is better for reputation to fail conventionally than to succeed unconventionally'. It is therefore no surprise that dissenters who take a different course are so often shunned and why the majority fail to make money trading the stock market. All that is known is discounted and reflected in the share price. Only lateral thinking or the ability to stand back and see the wood for the trees can provide an advantage. The suggestions of this book are already off the radar for the majority of investment folk. By following its logic well into the future, further scepticism will no doubt be invited. Nevertheless, precaution and pre-planning make for decisive action when others are floundering. If the advice proves to be incorrect then at least the reader will have gained comfort from being prepared. The object of the exercise is not to give an exact forecast of the future, but to stimulate a mental dress-rehearsal for what may lie in store.

The pattern of previous downturns does not follow an exact blueprint but does contain some commonalities. A domino effect is too neat a description with its implication of discrete events in a tidy, sequential order. It is instead more like a motorway pile-up with multiple, but connected, collisions. The first harbinger of doom from financial markets has already been considered in the previous chapter. This is just about the best indicator of trouble in store. We should have had a much worse recession after the 2000 slump in technology shares. However, this was countered by a flood of debt-based liquidity which will prove to have been just a temporary stay of execution. The armoury is now empty to counter any crash in this cycle. The tipping point that signals the start of the sequence is that of risk aversion. Time will tell if the spring sell-off in 2006 was a healthy correction or, more ominously, the first tremor of a much bigger quake. One moment all is well with the world and speculators wallow in the warm waters of risk tolerance. Well-hidden or long-forgotten problems then emerge simultaneously when the crisis commences.

For the rest of the world, the after-shocks and resonance will be dramatic also. The feeble currencies of indebted countries will be first to fall as a vicious dislocation effect ripples from country to country. Investors will become very discerning about what they hold, particularly with a flight to quality. Stocks will slide and gain momentum as the crisis deepens. We cannot tell the order or time-frame of these events, but to debate the issue in this manner is to miss the point. You either prevent it or prepare for its consequences. This is the same problem that besets us on many vital issues: on global warming, scientists fight politicians, while left battles right on economic issues. All the time they squabble, the clock is ticking away.

A hit on the dollar will be hotly pursued by a commodity crisis. The debate will then rage over what currency to use for pricing common commodities. As rising raw material costs spill over into every aspect of our lives, the combination of high rates and excess debt will make the transition from recession to depression surprisingly swift. There will likewise be few places for investors to hide. In mid-2006 we saw how virtually every asset class, bar bonds, was beaten up. Even then, bond performance was particularly soggy, implying a severe oversupply of what are meant to be safe-haven assets. The classic diversification argument of combining commodity and hedge funds into a portfolio of shares and bonds was severely tested as stock markets sank. Over long time-periods commodities, shares and hedge funds should behave differently. However, previous assumptions and negative correlations were swept aside. They fell in tandem because speculative, indiscriminate risk-chasers had their fingers in every pie. This phenomenon is yet another smokescreen laid down by the market to trick weak investors out of good positions such as gold and commodities. Such short-term trends also have a habit of hiding the true long-term action. Once the dollar devalues, a disruption in trade and globalisation will be inevitable, both financially and politically. Should these events come to pass, we will be faced with two crucial questions. First, as the weaker-dollar, stronger-commodity story unfolds, will rising prices destroy demand? Second, where is the equilibrium point for commodity prices between a demand-destroying depression and supply shortages from trade disputes?

GLOBALISATION TO ISOLATION

In periods of plenty, national barriers fall and trade flows with relative ease, just as it did in Ancient Rome and before the Great War. In modernity, it has been the role of the World Trade Organisation to encourage international commerce. When times change and hardship is endured, nationalism emerges and the desire to go it alone takes precedent: blood is thicker than bilateral agreements. In a similar vein, capital courses smoothly around the world when there is a high degree of risk tolerance and optimism. Places in which one would never normally invest become fashionable and acceptable. In times of tension, that same money is swiftly withdrawn to home territories, just like blood to the core of the body in episodes of shock. When under duress, exchange controls are introduced in weaker economies to stop home-grown wealth from fleeing the country in hot pursuit of foreign withdrawals. Debt-ridden economies undergo the painful process of seeing their foreign exchange reserves dwindle as foreigners dump their currency and assets on the market. As the crisis unfolds, the nations that emerge strongest will be those with the least debt, the healthiest financial reserves and access to commodities (either directly owned or via treaties). The same principles should apply to individuals also.

Significant currency adjustments have been engineered in the past when well-planned and negotiated in advance, as we saw with the Plaza Accord. Sudden devaluation is, however, a beggar-thy-neighbour policy which on the face of it appears to give the culprit a competitive edge. By default it puts one's trading partners at a disadvantage because their goods and services become more expensive to import. Naturally, such behaviour is not appreciated, even when it is not the chosen policy of the government. The worst scenario is where one country devalues and others follow suit in what is known as a round-robin effect. In such circumstances one could make a rough forecast of how the political map might unfold internationally. The downturn in trade will have a tendency toward isolationist policies. This would be followed by a rearrangement of alliances based on old friendships and future sources of commodity supply. Like twisting a kaleidoscope, we may see an entirely new pattern of trade emerging.

The scramble for commodity and energy supplies will no doubt be another source of tension. Like the generations before us, we like to think that we are rational, easy-going people who would never go to war over some petty squabble. However, we appear to be following the notions of our forebears who were swayed by the simplistic notion that tariffs on imports will magically protect our jobs and standard of living. This policy of isolation was prevalent in the USA after World War I. The consensus mood of the day was that self-sufficiency would avoid America's embroilment in future European wars. In 1922 the Fordney McCumber Tariff Act was introduced to preserve the dominance of US agriculture and industry following the war-related increase in demand.

European countries predictably countered with their own reprisal tariffs, specifically targeting American cars and wheat imports. US isolation was broad-based as it refused to join the League of Nations and the International Court of Justice and would not ratify the Treaty of Versailles.

On the social front, immigration quotas were introduced which favoured WASPs (White Anglo-Saxon Protestants). By 1929 just 150,000 immigrants per annum were allowed to enter,[1] under a complex process of racial categorisation. In future we may see religious affinity rather than race as the new determinant in who will qualify for immigration into western countries. Then again, this influx may not be a problem in future given that any immigrant worth their salt would head for the new Eurasian world rather than the old, decaying West.

In the Great Depression we saw that import levies were introduced prior to the dollar's devaluation against gold. Such tariffs are typical in downturns[2] having occurred in the depressions of the 1780s, 1840s and 1890s. The Smoot-Hawley Tariff Act of 1930[3] stuck another stick in the spokes by raising tariffs on a multitude of items to protect American farmers. Coming in the wake of the 1929 crash, it probably deepened and extended the Depression. Should similar tariffs arise either before or after dollar devaluation then the world will not be a pretty place. This is because Asian manufacturing has minimised inflation for years. Should trade wars limit the supply of their goods then the likes of Wal-Mart and the West in general will be in for some bleak times ahead. During a downturn, self-defeating paranoia can grip a nation as the populace bites the hand that feeds it. The hurdles for replicating Asian production capability in our abandoned factories do not bear thinking about. Apart from the sheer logistics, the delays and shortages entailed would be hugely inflationary.

Looking to the future, we may well see a resurrection of isolationist policies in a world of increasing tensions, tariffs and taxation. Unemployed immigrants would be viewed as a drain on the precious tax pot while those that worked would be accused of taking 'our' jobs. It will be conveniently forgotten that their younger age-profile is helping to offset our self-inflicted demographic time-bomb. The age-old argument may re-emerge that newcomers are feasting on the reserves accumulated over generations by the indigenous population. The thing is, what few reserves are left in the West are dwarfed by accumulated debts. The assets that were supposed to have been amassed in the good times have been usurped by future unfunded liabilities. It is not just this generation that is mortgaged to the hilt, but the next one also. In Britain, once public sector debt is combined with public pension deficits and PFIs (Private Finance Initiatives) then the total comes to £1.34 trillion, or £53,000 per household: a figure remarkably close to private debt levels. Tax rises appear inevitable given the state of welfare system deficits, the increasing need for economic stimulation and maintenance of the burgeoning government workforce. Just when taxes need to be cut they will inevitably escalate and burden an already battered economy. There could even be calls for a reversion to centralised planning in a bid to shield the populace from the ravages of market forces. No doubt the political pendulum, so long frozen in the centre, will swing further to both left and right.

POLARISATION OF POWER

Empires come in all shapes and sizes and differ in their longevity and impact. Some may be based on migrating populations in search of resources while others expand outwards from a secure base with pillaging in mind. While food and water shortages have been the cause of conflict and relocation in the past, one can only hope that any modern equivalent will be more benign. If the dollar devalues and commodity prices continue to escalate, we will then see if we are indeed any different from our ancestors.

In terms of future superpowers, if it were simply down to a weight of numbers then Asia would already have a strong and strengthening position. Over half of the 2020 population of 7.6 billion will be Asian,[4] 5 per cent Western European and 4 per cent from the USA. Aside from the numbers, Asia has credence in the form of financial reserves which tower over those of the developed world. It is therefore no wonder that America spends so much on military personnel and technology. Military strength is its greatest edge given that many of its commercial advantages have been eroded in just the last decade. While a defence budget of 4 per cent of GDP may not sound excessive, the actual figure dwarfs other countries' expenditures at over $500 billion for 2005. With some 120 outposts to pay for, the printing presses need to roll ever onward. In the modern sense, it is not printing presses in action but keyboards, red-hot from excessive use, which create electronic dollar debt. US military outlays are seven times that of China (in second place) and account for two fifths[5] of the world's total. Perhaps George Bernard Shaw was right when he said 'capitalism has destroyed our belief in any effective power but that of self interest backed by force'.

As we know from the rise and fall of the Roman Empire, military might requires financial muscle. When the highly indebted Julius Caesar embarked on the conquest of Gaul, it was no coincidence that these Celts were the overseers of hundreds of gold mines. The same exercise was carried out by the Emperor Trajan when Dacia (modern Romania) was invaded in the dawn of the second century AD. The gold mines of Transylvania were just too tempting a target for those cash-hungry Romans. As Rome produced little on its own merit, its armies were forced to invade and steal treasures, then collect taxes and tribute. That booty would then change hands in exchange for imports, both essential and extravagant from further afield. The Spanish were much the same in their conquest of South America. The vast quantities of gold and silver wrenched from the indigenous tribes caused an inflationary import boom which, paradoxically, bankrupted the nation.

Throughout history one finds that wherever geological resources are concentrated, the ruling power of the day will be drawn in. The American presence in Iraq is a simple repetition of this principle, in the finest traditions of imperial rule. Once it was yellow gold, and in the modern era it is black gold as world powers are being drawn head to head in the Middle East. Clashes may crop up in future at any number of strategic choke-points for oil transportation or exploration: anywhere from the Straights of Hormuz to the Panama Canal is possible. Tensions could arise in any place on any pretext, given the complex network of informal alliances built up by Asia and Russia.

If a phrase could sum up China's long-term strategy, it would be 'rivalry for resources'. To achieve those aims, it appears that China is waging not a cold war but what may become known as a warm war. Like the flow of the Gulf Stream, their influence is creeping unseen below the surface and from continent to continent. It is one where loans and assistance do not come with democracy clauses or 'advice'. In the first half of 2006, three top Chinese officials toured a total of 15 African states. China has supplanted Britain's rank as third biggest trader with the African continent.[6] Over the ocean, China has also signed cooperation accords with several South American states.

Like an observer unfamiliar with the rules of a board game, the players' motives and moves are hard to comprehend until the contest nears completion. This is very similar to the way that developing countries with financial reserves are courting the limited number of commodity producers. Unseen by many westerners, this network is spreading as China and Russia extend their influence far and wide, like markers on a campaign map, to secure long-term access to supplies. It is only after the forthcoming financial crisis that we will truly understand how smart they have been over the last decade. While they have been bonding with friends and building their wealth, we have squandered ours and made enemies along the way. Like a stereograph, only those who adjust their eyes to the hidden 3D image can comprehend the true underlying picture. While it would be easy to equate this diplomatic activity to networking at a tedious business conference, there is a far more serious side. Many have become disenchanted with western economic models and reforms, ending up with large debts and white elephant projects in the process. Having enjoyed decades of overseas goodwill, the grating nature of America's neo-conservative policies is wearing thin on its recipients. Meanwhile, our dwindling influence and limited access to strategic supplies will make the West appear an irrelevance in the years to come. It is reminiscent of Britain at the wartime Yalta Conference, where Stalin and Roosevelt dominated proceedings.

The commodity coalition that is being formed right now is one of subtle courtship. It is being well-received by developing nations who previously had little economic clout. The rise in commodities has changed all this: now they have something the world wants. They will not be quick to forget just who has shackled them, with iron chains in history and the manacles of Third World debt in modernity. The Chinese and Russians are masterful and often indefatigable negotiators who know how to pressure as well as pamper. Given the Russian influence on gas distribution and prices – as shown when supplies to the Ukraine were cut off in January 2006 – they will be a harsh adversary should relations (quite literally) turn frosty. Meanwhile, in South America, Bolivia's President Evo Morales has called China an ideological ally. He is also close to Venezuela's President Hugo Chavez: both seemingly united on an anti-US platform. Morales' orders to nationalise foreign oil assets has sent shivers through the West.

The mistaken approach of western powers is one alluded to in Bill Bonner's book *Empire of Debt*.[7] When nations get a taste for imperialism they have an almost involuntary habit of assuming that their way is the right way. Their culture and religion must be exported as a model for all to follow, no matter how inappropriate for the local climate and culture. The Roman's imported their Mediterranean villas to the windswept British Isles. The Spanish conquistadors erected their cathedrals in quake-hit South America, while the English built their mock-Tudor mansions on the weevil-ridden African continent. Perhaps the American footprint is characterised by a burger bar in every town.

But the Chinese are different. Their behaviour is much closer to that of the three wise monkeys whose maxim was 'see no evil, hear no evil, speak no evil'. While one can see China's vicious streak in its dealings with Taiwan, it is a different story away from their own backyard. Their way of doing business with favoured developing nations is one which avoids casting judgement or irritating what will be its future trading partners. They understand that influence is won by subtle moves and alliances: using signed deals rather than the sword to capture precious wealth. In the period to come, real wealth will be real resources.

It is not just a case of making pacts with foreign powers to ensure future material supplies but also one of using old-fashioned capitalism to snap up assets. In October 2005, a Canadian court gave approval for the $4.2 billion bid by state-owned CNPC (Chinese National Petroleum Corporation) for Alberta-based PetroKazakhstan. A rival bid by Russia's Lukoil was turned down. Chinese interest was not so well received south of the Canadian border some two months earlier. In one of the largest overseas takeover attempts by a Chinese company, CNOOC (China National Offshore Oil Corporation) made a bid for Unocal, America's eighth largest oil business. It was met with fierce opposition in Washington. The sum of $18.5 billion was offered by CNOOC, but an inferior bid of $17 billion was instead accepted from US oil giant Chevron. Whatever happened to market forces? Along with the CNPC, these state-owned companies act as a tool[8] of the Chinese government.

The reaction to this acquisition threat shows just how sensitive the Americans have become to foreign ownership of their strategic assets. Overseas, the intricate web of deals is even hampering the US war of words over Iran's nuclear development. The fact that Russia and China are close to Iran politically has meant that Washington has had to tone down its threats. In late 2004, Sinopec (China Petroleum and Chemical Corporation) signed a preliminary agreement with Iran to develop the Yadavaran oil field[9] in a deal worth $70 billion. In return the Chinese will receive guaranteed supplies of liquefied natural gas and crude oil. Iran has also expressed an interest in joining the Shanghai Cooperation Organisation,[10] wanting closer allegiance with a body that includes China and Russia in security issues.

During their 1980s boom, the Japanese went out to buy trophy items such as the Rockefeller Center in New York. This caused consternation as it was symptomatic of Japan's ascendancy, when America was just emerging from industrial stagnation. The difference in this case was highlighted by Irwin Stelzer in his June 2005 *Sunday Times* article,[11] as China is now a bigger rival for natural resources, worldwide influence and intellectual property. Japanese overseas activities were driven by private companies and not state-owned industries. Their status as an American ally was in sharp contrast with China's competitive threat today.

The most crucial idea to contend with in the coming decades is that of a rebalancing of power. As the West sinks under the weight of its amassed debts, commodity countries will naturally float with the buoyancy of wealth accumulation. For many westerners, this contraction in their living standards will undoubtedly be seen as a tragedy for cultural living, in the same way that the Romans viewed the sacking of Rome by the Barbarians. For developing countries, it will be seen as a form of justice after centuries of colonialism followed by decades of financial repression. Many of these countries have endured unfair price competition, fighting an uphill struggle against subsidies to western farmers, which in turn have depressed soft commodity prices. The burden of debts owed to foreign institutions – paid many times over thanks to high interest rates – has been a further fetter. In spite of these impositions on developing countries, they are fighting back by paying down debt. Their gradual recovery is of course presented with a positive spin. Surely as they become consumers they will import luxury goods and services from the West? While this may initially be the case, such optimistic expectations should be reconsidered over the long term. The symbols of previous empires are often despised or discarded by their ex-subjects, as the crumbling statues of the British Raj bear witness.

While one can only hope that we are not entering a new phase of militarism and conflict, we should nevertheless prepare ourselves, at least mentally, for such conditions. With the surge in population growth since the war, there will be few countries that are entirely self-sufficient on the food front. As the world polarises into power blocs, trade is likely to follow in the same course. Each area will need to work out who its friends and trading partners will be. While Europe and Japan still have worthwhile manufacturing to speak of, this is no longer the prevalent position in Britain or America.

As western populations age and lifespans increase, so our liabilities will escalate. With fewer young people to support the tax burden, the system will eventually break. Not only will we have to endure a downturn but the pension rights we had taken for granted will evaporate. For a change, it will be us who have to get used to poverty: our currencies will be weak, our investments decimated and our retirement dreams shattered. The assets that were inflated on the incoming tide of liquidity will be broken on the rocks when it ebbs away. Only those who divest themselves of debt while accumulating cash, gold and commodities (both real and financial) will be saved to a degree.

In past depressions, workers' purchasing power increased as prices fell. Even when unemployment rates hit 25 per cent, it still meant that three quarters of the workforce was earning. This has been the case for the last two centuries where downturns were eventually followed by upturns. This time round the boom period has been stretched and extended beyond repair. Like a steel spring that is pulled too far and distorted, it can never regain its original ability to bounce back. The next economic bust may not be treatable, leaving us permanently deformed financially. The classic tactics used for bailing out a weak economy have already been applied in the good times – there are no more aces up the sleeve. The whole point of slashing interest rates post-9/11 was the hope that the cycle would continue under its own steam. The recent upturn is more a product of greater debt than organic growth. Soon we will see that the supposed prosperity of the last five years has in fact been a mirage. Rising interest rates are lifting the veil of deceit: too late, we will realise the shakiness of the foundations upon which we built our dreams.

SELF-SUFFICIENCY AND SUBSTITUTION

Self-sufficiency in terms of energy and agriculture will likely become the dominant theme of the next two decades. Once the Asian economies of the future have emerged and become consumers in their own right, they will no longer need the West, perhaps following the 1920s American model by moving into isolationist mode. They could even create their own trading and financial blocs, forming a reserve currency in the process.

We have become accustomed to a globalisation where every basic item can be imported. The problem will come when international relations are not so good and trade is not free-flowing. The era of cheap produce will then be drawing to a close. Flying out-of-season fruit halfway around the world will no longer be an option. Home-grown produce should be more appealing from the price angle as transport costs surge. If one has little by way of a farming industry then that is a problem. Even by World War II, Britain was no longer self-sufficient, depending on Atlantic convoys to feed the populace. It is curious to note that – like generals fighting the last war – we spend billions on defence systems[12] yet have little provision for securing our basic food supplies.

The most pressing area for autonomy will be oil and energy. Aside from the supply quality and shortages alluded to earlier, there is also a political angle. Commodities will be the weapons of the next trade war, and if thought of in those terms, it is clear that we have some serious rearmament to undertake. In the UK, many nuclear power stations have reached the end of their useful life and most will be decommissioned by 2025. Building new stations is lengthy and subject to many public enquiry delays. In the tough times ahead, it is likely that bottlenecks such as public opinion will be swept aside[13] in the race to become self-sufficient. We may find that the Asian practice of building nuclear plants within five years becomes commonplace.

Whatever one's views on nuclear energy, the principal positive is the lack of carbon dioxide and particle emissions. This is of course offset by the radioactive waste issue which, quite literally, will not go away. Given the scale of ice-cap regression then atmospheric carbon reduction would appear to be the priority. This has been the opinion of the British government which has opted for nuclear power. It is also the view now supported by the International Energy Agency[14] which has backed the nuclear option for the first time in its 30-year history. Although no new supply is due until 2018, it is likely that a building programme will be fast-tracked as energy shortages kick in. One problem with nuclear power generation is that the degree of indirect financial support could have gone into alternative energy, perhaps with more sustainable results. UK companies involved in the nuclear industry have had a poor time of it financially, such that British Energy had to be bailed out by the government[15] in 2002. Much of the benefit of building a nuclear infrastructure is likely to fall in the hands of French, German or even South African companies. Subsidies for wind-farming are also distorting investment[16] away from areas such as wave and tide technology. We should also bear in mind that electricity is just a small part of Britain's energy requirement, with alternatives barely meeting a fraction of demand.

Every debate on the topic throws up huge controversy and polarity of thought. While the weight of scientific opinion favours the reality of global warming, some take the business-as-usual approach, which is one emphasised by Bjorn Lomborg in his well-researched book *The Skeptical Environmentalist*. Other works, such as the beautifully written *The Revenge of Gaia* by James Lovelock, make the case that global warming is genuine, and suggest a mix of alternative energy resources including nuclear power.[17] It is not the job of this book to become overly involved in the debate, other than to emphasise the strong interdependence between financial markets, commodities and energy use. Nevertheless, a few interesting points may be indulged in. One fascinating observation which favours the global warming theory came from the days following 9/11 when US air travel was suspended. An American climate scientist, Dr David Travis, noted a significant change in temperatures during the period. It was not just a case of them rising or falling more than normal; it was both. Temperatures rose more in the daytime, which was found to be brighter, while falling more with the clear night sky. The key factor was found to be the shielding effect from airborne particles generated from aeroplane and car pollutants high in the atmosphere that blanket the earth against harmful ultraviolet radiation.

From the results of that period without air travel, it appears that the potential problems of global warming may be worse than initially thought. While particles and jet vapour trails are providing cosmetic protection, they also mask the state of the underlying predicament. In a frightening paradox, we could be fighting to reduce particle emissions (giving a cooling effect) while doing little about greenhouse gas emissions (giving a warming effect). Removing one without the other may indeed speed up the heating process. The two should therefore be tackled in tandem if this conclusion is correct. Scientists have coined a new phrase, 'global dimming'[18] to describe the phenomenon. The particle pollution in the atmosphere is not only reflecting ultraviolet light away from the earth but actually reducing the penetration of the sun's rays. It has been observed that the amount of sunlight hitting the earth's surface has dropped by 10 per cent over half a century.

There are still many sceptics concerning climate change. The study of ancient tree rings shows that there were extreme periods of hot and cold well before mankind had any impact on the environment. Some argue that the complex behaviour of clouds and water vapour has a greater influence than that of atmospheric carbon. Countering this we know that core samples from Arctic ice can demonstrate a positive correlation between carbon dioxide (CO_2) levels and temperature variations. Before the Industrial Revolution took hold, CO_2 concentrations were just 280 parts per million (ppm). They now stand at 381 ppm, and if current trends are extrapolated they will reach as high as 550 ppm by 2050. The effect of new and latent atmospheric carbon could raise temperatures above the crucial 3° Centigrade by the end of this century.[19] In pure financial terms, the 2006 Stern report estimated that the cost of climate change in today's terms would amount to almost $10 trillion, which equates to one fifth of world GDP.

Meanwhile, Professor Bob Carter, an Australian geologist, points out that the climate has been much colder for some 90 per cent of the last 2 million years.[20] While 1970–98 demonstrated a warming phase, the period from 1998 to 2005 was static. He also emphasised that warming occurred during periods of weak economic activity (from 1918 to 1940) while cooling occurred when emissions were high (1948–65). This may back the dimming theory. There is also debate as to whether ocean currents or tropical regions drive changes in temperature. In short, the whole topic is beset with claims and counter-claims. The real question is whether we are prepared to take such an enormous risk in ignoring it altogether. If the sceptics are right then we will expend inordinate amounts of money and resources to resolve a problem over which we have little influence. If the global warming theory is correct then we are just 'three degrees from disaster'. Most large cities are situated at sea level, having originally been established with port facilities in mind. If the ice caps continue to melt at the current rate then a major transformation of our way of life may well be in stall, even in our own lifetime. It is just one of those ironies of history that the most powerful person in the world who can influence change is also from an oil family and may have financial and political interests to protect. If climate change leads to crop failures and water shortages then war and mass migration may well follow – unless, of course, it's different this time and we all communicate and cooperate in a supportive manner to share our resources. Given our track record for building up food mountains while others starve, it would appear unlikely.

Dollar devaluation and a global slowdown will have two unexpected spin-offs which will eventually be for our own good, even though we will not appreciate them to begin with. First, a weaker dollar will push up oil prices. As energy costs soar, fossil fuel demand should eventually fall as its use becomes a luxury. One can argue that a slowdown in global growth will lower oil prices, but we already know that this resource is dwindling, come what may. The second positive aspect is that these rises will do what no government or regulator could ever achieve: they will lead to greater research and usage of non-polluting energy sources. Indeed, the shares of companies involved in this field have already surged. The hotbed of venture capitalism in California's Silicon Valley is humming once again. Firms that once financed Internet start-ups are doing much the same thing[21] with alternative energy companies. Let us hope that this is not the beginning of a fanciful bubble but the start of a brave new world in human endeavour where the innovative elements of capitalism are harnessed for the common good. Another beneficial effect of a slowdown is that of energy conservation and recycling. When we are wealthy and wasteful we dispose with abandon. When times are tough we naturally reuse and recycle. Price may be the master of our destiny to help us save ourselves.

Solving global warming is a process that will require global cooperation. If economies are undergoing turmoil then this is harder to achieve when trade disruptions are in place. There is likewise the problem of pollution arbitrage. If one country regulates and another does not, then industries will switch to the latter area, and will pay a premium to do so. These industries will also provide much-needed jobs, which is the American dilemma. It emits a quarter of the world's greenhouse gases with Bush's home turf of Texas being one of the worst offenders. As the workshop of the world, China is likewise a major culprit where pollution is concerned. Unlike America, they have acknowledged the problem and are taking steps to reduce it. In a centrally planned economy they are more likely to tidy their mess more quickly, without commercial lobbyists to block progress.

While the debate rages on, we know that 2005 was the hottest year on record for the northern hemisphere, while in the UK, 2006 was the warmest year since 1659. Compounding this, particulate deposits have darkened the ice caps and diminished their white, reflective qualities, leading to higher rates of sunlight absorption and melting. The resulting water then soaks up solar energy which in turn tends to discharge dissolved gases like CO_2. As sea temperatures rise, this is likely to increase the intensity of hurricanes,[22] according to Dr Tom Hutson, a research meteorologist. Meanwhile, trapped methane gas, frozen for thousands of years, is being released from ice caps as well as the frozen tundra. Higher temperatures also promote greater activity in soil bacteria which in turn produces more CO_2. In Britain, the lack of winter rainfall has created the worst drought since 1933. Coincidentally, the early 1930s were not just the era of the Great Depression – there was also an international famine. The European heatwave of 2003 brought about the biggest decline in agricultural output in a century. Simultaneously, greenhouse gases were generated from multiple forest fires while low crop yields meant that less carbon dioxide was absorbed compared with normal years. Nature appears to act like the stock market, where ghastly events beget others.

As well as big-picture solutions there has also been a good deal of debate about what we can do to produce our own energy as individuals. Given that centralised power generation loses two thirds of the energy through heat loss and distribution, then it makes sense to generate some of our requirements closer to home. Examples include micro wind turbines, water turbines, solar cells, photovoltaic cells (producing current via electromagnetic radiation), deep-soil heat pumps, biomass boilers[23] and much, much more. The use of alternatives on a small scale highlights the problems shared by large-scale producers: high levels of initial capital are required for minimal output while the financial payback is very long term. Whatever we do, there will still be an energy gap that will occur when the UK's coal and nuclear power stations are decommissioned in the coming decades. We may even have to import French (nuclear) electricity and depend on foreign gas supplies through continentally owned pipelines.

Following the Kyoto Protocol for industrialised countries to reduce greenhouse gas emissions there is at last an incentive for large-scale investment in renewable energy. The Protocol was ratified in February 2005. The US refused to sign up to it, but Russia bought into the deal, so the 55-signatory threshold and emissions target was achieved. These 55 signatory states were jointly responsible in 1990 for over 55 per cent of global CO_2 emissions. Industrialised nations have to reduce their 1990 baseline level of emission by 5.2 per cent by the year 2012. The problem with the Protocol is that it does not account for all emissions, so it will slow, rather than solve, the problem. A system of carbon trading[24] was also introduced by the European Union to allow successful countries to sell their negative carbon quota to those who had not hit their target. The same applies to companies. In this way, those who reduce emissions are rewarded while those who miss their target effectively have to pay to pollute. The success of emission reductions has led to a substantial fall in the price of carbon certificates. Without a shortage, the market price will logically decline and lose its *raison d'être*. With more sellers than buyers, the scheme does not have the financial incentive that had initially worked so well.

Other developments include hybrid cars that use a combination of electric power (at low speed) and conventional fossil fuels (at high speed). Unfortunately, such vehicles require greater energy input in their production that offsets the fuel benefits. An interesting comparison can be made with sea travel where combined engine and sail is already utilised on some tourist vessels. It was not too long ago that wind-driven clippers raced across the Atlantic to deliver goods at high speed. Perhaps we can also couple natural power with man-made engines to provide a solution for goods transportation. One of the great hopes for future car fuel is the hydrogen cell. Hydrogen and oxygen are passed over electrodes such that electricity, heat and water are produced. The principle is based on the reverse of a battery. While the mechanics of the hydrogen cell were first observed in 1839, they are still in the embryonic stage commercially. The curse of all such solutions is that for now, the energy input is greater than the energy output from the process.

Ethanol or pure alcohol is already in the mainstream as a complement to petrol. While it can be produced from corn (starch), this also requires significant energy input. Ethanol production from sugar cane is much more efficient. Brazil has become a leading player in its manufacture and roughly half its sugar crop goes into ethanol production. The World Trade Organisation has ruled that the European Union must cut subsidies on its sugar exports, which will further empower Brazil's producers. Some 70 per cent of Brazilian car sales[25] are for vehicles that can run on petrol, ethanol or a combination of the two. The advantage of ethanol is that it is renewable, clean and improves combustion without polluting groundwater. The disadvantage is that there is less energy produced from its combustion, so double the volume has to be supplied to travel the same distance compared with petrol. Also, the growth in its use may eventually encroach upon crop production for human requirements. It may also entail further rainforest destruction in the race to increase farmland and crops to meet higher demand.

There will be a spill-over from falling financial markets and dollar devaluation into every aspect of our lives. The downturn will bring a marked shift in politics both domestically and internationally. Having been through a period of high interdependency, we are on the edge of a withdrawal phase where trade and relations will polarise and turn inward. The pre-planning and preparation work of countries such as China and Russia will pay dividends. Having milked the West of its last assets, they will emerge as the new leaders. The rebalancing act will bring about an end to our apparently never-ending prosperity as Asian countries resume their past position as world leaders. One of the few bright spots is that we may be at the starting point of reversing our dependence on fossil fuels and slowing global warming.

10

PURITANS AND PENITENCE

For whosoever hath, to him shall be given, and he shall have more abundance: but whosoever hath not, from him shall be taken away even that (which) he hath.
Matthew 13:12

Although the biblical passage above has been quoted out of context, its sentiment can be applied to the giver and taker of interest. Those who accumulate cash will earn more and prosper. Those who are beholden to debt will lose all they own, and more, in the black hole of usury. As the debtor's ditch gets deeper, the lender's spoils pile ever higher.

When the days of conspicuous consumption draw to a close it will no longer be tasteful to flaunt one's wealth, assuming there is any left. This time around, the resurgent zeal of our Puritan ancestors will not be visited on sinners but on those who appear to be unscathed by the downturn. Political commentator H.L. Mencken once described Puritanism as 'the haunting fear that someone somewhere may be happy'. There will be little chance of that when recession turns into depression. In future, anyone beating the bailiff and not seen to be suffering will be viewed as a cheat or the equivalent of a black marketeer in World War II. The fact that they had been frugal and conservative in the good times will matter not. When the Puritans stripped churches of all their finery, adopted plain garb and plainer lifestyles, it was not just a religious phenomenon but a rebellion against the old ways. Adopting a basic way of life will therefore be nothing new.

In a downturn, someone somewhere must be brought to account. For Mid West farmers in early 1930s America, a combination of inappropriate land use and drought conditions led to a devastation of the farmland. Dust bowls smothered the once fertile plains as agriculture slumped after the boom times of the Great War. The peace dividend turned into a rights issue (a call on investors for extra cash). While some farmers stoically accepted this double blow, others lobbied the government for protection, leading to the self-destructive tariffs discussed in the previous chapter. A minority even blamed their woes on speculators in cities who were 'manipulating' crop prices at their expense. The belief that honest country folk were used by conniving city-dwellers was an underlying theme of Frank Baum's original book[1] *The Wizard of Oz*, published in 1901.

Whenever a crash occurs in financial markets, much effort is wasted on chasing shadows after the event. It is always assumed that someone has profited greatly from the collapse and that 'they' were responsible for wiping out our investments. In the 1987 crash, so-called programme trades were held responsible. 'Circuit breakers' have been introduced that shut down the market temporarily (or even close it late in the day) should prices fall too far, too fast. No doubt hedge funds will be called to account for the next crash. While such funds have exacerbated the speculative build-up, the ensuing rout in markets will be a reflection of debt accumulation in all walks of like: as inevitable as the fall of children's bricks when piled too high. America will not give up its superpower status without a fight and every lever will be pulled and strained to engineer a restoration of the good old days. No doubt determined efforts will be made to bail out the economy yet again with further doses of debt. However, there will come a point where it becomes too numb to respond to stimulation, like the frazzled pleasure centre of a cocaine addict's brain. It will be some time before we come to realise that it was the guardians of our central banks who created the conditions for speculation to thrive and for money supply to surge. America's downfall will not have been caused by the terrorist without but by the inflationist within. We will then wonder why we did not heed the Latin phrase '*Quis custodiet ipsos custodes*': 'Who is guarding the guards?'

RETRIBUTION AND REMORSE

We have so far considered a short-term crash coupled with long-term rebalancing. There now remains a hinterland of time between the two that must be filled with a feasible forecast. For the minority that thinks a downturn is inevitable, their efforts are often wasted on debating its sequence and timing. Too little is focused on who it will hurt in the process, let alone identifying the follow-through effects. This section deals with the aftermath of a stock market crash when risk aversion will spread like a virulent plague. Crashes have a variety of direct and indirect effects. Bad news can be self-fulfilling and can severely impact on consumer confidence. The negative blow from falling share prices is most likely to coincide with that of a deteriorating housing market – a double whammy. Given the property and equity market ownership culture of both Britain and America, these two countries will suffer the most from the wizened wealth effect. Since 2003 we have seemingly had the best of everything: low inflation, high employment, strong markets and rising house prices, with cheap and easy access to a proliferation of short-lived goods. Imagine the reverse of the recent sweet-spot and one can see why spending will slump and savings will surge.

As with previous problems in the banking system, too much debt has been secured against overinflated assets. In depressions banks become desperate to insulate themselves from losses on existing loans and demand more security or cushioning for their overly aggressive advances. If asset prices get close to the value of the debt then banks will force liquidation in a bid to protect themselves. Selling begets selling, and in a debt-based economy a lack of fresh lending grinds activity to a halt. As a slowdown squeezes nation after nation, a multitude of easily granted loans will turn into bad debts. Only then will the weakness of the banking system be revealed. One collapsing company has many knock-on effects that choke local activity. Much like breaking the chain in a house purchase, the system is only as strong as the weakest link when it is under duress. Reckless lending will come back to haunt many a greedy banker and catch up with those directors that set excessive sales targets, forcing bank employees to fund unsuitable projects, chase ever-riskier clients and sell inappropriate investment products.

In spite of the dominance of consumers, we should not forget the impact of corporations. Abstemious at first in the face of easy borrowing, they gave way to temptation as merger mania took hold. Bond issuance surged in 2006 as companies geared themselves up to magnify performance and buy back their own shares. This was partly performed as a survival mechanism to fight off predatory private equity funds. In a crunch they will find it harder to endure an environment of high rates and risk aversion. As trend-followers, business people will shelve investment plans and put recruitment on hold. There will also be a cutback in corporate spending and entertainment. All those freebie hospitality days will be but a fond and distant memory. Media and advertising will likewise suffer. This serves to remind us how lemming-like the boardroom mindset can be. The very time that one needs to keep a competitive edge and communicate with customers is during a downturn. Yet advertising budgets are slashed at just such times. This is exactly the point when customer loyalty can be won for life – not when conditions are easy but when they turn tough. If you continue to advertise when others are keeping quiet then you are not just grabbing more of the airtime but doing so at bargain basement prices. It is much the same in the investment business. When the markets are alight you cannot get the broker off the telephone, but when those hot tips turn into damp squibs the sound of silence is deafening.

For many in the Anglo-Saxon arena, the very jobs that made us think we were special will instead make us surplus to requirements. We are talking here about superficial service industries. We think that we are smarter than our forebears and ancestors because we can send e-mails and use computers. Students and graduates must therefore understand that the career that looks a dead cert today will be the dead duck of the next era. This is not to say that students are sheep: it is just that they have not had the experience to understand that the most talked-about area has had its day. It is the lonely, unpopular choice that is the next big thing. The skills learned in the tough courses that no one wants to touch will be in most demand: namely, engineering, science, geology and energy-related fields.

Much like investing, a contrarian philosophy should be adopted to find the right career path. More important still, this philosophy should be utilised to avoid the wrong one. Anything that has thrived in the new millennium is likely to be a casualty. These careers would typically include[2] law, accountancy, surveying, stock broking, corporate finance, property development, construction, public relations, advertising and much, much more. Superfluous and pampering activity, especially in retail, will be hammered. Luxury and extravagance will not just be unaffordable, they will be unfashionable. It should also be remembered that rising fuel costs will be disadvantageous to those who must commute or use transport for their business activities. As ever, the poorest will be hardest hit as travel costs and utility bills eat up a higher proportion of their wages.

BOOK OF REVELATIONS

It is all too easy to be excessively radical when attempting to forecast or contemplate the future. In the 1970s, television series such as *Space 1999* caught the mood of the day. There was a feeling then that in a quarter of a century, we would be in flying saucers wearing silver suits. Yet here we are sporting retro 1970s fashions.

It is now time for us to grow up from the hedonism that debt has fostered and recognise it for what it truly is: a self-indulgent phase. Much like a forty-something's attempt to extend their youth, it is not cool but sad. The baby-boomers have not just squandered their parents' inheritance, they have blown their own savings and mortgaged their children's too. The age group that had it all has spent it all, and more. They now expect the next generation to clear up their financial and environmental mess, and then fund their pensions and healthcare to boot. This is an era where a new breed of radical philosophers will have to ignore the 'wisdom' of their parents and grandparents and think for themselves. They will have to earn their crust in a much tougher world.

In the introduction we compared our apparently easy lifestyle with that of the well-fed human cattle in the film *The Time Machine*: duped into slavery under the yoke of the man-eating Morlochs. We can use the same film to envision our lifestyle in the future. To adapt and survive, we need to sit in a quiet room and imagine how bad life could be should our scenario unfold. Only when we make this journey can we understand how we must gather what we have today for the shortage of tomorrow. To undergo this voyage of discovery one must analyse the aspects of one's daily life that do not usually bear a passing thought. As a rough guide one can consider them as follows: house, garden, food, energy, transport, work, leisure, education, politics, religion and relationships (in no particular order). As the lever on the time machine is pushed forward and the years fly by, we can unleash our imagination. We see stock markets crash, house prices fall, second homes deserted, unemployment rife, food running scarce, big cars abandoned and shortages proliferating. All the while global tensions mount. No one plans for the worst because we 'hope' that all will be well. The government will bail us out or some smart economist will come up with a cute and painless plan. Maybe not this time. The longest-ever expansion is likely to be followed by the longest-ever bust. If we get used to this scenario right now then we can take the edge off the worst to come. Before the eighteenth century, living standards across the world were relatively even. If a rebalancing occurs then it is us whose lifestyles will suffer as the developing countries improve: reversion to mean is not just an investment phenomenon.

Before we visit the future we can take a trip down memory lane. During the global party – or Jazz Era – that was the 1920s, traditions and conventions were brushed aside. Women were liberated and held their own in the smoking, drinking and drug-taking of the time. Property and stock market speculation was rife and a consumer boom in cars and gadgets raged. Once the 1930s Depression took hold, the realisation dawned that free market forces were too powerful to be left unfettered. The mood between the decades changed from migration and globalisation to nationalism and centralisation. The planned economy became the acceptable norm as the likes of Stalin rolled out his Five Year Plans with colossal construction in mind.

As the Roman Empire collapsed and its worthless, tinny coins ceased to make their way to Britain, urban existence in many areas ground to a halt. Entire towns were abandoned as they depended on the flow of currency to function. Without money, the population had to grow food or produce something relevant with which to barter. The case is often made that we can never go back in our living standards because of technology. Inventions cannot be un-invented. However, that technology can become superfluous or too expensive, as we saw with Concorde. Alternatively, it may not be realisable on such a large scale for centuries to come – just look at the sophistication of water and sewage systems of Ancient Rome. Such standards were not achieved again until the twentieth century: some would argue they have still not caught up, given the leakage rate from modern water pipes.

While such thoughts of a second Dark Age are too extreme for most tastes – and in any case extremely far-fetched – it should not stop us from reviewing a softer option. If a commodity crisis unfolds we could be left to cope with much higher fuel and food prices. Aside from having to conserve energy at home and work, we will need to be responsible for some of our own supply, either domestically or communally within our neighbourhood. A return to this quasi-country living is again unlikely, if only because the population is now so much larger. However, there may be ways that communities can come together to share a common energy point that would otherwise go to waste. While wealth allows us to stand alone, a lack of it will mean we will need each other for support. It really isn't such a bad thing – our ancestors seemed to cope with it.

Like the populations they represent, governments will be desperately short of money. The tax take will dwindle just as the demand for state aid begins to soar. The tax collection tactics of the future may well make King John look like a charity worker. One striking undercurrent that has been at play in both Britain and America has been the relentless quest to gather and store information about us. Every move we make leaves some kind of electronic imprint, while databases and DNA records abound. The actions of democratically elected governments are putting an infrastructure in place that would do any dictatorship proud. Anti-terrorist legislation has already been abused and legal parameters called into question as British business people have been extradited to America to face charges in that country. Perhaps we may one day see authors and journalists arrested in their own country and dragged across the Atlantic for anti-American sentiment. The 'War on Terror' feels more repressive by the day, just as we are informed that such legislation is put in place to protect our freedom. Future generations may well demand why we sat round and failed to protest or react in time.

Like refugees on the run, international investors will snatch every liquid asset and take it with them. In time-honoured fashion, the knee-jerk response to a financial meltdown would see the introduction of exchange controls. They will no doubt appear hand-in-hand with tariffs on imports. Every move will be made to prevent capital flight out of each country. Often introduced as a temporary measure, these interventions have a habit of becoming a permanent feature, as yet another mechanism for control. In this environment, finance centres such as Switzerland and Singapore will be pressured by external governments as their currency and banking system will be in huge demand as a safe haven. Tax amnesties will be waved in front of the world's wealthy, as a way of bringing more taxable wealth onshore. It is unlikely that many would comply as money is placed offshore for a purpose: not for mere status or tax avoidance, but as an insurance policy against disaster or dictatorship.

A strange paradox could emerge where businesses are given far more freedom to create jobs yet central planning becomes much more influential. There will be the age-old argument of private sector versus the state in terms of efficiency. While westerners point to the shortages in the former Soviet Union as an example, there are some Muscovites (even those that have since become multi-millionaires) who will tell you that the deficiencies only appeared after *glasnost*. Retailers of every hue will face a serious squeeze. Commercial landlords will be left with a lack of cashflow to cover their costs when tenants default. The geared nature of commercial property prices will leave them with a big capital loss, assuming they can even find a buyer. No doubt pension funds and insurance companies will attempt to offload their shopping malls and office space all at the same time: just as they did in the early 1990s. The buildings and systems that we use will in any case need an overhaul. Although the latest designs have taken energy usage into account, there is no getting away from the fact that these edifices require huge energy input for lighting, IT systems and climate control.

On the subject of houses, the proliferation of second homes may be too tempting a target for commandeering or taxation. In the USA, 40 per cent of house purchases in 2005 were for second homes, so there will be plenty of stock to go round. Buy-to-let developers will no longer be investors but will be labelled as greedy landlords. If we see a re-run of the Great Depression then there will be many homeless and unemployed people to house and feed. Second-home owners may face a carrot and stick approach: lease out your spare home to the government for a peppercorn rent, sell under compulsory purchase orders or face being squeezed with a big tax – given the lack of buyers, many people with second homes might jump at the offer. Banks that had lent recklessly will be left with the keys to thousands of premises, as they were after the last property slump. No doubt these paragons of the free market will look to the government to offload their past errors.

Away from the cities and into the country, it is unlikely that American and European agriculture will receive the same degree of subsidy that it enjoyed in the past. In spite of the failure of the World Trade Organisation talks[3] in 2006 – to break the subsidy system for these farmers – the writing appears to be on the wall for such support. As with the IMF doctrine on developing world trade deficits, America has failed to practice what it preaches[4] where subsidies are concerned: acceptable at home but not in target markets. This is not to say that the farmers were getting rich from them. They have often been the difference between survival and bankruptcy. This is another industry cursed with the life and death struggle of heavy debts, where economies of scale override sustainability. There is also a downside for the developing world in this scenario. When transport costs and trade disputes are increasing, it will be harder for them to sell agricultural produce overseas. Then again, if subsidies are reduced, they can at last compete on a more even footing, transport costs aside. Pride in regional produce and dishes may also reappear. The joy of domestic produce comes with the anticipation and tantalisation that seasonality brings. This should help reduce the ridiculous mileage that some food is undergoing to make its way to our shelves in the depths of winter. Higher fuel costs should make home-produced provisions much more attractive.

When governments run short of money, a variety of schemes may come to fruition that would otherwise be unthinkable today. Rather than allowing a black economy to flourish, which it typically does in a slump, we could see the elimination of high denomination paper cash, with only coins maintained for the smallest of purchases. By making all transactions recordable there is less scope for tax evasion or for the proceeds of crime to circulate underground. This would not be for any moral purpose but to bring 'under the mattress' money back into circulation where it can be taxed.

Whipping up hatred against a common enemy is a cynical trick used by politicians down the ages. Rather than demonising individuals or nationalities, we could instead turn our fighting spirit against poverty and pollution. While there is still debate as to whether global warming truly exists, it could still be used in any case as a way of bringing us together. In World War II, Lord Beaverbrook came up with an inspired move by imploring the public to deposit their spare aluminium utensils to go toward the war effort. The conversion of pans to planes was not that clear-cut, but the mood of wanting to help caught everyone by surprise. It may not have been the intention to strip every park and public building of their ornate iron railings, but this is just what happened. Whether or not it was a public relations move was not the point – by involving everyone from the grassroots upwards, it moulded the country into one. Many who endured the horrors of the war years also point to the paradox of this period. One feature they noted was the satisfaction felt when working together for a common cause and the selflessness of the majority of people. At heart we are communal animals that love to sing along at concerts or scream our team to victory. When that undercurrent is tapped, unimaginable results can be realised. If a message is spread by the right people in the right context, new ideas can spread as vigorously as a virus through a population. This was the theme of Malcolm Gladwell's wonderful book *The Tipping Point* which emphasised that small changes can make a big difference.

In a downturn there is likely to be a much greater involvement in voluntary and charity work. The ever-growing ranks of jobless will be employed on infrastructure projects, most likely involving energy conservation and generation. The more that oil supply is used as a tactical weapon, the more widespread and surprising will be the alternative energy solutions. Human initiative is awe-inspiring, especially when applied creatively and peacefully. The agony of childbirth is the price paid by women for the genetic investment in larger human brains; let us hope that we use them to good effect.

Tourism is another area that is likely to bear the brunt of bad times. Not only will there be a lack of disposable income for taking a holiday, but there is the energy aspect that will curtail the era of cheap and regular flights. This will doubtless have a knock-on effect for all those holiday homes or 'investments' in rough and ready properties across old and emerging Europe. Locations that are easily accessible via localised sea-travel would become more attractive, with less risk of terrorist attacks. Just as hoteliers race to turn hotels into flats in the Channel Islands, so a surge in tourism will catch them off guard. From a cost and environmental angle, local destinations provide a double benefit. While many in Britain sneer at the old seaside resorts that our grandparents loved to visit, they may well become the destination of choice. It is on this subject that a downturn offers us the greatest hope for the future: not in wealth but in health. A decrease in unnecessary demand, industrial production and transport will reduce pollution, as will the higher price of fossil fuels. What we at first take to be misfortune will turn out to be our salvation. Only the passage of time will show us how fate has done us a favour and steered us away from a doomed course of action. We cling to our old, familiar way of life because we think it is what we want and fear the unknown alternatives. However, the next phase will be different, but better than before.

PIETY AND FRUGALITY

Once the depression is under way, we will come to understand that we really weren't that smart after all. While effortless borrowing provided a free and easy lifestyle, the weekends of buying up boutiques or bingeing in bars will seem like a distant memory from a past life evoked under hypnosis. Job insecurity and a lifetime of debt repayments will soon wipe away our smug attitudes. Celebrity status will mean little as substance will be valued over trivia and gloss. Humility, conservative appearance and conformist behaviour will become the order of the day. This is not to say that the public will become easily-led automatons. If anything, there will be a surge of interest in political topics and debates.

Having depended on immigration to make up for a declining birth rate in the West, the lack of opportunities will drive immigrants to greener pastures. To encourage the production of offspring, some tax breaks, cash rewards or working improvements may well come to pass. There is also no reason why house husbands could not take a leading role in child-rearing – times have changed since the Great Depression. It is the catch-22 of developed nations that economic growth encourages more women to work, which in turn reduces the birth rate. Perhaps 'encourage' is the wrong word given that few women have any choice in the matter as many couples must work simply to survive and service their vast mortgages. The debt-driven deterioration of purchasing power has forced many of us into the drudgery of rule-bound office environments, whether we want it or not. Everyone now has a 'career', no matter what they do. Such platitudes offer us hope that we are doing something worthwhile. A depression will paradoxically provide us with genuine autonomy, as we are freed from debt's shackles over the long haul.

Television series and movies will undoubtedly alter their emphasis. The programmes that focus on property speculation, luxury and antiques will vanish, while those on a theme of frugality will flourish. Areas of interest will include DIY, recycling, home growing, home cooking, home brewing, debt reduction and repair. In the garden, ornamental aspects will be overturned by their utility function. Vegetable patches will spring up where once were blooming borders. There is likely to be greater interest in the use of allotments: growing vegetables to further stretch the family budget, which is commonplace in France today.[5]

Elsewhere we may become a nation of food fanatics but for all the right reasons as the downturn allows us to rediscover the joys of home crops and cooking. This is not meant to portray a quaint impression of a 1950s throwback, of housewives with ribbons in their hair and an apple pie baking in the oven. This time both adults and offspring could be involved in home growing: sharing activities instead of being glued to electronic games and gadgets. To use France as an example once more, one can still see families in hedgerows, fields and forests, foraging for the fresh pickings on offer. This is not because they are poverty-stricken peasants but because the act of harvesting nature (for free) is a highly nutritious and satisfying activity. Depending on where one lives, this may involve gathering from the seashore or countryside. Farmers' markets will continue to flourish as local produce at last competes with the transport-laden costs of goods in centralised supermarkets. Endless rules on food standards will become obsolete as the source of our nutrition will be more localised and less mass-produced. The need for uniformity of fruit and vegetables will no longer be relevant as we become less neurotic and savour such quirky and flavoursome offerings.

Where building and property is concerned, first-time buyers need no longer fret about getting on the ladder. The time to buy is when the braggarts go on about how dumb it is to do so and why they are so smart at having chosen to rent. This may be many years away but it will pay to be patient. In a downturn, it makes sense to share and we may once again find generations of the same family under the same roof to minimise costs. It may also lead to a greater degree of care and respect for the elderly; that rare breed which is not mortgaged to the hilt and whose life's work is taxed into oblivion upon their death. If staying under the same roof as one's in-laws invokes feelings of angst, then that will indeed be a tough prospect. Nevertheless, with as many as one in three people living alone in some areas, it can only be healthy to have a little more human contact.

On the leisure front, collective activities were common in the 1930s and this may well reappear, albeit with some modern spin. Lidos were all the rage for public bathing and all kinds of communal activities flourished. Amateur dramatics, cycling, camping and outdoor activities were likewise popular. Anything that was inexpensive to organise was the overriding factor. The combination of more exercise and outdoor living is the upside of a depression. The emphasis on amusing ourselves instead of being spoon-fed entertainment could also lead to greater fulfilment and involvement.

Where religion is concerned, this has a much greater undercurrent in America than in Britain today. The Protestant work ethic and Puritan roots were never far below the surface across the Atlantic. These qualities may indeed re-emerge as Americans follow the lead of their New England ancestors – rejecting worldly temptation for a life of piety. An economic crunch may also lead to a renewed interest in nature and the spiritual side of our being as feelings of self-reliance dissipate. In the early days of British Christianity there was a harmonious mix of ancient and modern in the form of the Celtic Church, which combined the pagan traditions of the Celts while adopting early Christian teaching. Perhaps we will revert to a similar style of religion where nature is respected and men and women are equal – like the sun and moon of the cycle: opposite yet complementary.

DEPRESSION SUPPRESSION

Having reviewed what may come to pass on both a personal and national level, it then begs the question of what it is that we can do in practical terms. Put simply, one should spend less and save more, but this is about as helpful as thin people saying eat less and exercise more. There are many parallels between debt and the deterioration of our modern industrially-produced food, in that the latter gives one a sugar rush but no nutrition, which in turn creates further cravings. Like dieting, there is no magic pill or potion to cure our debt dependency.[6]

The entrepreneur reading this book may be mulling over ideas and making mental preparations for this scenario. Money-lending pawn shops are the ultimate trade which thrives in bad times. It is no coincidence that since interest rates went up, the shares of pawnbroking companies have been on a tear in both Britain and America. A slump is likely to require a raft of loss adjustors to judge on a surge in real and phoney insurance claims alike. Anyone working in the field of debt collection, bailiff duties, auctioneering and credit rating will be spoiled for choice.[7] It would also be wise to learn some bargaining techniques.[8] Surviving a downturn is as much about working together with others as it is about accumulating cash and commodities. It is worthwhile building contacts in an unselfish way: clubs and societies already abound.

Having been in the doldrums for decades, farming may well make a comeback, albeit with fewer subsidies than in the past. The desire for a rural life coupled with higher food prices may once again make it a viable lifestyle of choice rather than one of subsistence. This could be the time to buy both farm and woodland: preferably in protected areas where property developers are restricted and have not already ramped up prices. Ethical investors should also consider investing in green technology or timber funds for their commodity exposure, if the idea of investing in mining runs contrary to one's conscience. As repossessions soar there will be a need for cheap storage space to place household possessions. The glut of commercial property should provide the requisite warehousing facilities. As industry and retail activity becomes more parochial, storage will become vital. Once the days of JIT (Just In Time) production fades from our memories then the emphasis will fall on holding some degree of stock to minimise transport costs. Discount stores will thrive but, depending on international relations, they may use local suppliers instead of those further afield. We will need to trade closer to home because of the political and transport problems involved with distant imports. One day it may only be the wealthiest who can import items from such regions as China comes to dominate both luxury and high-tech manufacturing in decades to come.

On the subject of Asia, this is one area where antique dealers could do themselves a favour. When the likes of India and China were colonised, their prized possessions were shipped back to Europe. As these countries return to their former glory, there will be a strong desire to bring home their ancestors' inheritance. As western economies founder, this will be the time to snap up these items for export to the new rich in the East. This is no supposition as there is already a precedent for it. Samurai swords were banned in Japan and were sold abroad in the 1870s. With the onset of the Asian boom a century later, wealthy Japanese businessmen came back with a vengeance to repurchase their national artefacts at a serious price premium. There are likely to be other advantages accruing with the moneyed folk of the Orient. Having endured prolonged colonial occupation, there may be a niche in the tourist market for Chinese and Indians to lord it over their old imperial masters. Tours to New York and London will be equivalent to our trips to Rome today – a visit to the heart of a once-great empire. As Britain moves from peak to trough in little more than a century, Asian visitors will marvel at how short-lived the dominance of the West proved to be. Learning a foreign language may give the competitive edge one needs for future careers. Ideally, it should be one that is used in the likes of Russia, China, India or Brazil.

The modern mantra of 'speculate to accumulate' will reverse. For those who care little about community and networks, they may be more concerned with the monetary angle. The most important element of building a cash pot is to keep it in a safe bank. Make yourself familiar with what it is your bank is doing in the background. How exposed is the bank to the mortgage market, for example? While wealthier clients will already be catered for, it should look for a private bank with limited debt which is not involved in the merry-go-round of credit derivatives. When the final crash comes, every asset will be caught up. However, gold and commodities will be a good medium-term play working as insurance rather than investment. They should be bought from a scarcity and chaos point of view rather than being a play on global growth. This will help one psychologically when a downturn initially hits these investments. Gold is good – until it becomes highly speculative – but must be held in various forms to achieve geographical spread and diversify risk. It should be considered as a temporary antidote rather than a long-term cure. Fixed income securities must be top quality in nature, preferably issued by governments. While longer-dated bonds will perform very well in a slump, one should hold a variety of maturities to provide cashflow and dampen the price volatility. Stable currencies such as the Swiss franc and the Singapore dollar are safe havens, but they pay low interest rates as a result.

While it will be tempting to buy shares after a crash, it is best to wait for the after-shocks and later sell-off to work through the system. In any case, one should only consider defensive companies with good dividends. These include consumer staple stocks (those that sell essentials), utilities and perhaps pharmaceutical companies. Although dividends are a good feature, one must remember that in a downturn any company can cut them back or even demand fresh funds from shareholders. While banks are tempting in terms of dividend yield, it must be remembered that they are one of the biggest single sectors in world stock markets. Although their dominance is not as extreme as technology shares in the TMT bubble, the largest sector today often becomes tomorrow's dud. The growth of the banks is a reflection of increased speculation, consumerism and debt – the three prime casualties of the future environment. They generate a quarter of the stock market's earnings and their share of market capitalisation has risen five-fold since the early 1970s. It is hardly the time to be adding them to a portfolio.

Regular savings plans with top fund companies or investment trusts (in the case of the UK) may be worthwhile because they nibble at the market and gradually accumulate shares at a variety of prices and varying conditions. As higher-risk investments, shares will in future be used to generate a higher income than deposits but will not be expected to provide capital growth. This is the curse that has led to so many conflicts of interest in the past. By cutting taxes on dividends and penalising capital growth and speculation, the emphasis will encourage income generation as a way of bringing real – not borrowed – cash back into the economy. Genuine cashflow and dividend payments to shareholders are much harder to fake than manipulated earnings per share figures. As western markets diminish in importance, one should also consider emerging stock markets. They have already blossomed but the depression will create opportunities as the good is thrown out with the bad. There are plenty of funds that invest in such areas which will benefit from commodity strength and dollar weakness.

A devaluing dollar will drive up US interest rates in an effort to stem capital flight. Like a faulty water-pump, the suction effect of the raised rates will not hold the liquidity for long: soon it will gush back out from whence it came. As highlighted by James Turk and John Rubino in *The Coming Collapse of the Dollar and How to Profit From It*, the more the dollar devalues the more gold rises. It could then become viable to introduce a new gold standard and revert to the financial discipline of the past. While the gold standard brought periods of great stability, it also caused unnecessary austerity with 'poverty amongst plenty' – a veritable sledgehammer to crack a nut. There seems little reason to arrange our finances based on geology when we have the technology (but not yet the philosophy) to organise money flows.

MASTERING THE MORLOCHS

It is a frequent human fault to pigeonhole or demonise individuals, religions or nationalities during times of economic stress. This book is not aiming to whip up hatred against any group, be they bankers or business people, as the author in any case fits both these categories. We are all trapped in a lousy system which has fooled us into believing that more work and possessions will make us happy and fulfilled. At the same time we should not hark back to the 'good old days' as the current period is the best era in which to be alive relative to many episodes in history.

We should not fear the turmoil that faces us but instead should think deeply about the meaning of words such as 'apocalyptic' or 'Armageddon', which will no doubt be used by critics of this book. The word 'apocalypse' means 'unveiling', while the result of the biblical Armageddon is a 1,000-year period of peace. While there is little that can be done to prevent the forthcoming downturn, which is in effect a form of healing, we can at least jump one step ahead to think of solutions, if indeed any exist. It is always tempting to make the case for a system that worked in the past, albeit temporarily. We have followed a variety of regimes down the ages which have all come and gone. Time and again our leaders have taken the inflationary path to court popularity. With the advent of debt-based banking, bouts of currency devaluation have become the norm. In modernity we have tried fiscal austerity under President Clinton followed by the exact opposite under President George W. Bush with the debt-driven dilution of the dollar. Surely there can be no more options open, otherwise they would have been tried and tested?

In reality they have already been thought of but rarely countenanced because they appear counter-intuitive. If one swaps the latter word with 'contrarian' then all of a sudden this should make one stop and think, bearing in mind the success of this strategy in investment. We frequently find in history how eccentric or revolutionary thought can one day become the established norm. There is also an old saying that 'the problem is the solution'. Rather like being stung by a nettle, one will often find a soothing dock leaf in the same area. In an economy based on bank debt there is a constant burden of catch-up for both companies and consumers, like jogging up a downward escalator just to stand still. By stepping off the conveyer mechanism, and moving the economy onto a firm debt-free footing, then more leisurely progress can be made with less effort and pointless production. If the problem is debt, spending and speculation, then the solution is likely to be one of credit, saving and investment. As consumers save more and bank lending is curbed, greater savings have a propensity to lower interest rates and ease the burden of existing debt.[9]

Before concluding this book, it is worth considering some 'what if' scenarios that may one day be possible if we open our minds to monetary reform. What if we could pay wages and capital expenditure for healthcare and hospitals, education and infrastructure projects yet minimise budget deficits and inflation. Would that be attractive? Could business start-ups, first-time buyers and students break the debt trap with a whole new generation freed from its tyranny? Can companies really be good employers and make products based on quality and longevity, without having to pass on previous debts through higher prices? Could banks act as stewards and mentors of business, matching investors with entrepreneurs, rather than indebting both parties? Could they loan money and provide mortgages, according to need and not speculation? Imagine a process that would satisfy some (but not all) of the philosophical differences between left and right. Could one be social without being socialist and engage elements of capitalism without the usual cronyism? Such a system could sample the best of both worlds with the government providing public services while allowing businesses to be innovative and be rewarded for advancements in engineering and technology. It could give the customer the quality they deserve on items that actually last, without having to ship goods from the ends of the earth.

Michael Rowbotham has suggested that a harmonious system can indeed be fostered by increasing the amount of true cash in the economy as opposed to bank debt and borrowing. It also appears that a strong currency can be compatible with having a social conscience. A faint echo may be discerned from the history books in this regard. During the crisis of the third century, the Roman Empire was beset by external invasion and civil war as well as hyperinflation as the coinage was debased. It took a strong general like Emperor Aurelian to turn the tide. Although his reign was brief, he fought campaigns up and down the country to restore order. He even fought a pitched battle against the corrupt Mint workers in Rome who were extracting precious metals during the production of coins, thereby creating inflation. It may not be a fluke that after he improved the precious metal content of coins, he was still able to pardon debts and be generous with food handouts to the poor.

Like the classroom experiment of dropping detergent on a film of oil, we can indeed break the layer of debt that is choking us, allowing it to be dissolved in the process. By an incredible coincidence, an application of just such a financial experiment occurred in the Channel Islands in the early nineteenth century. On Guernsey pound notes, the clue is provided by a miniature print of the beautiful town market building, with the date 1822 over the entrance. Known as the Guernsey Experiment, unemployed troops returning from the Napoleonic Wars were set to work on restoring the sea defences and building a school and new town market, all of which still stand today. Like many projects in the past, labour and materials were available but no funding could be found. By issuing notes that were not repayable on demand, the States, as the island government is still called, was able to pay for the exercise then recall the notes in years to come. No deficits were created, no interest was paid and no inflation resulted. This exercise was repeated several times over the next century. Money became what it always should have been: a bland token of exchange to aid transactions in the real world, and not a means of making more money through interest.[10]

Authors often talk of a voyage of discovery in their research. For me it has been more like space travel. At first I thought I was reasonably smart, but I have since been humbled, realising that my education, training and experience of markets was simply a product of our time. It likewise never crossed my mind that my ambitions for my own children might one day provide a partial solution to a big-picture problem. My aim is to give them a start without the slavery of student debt and a property without the millstone of a mortgage. It is a tall order that will entail much sacrifice and foregoing of luxuries. This gift will not give them a leisurely life but will remove the burden of a lifetime of liabilities. It provides liberty to pursue a vocation that satisfies them, whether it makes money or not. This freedom of choice is most surely the greatest legacy one can offer: enough to encourage industry but not too much to spoil them.

I am fortunate in that the Channel Islands, my home, have not been beset by the injustice of inheritance tax that would otherwise make the task insurmountable. The most inequitable element is that it appears envious. Worse still, the very people it is meant to ensnare are rarely caught. For the super-rich it is effectively a voluntary tax, as they can in any case pick and choose their residence and tax jurisdiction. This is why the cream of Russia lives in Britain – the ultimate tax haven for moneyed foreigners. The new aristocracy can even negotiate with the relevant fiscal authorities around the world to pay a special tax rate or a fixed amount of money. It is noticeable that countries with minimal or no inheritance tax have sound finances, such as the Channel Islands, Singapore and Switzerland. While it may be argued that they are also major financial centres, this has not always been the case. This issue goes to the heart of the problem highlighted in the introduction. Where there is no incentive to save – and such action is penalised during one's lifetime – then it is no wonder that debt is so tempting. Why bother to accumulate assets for one's old age, only for them to be sold to pay for nursing home fees? Any action to invoke monetary reform after a crisis must also include a simplification of the existing complex tax regime, which has created an industry for accountants in its own right.

Rather than vilifying the international wealthy we should instead learn from them. They often set up offshore trusts which allow the distribution of their assets in a sustainable manner for many years, or even generations, after their death. Depending on the wishes of the settlor (the wealth creator), trustees disburse the money in a controlled fashion which minimises the chance of the beneficiaries (usually their children) from becoming wastrels. We can follow this model to provide the next generation with a head-start rather than a handicap. The housing slump will provide an incredible opportunity for the government to buy up housing stock on the cheap, preferably through a credit-based rather than a debt-based mechanism. Instead of taking on huge mortgages, our offspring can be provided with no-cost housing. Rather than paying rent or mortgages, they can pay into a trust fund to finance their own pension or portfolio (which banks could not use as collateral for lending). The hand-up given by the state would paradoxically reduce government debt in the long run as people become less state-dependent over time. There would still be the issue as to whether there would be enough bonds in existence for pension funds to meet liabilities for their pensioners. However, as debt is whittled out of the system, inflationary pressures would be curtailed and allow cash to be used as a store of value without the need for fixed interest investments with their certainty of cashflow. There would need to be a curtailment of debt creation, and the first place to start would be bank lending such that any fresh lending would have to be matched with deposits on a one-for-one basis. There are so many methods of gearing up and leveraging in all walks of banking and investment that no sooner has one created a rule than someone will discover a loophole, like an addict who can always find money for a fix.

Would a no-cost housing system be abused? Of course it would. However, if we trust the next generation then we may well be surprised by the communal buy-in. Like weddings where there is a free bar, most guests feel embarrassed about going overboard. There will always be those who take advantage, but they will be despised by the majority. The object of the exercise is not to suggest a perfect system at the end of a relatively short book, but to stimulate a philosophical debate. Once we have a dream or set of ideals to follow, the mechanics of the process can be determined in its wake – the method should follow but not lead reform and must not be used as an excuse to avoid it. The automatic reaction to such proposals will no doubt be cynical and a case of 'it will never work'. This is exactly the same manner in which such ideas were greeted two centuries ago in Guernsey, but once the building projects were completed, the populace were delighted. The constraints are there to be conquered, but first we must be sure about what it is that we want for ourselves and our offspring. The Founding Fathers of America had a very clear idea of the way forward, learning from past mistakes to seek equality and opportunity. It took a bloody revolution to establish such principles – let us seek a bloodless one.

By adopting these philosophies, we could satisfy the many aspects of our life that are so lacking: the freedom to follow both personal and national goals without the necessity to indulge in a rat race or tension-inducing trade wars. We should reward good behaviour and foster the savings culture rather than taxing economy. The earlier this starts the better. Instead of compounding debt we can compound interest. During his office, President Clinton discussed ideas of taxing bad things like polluters[11] while leaving the likes of saving well alone. This approach was blocked because lobby groups in the car and energy industry crushed the idea. We will look back in horror at how vital policy decisions could possibly have been influenced by such narrow-minded and selfish constraints based on greed.

We began the first chapter with the visionary foresight of the US President and Founding Father, Thomas Jefferson. It is now appropriate to use two further Jefferson quotes at the end of the final chapter. First, 'I like the dreams of the future better than the history of the past'; second, 'and to preserve their [the people's] independence, we must not let our rulers load us with perpetual debt. We must make our selection between economy and liberty, or profusion and servitude.' The downturn will make us financially poorer and we will just have to get used to getting by. However, the benefits will be well beyond our imagination or expectation, but different from the material goals relentlessly pursued with little thought for others. We are likely to be happier and more fulfilled both communally and spiritually.

Throughout my research it has been clear that every profession is dogged by entrenched extremes of factional fighting, as great as any religious divide. 2006 has witnessed the deaths of two great though opposing economic thinkers: namely, Milton Friedman and John Kenneth Galbraith. The latter was a liberal and an advocate of Keynes, believing that government spending and control through taxation provided social justice and sustainability. Professor Friedman was the driving force behind the Chicago School of economics that promoted the laissez-faire approach of allowing market forces and capitalism to call the shots: a view followed by both Ronald Reagan and Margaret Thatcher. He argued that deficit spending by governments was inflationary and that the quantity of money determined economic activity. By limiting money supply, inflation would be controlled and there would be greater economic freedom. The role of government would be reduced and result in lower levels of taxation.

Perhaps both economists were right in their own way; only their theories should not have been applied universally, but to different areas of the economy. When the state is dominant, it tends to loosen the purse strings while smothering private enterprise and individuals with excessive regulation and taxation. This can frequently be inflationary. When market forces are applied to public services, cuts abound and inappropriate business practices of targets and 'efficiency' measures lead to poor service and an ever-greater bureaucracy. Such market-driven solutions are often deflationary. Perhaps the reason that the two have never been able to coexist is because of debt. Government deficits balloon because they are compounded by interest and are rarely paid off. If credit could be created without interest, then later withdrawn, inflation would not take hold. This would appear to be ideal for government projects and public services. Meanwhile, the curbing of debt creation by banks would suppress price pressures and preserve purchasing power for individuals and corporations. The latter could both do with less tax and regulation, but this could only exist where inflation was low and income generation took priority over the misplaced inducement for capital growth and ever-increasing profits. Financial sustainability will come from organic growth rather than artificial stimulation which so often benefits the minority at the expense of the majority.

The coming depression will convince economists, business people and politicians to accept that the current system is now bust and that the old orthodoxy no longer applies. The solution will not be found in bland consensus or compromise but in a revolutionary revision of thinking. Nothing has to be reinvented as the tools already exist that can do the job, albeit with some alteration in emphasis, like swords to ploughshares. Just as we mix uncorrelated investments in a portfolio – to achieve the optimal level of risk and reward – so we can incorporate a broad range of opinions into the same solution, creating a portfolio of thought that is not myopic or polarised. We frequently see in nature how diverse species make strange bedfellows that cooperate and complement each other through symbiosis. As psychologists will confirm, it is the use of diverse psychometric profiles and talents that has created some of the greatest success stories in business and human history, much like opposites attracting in a marriage. Good ideas can be apolitical and should not be pigeonholed or dismissed just because they appear to be on the left or right politically, or contrary to one's own ingrained viewpoint. Perhaps one day we will run two financial systems in parallel for everyone's benefit which taps the best of both the public and the private sector. This can only be contemplated with the destruction of debt, which will be the greatest achievement of the forthcoming and final crash. We can and will work together for a better future. It is just a pity that we have to endure so much pain before our heads are banged together and we come to our senses.

NOTES

CHAPTER 1

1. <http://www.ofheo.gov/media/pdf/2q05hpi.pdf#search='office%20of%20federal%20housing%20house%20price%20inflation%202005>.
2. Kathleen M. Howley, *Bloomberg News*, 'U.S. home price may fall as inventories favor buyers', 7 September 2006.
3. ABN Amro, *Overnight Report*, 'Bursting bubbles', 1 December 2005. National Bureau of Economic Research, working paper 8992.
4. John P. Calverley, *Bubbles and How to Survive Them*, London: Nicholas Brealey Publishing, 2004, p. 13.
5. For further historical examples, see Charles P. Kindleberger, *Manias, Panics and Crashes: A History of Financial Crises*, 4th edn, New York: John Wiley & Sons, 2000.
6. Joseph Stiglitz, *The Roaring Nineties: Why We're Paying the Price for the Greediest Decade in History*, London: Penguin Books, 2004, p. 7.
7. Gretchen Morgensen, *New York Times*, 'After the debt feast comes the heartburn', 27 November 2005 (re-published on Richard Russell's newsletter).
8. Richard Russell, *Dow Theory letters*, 9 June 2006.
9. Terry Savage, *Chicago Sun-Times*, 'Look before you leap on Greenspan's ARM plug', 4 March 2005, <http://www.suntimes.com/output/savage/cst-fin-terry045.html>.
10. Stephen Schurr, *Financial Times*, 'Bernanke gets a tough grade from hedge fund alpha males', 19 May 2006.
11. ABN Amro, *Overnight Report*, 'Perpetual motion', 20 January 2006.
12. ABN Amro, *Overnight Report*, 'The warm California sun', 18 April 2005.
13. Richard Russell, *Dow Theory Letters*, 4 April 2005.
14. ABN Amro, *Overnight Report*, 'US house price inflation' 18 April 2005.
15. ABN Amro, *Overnight Report*, 'Euphoria', 5 December 2005.
16. <http://www.in2perspective.com/nr/2006/04/another-record-smashed-us-second-homes-sales.jsp>.

17. Christopher Swann, *Financial Times*, 'Housing boom brings record loan debt, says Harvard', 13 June 2006.
18. Richard Russell, *Dow Theory Letters*, 28 March 2005.
19. Robert C. Beckman, *The Downwave: Surviving the Second Great Depression*, London: Pan Books Ltd, 1983, pp. 106–7.
20. ABN Amro, *Overnight Report*, 'Another look at US housing', 29 March 2005.
21. Morgensen, 'After the debt feast comes the heartburn'.
22. Richard Russell, *Dow Theory Letters*, 9 June 2006.
23. For a full explanation of the risks in the American mortgage market along with the inherent concerns over Freddie Mac and Fannie Mae see John R. Talbott, *The Coming Crash in the Housing Market*, New York: McGraw-Hill, Inc., 2003, pp. 119–39. For the British version see Fred Harrison, *Boom Bust: House Prices, Banking and the Great Depression of 2010*, London: Shepheard-Walwyn (Publishers) Ltd, 2005.

CHAPTER 2

1. <http://www.bankofengland.co.uk/statistics/mew/2003/2003Q4.xls>.
2. <http://www.acadametrics.co.uk/FTHPI%20Historic%20Series%20from%201995%20June%202006.pdf>.
3. <http://news.bbc.co.uk/1/hi/business/4488432.stm>.
4. Chris Giles, *Financial Times*, 'Mortgage debt exceeds £1,000bn as house price inflation edges up', 30 June 2006.
5. ABN Amro, *Overnight Report*, 'Unsettled', 17 January 2006.
6. <http://www.hbosplc.com/media/includes/Scotland%20FTB%20Review%2005.doc>. HBOS First Time Buyer Annual Review 2005.
7. <http://www.ft.com/cms/s/ab5e8f72-b7b6–11d9–8f87–00000e2511c8,dwp_uuid=d4f2ab60-c98e-11d7–81c6–0820abe49a01.html>.
8. Sean Poulter, *Daily Mail*, 'Houses hit eight times average pay', 19 May 2005.
9. <http://www.finfacts.com/irelandbusinessnews/publish/printer_10003207.shtml>.
10. ABN Amro, *Overnight Report*, 'Boom and bust', 27 March 2006.
11. Sean Poulter, *Daily Mail*, 'Mortgage madness', 15 October 2005.
12. Josephine Cumbo, *Financial Times*, 'House price bonanza has reaped revenues for No 11', 23 March 2006.
13. Chris Giles, *FT.com*, 'FT index shows house prices up in 2005', 13 January 2006, <http://www.ft.com/cms/s/dd92d00c-8376–11da-9017–0000779e2340.html>.

14. <http://news.bbc.co.uk/1/hi/business/3750603.stm>.

15. <http://www.registry-trust.org.uk/Default.aspx?grm2catid=4&tabi d=62>.

16. Ian Cowie, *Daily Telegraph*, 'Home repossession orders soar by 66 per cent as debt mounts', 27 October 2005.

17. Sean Poulter, *Daily Mail*, 'Nine in ten credit cards "fail to check on income"', 23 January 2006.

18. Jon Land, *24.com*, 'Banks should be more "responsible" over credit card lending', <http://www.24dash.com/content/news/viewNews. php?navID=34&newsID=2520>.

19. Jim Pickard, *Financial Times*, 'Portman refuses to lend on buy-to-let new flats', 8 December 2005.

20. Steve Doughty, *Daily Mail*, 'Ballooning public sector gets 95,000 more jobs in a year', 1 October 2005.

21. ABN Amro, *Overnight Report*, 'Nobody home', 3 July 2006.

22. <http://www.debtadvicebureau.org.uk/news/2005/20050112-more-borrowers-plan-to-reduce-their-debts.shtml>.

23. Becky Barrow, *Daily Telegraph*, 'Families spend 20pc more than they earn', 10 June 2005.

24. Sean Poulter, *Daily Mail*, 'The £50,000-a-year high fliers trapped in a cycle of debt', 19 May 2005.

25. Becky Barrow, *Daily Mail*, 'Bankruptcy boom is blamed on easy credit', 31 October 2005.

26. Cowie, 'Home repossession orders soar by 66 per cent as debt mounts'.

27. Joe Morgan, *The Times*, 'Lenders target homes in move to recover debt on credit cards', 24 October 2005.

28. Sean Poulter, *Daily Mail*, 'Repossessions up by 50pc in a year', July 2005.

29. <http://www.insolvency.gov.uk/otherinformation/statistics/200608/ index.htm>.

30. Jane Croft and Peter Thal Larsen, *Financial Times*, 'Bank chief hits out at insolvency industry', 1 August 2006.

31. Grant Ringshaw, *Daily Telegraph*, 'Barclays plastic bent by bad debt', 4 August 2006.

CHAPTER 3

1. Remarks by Governor Ben S. Bernanke, 'Deflation: Making Sure "It" Doesn't Happen Here', before the National Economists Club, Washington DC, 21 November 2002, <http://www.federalreserve. gov/boarddocs/speeches/2002/20021121/default.htm>.

2. Craig Torres and Alexandre Tanzi, *Bloomberg News*, '"Hourglass economy" divides Americans, defines U.S. politics', 3 August 2006.
3. Robert Beckman, *The Downwave: Surviving the Second Great Depression*, London: Pan Books Ltd, 1983.
4. James Turk, *The Freemarket Gold and Money Report*, 'Economic suicide', 15 March 2006, <http://news.goldseek.com/JamesTurk/1142438460.php>.
5. Congressional Budget Office, 'The Budget and Economic Outlook: An Update', August 2005, <http://www.cbo.gov/ftpdocs/66xx/doc6609/08–15-OutlookUpdate.pdf#search='congressional%20budget%20office%20August%202005'>.
6. Edmund Conway, *Daily Telegraph*, 'US "could be going bankrupt"', 14 July 2006. Also Thakor Anjan, Federal Reserve Bank of St. Louis, *Review*, July/August 2006, pp. 251–7, <http://research.stlouisfed.org/publications/review/06/07/Thakor.pdf#search='professor%20kotlikoff%202006'>.
7. Joseph Stiglitz, *The Roaring Nineties: Why We're Paying the Price for the Greediest Decade in History*, London: Penguin Books, 2004, p. 43.
8. John Cassidy, *Dot.con: The Real Story of Why the Internet Bubble Burst*, London: Penguin Books, 2005, pp. 344–5.
9. Stiglitz, *The Roaring Nineties*, pp. 64–5.
10. James Dora, *The Times*, 'Greenspan wins $9m for his autobiography', 8 March 2006, <http://www.timesonline.co.uk/article/0,,5-2075126,00.html>.
11. David P. Hamilton, *The Wall Street Journal Interactive Edition*, 'Time may cushion US from effects of bubble', 10 December 1996, <http://pages.stern.nyu.edu/~nroubini/articles/StMkExub1WSJ.htm>.
12. Richard Russell, *Dow Theory Letters*, 10 February 2006.
13. ABN Amro, *Overnight Report*, 'Full of many cronies', 15 February 2006.
14. Jennifer Hughes, *Financial Times*, 'Bernanke remarks leave analysts bemused', 3 May 2006.
15. ABN Amro, *Overnight Report*, 'Federal kill', 27 July 2006.
16. Stiglitz, *The Roaring Nineties*, pp. 116–17.
17. Robert Schmidt and Otis Bilodeau, *Bloomberg News*, 'Options scandal may ensnare dozens more companies, executives', 3 August 2006.
18. For further information on the workings of Third World debt, see Michael Rowbotham, *Goodbye America!: Globalisation, Debt and the Dollar Empire*, Charlbury: Jon Carpenter Publishing, 2000.

19. Michael Rowbotham, *The Grip of Death: A Study of Modern Money, Debt Slavery and Destructive Economics*, Charlbury: Jon Carpenter Publishing, 1998, pp 45–72 (second printing, 2000).
20. Gerard Minack, *Downunder Daily*, 'Bonds bomb', 8 April 2006.
21. Gerard Minack, *Downunder Daily*, 'Would you credit it?', 29 April 2006.
22. Peter Thal Larsen and Chris Giles, *Financial Times*, 'Bank warns of risk in corporate debt levels', 12 July 2006.
23. ABN AMRO, *Overnight Report*, 'Signal failure', 25 August 2005.

CHAPTER 4

1. Kate Burgess, *Financial Times*, 'Regulators test hedge funds' formula', 11 March 2005.
2. Barton Biggs, *HedgeHogging*, Hoboken, NJ: John Wiley & Sons, 2006, p. 291.
3. Richard Hills, *Hedge Funds: An Introduction to Skill Based Investment Strategies*, Leighton Buzzard: Rushmere Wynne Ltd, 1996, pp. 30–2.
4. Gregory Connor and Mason Woo, 'An Introduction to Hedge Funds', London School of Economics, September 2003, <http://fmg.lse.ac.uk/upload_file/190_Intro%20to%20hedge%20funds.pdf#search='first%20hedge%20fund%20jones'>.
5. Alex Armitage and Miles Weiss, *Bloomberg News*, 'Disney taps hedge funds, investors to share film funding risks', 23 September 2005; also Mathew Lynn, *Bloomberg News*, 'Hedge funds, pro sports make a troubling team', 26 June 2006.
6. Connor and Woo, 'An Introduction to Hedge Funds'.
7. Christopher Cox (Chairman of the US Securities and Exchange Commission), 'Testimony concerning the regulation of hedge funds', 25 July 2006, <http://www.sec.gov/news/testimony/2006/ts072506cc.htm>.
8. Stephen Schurr, *Financial Times*, 'Investors keep faith in hedge funds', 24 October 2005.
9. James Drummond and Peter Thal Larsen, *Financial Times*, 'Study estimates banks made £13 bn', 11 March 2005.
10. Katherine Burton, *Bloomberg Markets*, 'High fees, low returns', April 2006.
11. ABN Amro, *Overnight Report*, 'No way out', 10 May 2005.
12. Burton, 'High fees, low returns'.
13. Robert Schmidt, *Bloomberg News*, 'Hedge fund fraud poses "emerging threat" U.S. regulator says', 7 July 2006.
14. Harry Kat, *FTfm*, 'Hedge funds are no panacea', 11 April 2005.

15. Simon Hayley, Capital Economics, *Global Economics Focus*, 'Investors run into the correlation trap', 22 May 2006; also Chris Hughes and Anuj Gangshar, *Financial Times*, 'Hedge funds fail to live up to their name', 13 July 2006.
16. Mathew Lynn, *Bloomberg News*, 'Hedge funds may be worth less than you think', 13 October 2005.
17. James Moore, *Daily Telegraph*, 'Top hedge fund and trader face FSA inquiry', 27 October 2005. See also Business Comment, *Daily Telegraph*, 27 October 2005, p. B2.
18. Mathew Lynn, *Bloomberg Markets*, 'Hooked on hedge funds', June 2005.
19. Editorial, *Financial Times*, 'Case for a closer look at hedge funds', 12 May 2005.
20. John Dooley, *Bloomberg News*, 'Derivative banks need systems to cut backlog, OCC says', 20 September 2005.
21. Hamish Risk, *Bloomberg News*, 'Credit derivative market expands to $17.3 trillion', 15 March 2006.
22. Gerard Minack, *Downunder Daily*, 'Taking a punt', 8 May 2006.
23. John Dooley and Hamish Risk, *Bloomberg News*, 'Fed calls in banks on derivatives paperwork backlog', 13 September 2005.
24. Gerard Minack, *Downunder Daily*, 'Hedged bets', 20 April 2006.

CHAPTER 5

1. Michael Rowbotham, *The Grip of Death: A Study of Modern Money, Debt Slavery and Destructive Economics*, Charlbury: Jon Carpenter Publishing, 1998 (second printing, 2000), pp. 292–9.
2. James Turk and John Rubino, *The Coming Collapse of the Dollar and How to Profit From It: Make a Fortune by Investing in Gold and Other Hard Assets*, New York: Doubleday, 2004, p. 48.
3. Jack Weatherford, *The History of Money: From Sandstone to Cyberspace*, New York: Three Rivers Press, 1997, p. 172.
4. <http://civil-war-time-machine.com/civil-war-plantations.html>.
5. Rowbotham, *The Grip of Death*, pp. 192–4.
6. <http://www.newyorkfed.org/education/frtea.pdf#search='original %20role%20of%20the%20federal%20reserve'>.
7. Weatherford, *The History of Money*, p. 205. Coinage Act 1792.
8. Peter Schiff, 'The U.S. Dollar's Days as the World's Reserve Currency are Numbered', 18 March 2005, <http://www.financialsense.com/ fsu/editorials/schiff/2005/0318.html>.
9. Hon. Ron Paul of Texas (before the House of US Representatives), 'The End of Dollar Hegemony', 15 February 2006, <http://www. house.gov/paul/congrec/congrec2006/cr021506.htm>.

10. Dania Saadi, *Bloomberg News*, 'Syria will end dollar peg, moves reserves to euros', 11 July 2006.

11. Paul A. Volcker, *Washingtonpost.com*, 'An economy on thin ice', 10 April 2005, p. B07, <http://www.washingtonpost.com/ac2/wp-dyn/A38725-2005Apr8?language=printer>.

12. Christopher Swann, *Financial Times*, 'US exporters fail to reap the full benefit of a weaker greenback', 21 March 2005.

13. Vivianne C. Rodrigues and Michael McDonald, *Bloomberg News*, 'Dollar falls after current-account gap grows more than forecast', 16 March 2005.

14. Alison Fitzgerald, *Bloomberg News*, 'Oil dollars return to US, holding down rates, helping growth', 3 January 2006.

15. Ben Bernanke, 'The Global Savings Glut and the US Current Account Deficit', 10 March 2005, <http://www.federalreserve.gov/boarddocs/speeches/2005/20050414/>. Accessed 20 July 2005.

16. ABN Amro, *Overnight Report*, 'Goldilocks – the end', 12 June 2006.

17. ABN Amro, *Overnight Report*, 'Debt, deficits and the dollar', 22 September 2005.

18. <http://www.york.ac.uk>.

19. Richard McGregor and Dickie Mure, *Financial Times,* 'China on track to exceed Japan reserves', 16 January 2006.

20. Nerys Avery, *Bloomberg News*, 'China's economy grew 9.9% in 2005, overtaking UK', 25 January 2006.

21. Charlene Barchefsky and Edward Gresser, 'Revolutionary China, complacent America', in Richard Russell, *Dow Theory Letters*, 15 September 2005.

22. ABN Amro, *Overnight Report*, 'Reindustrialisation', 2 August 2005.

23. Sandra Ward, *Barron's Magazine*, interview with Ray Dalio, Chief Investment Officer, Bridgewater Associates, USA, 11 June 2005.

24. ABN Amro, *Overnight Report*, 'Bretton Woods II RIP', 22 July 2005, and '2%, try 50%', 22 August 2005.

25. <http://www.senate.gov/comm>.

26. Edward Allen and Christopher Swan, *Financial Times,* 'US to shy away from tough line on China's currency', 10 May 2006.

27. Nerys Avery, *Bloomberg News*, 'China has record trade surplus, higher inflation', 12 June 2006.

28. <http://au.biz.yahoo.com/060422/33/o8zk.html>.

29. Bill McKibben, *Harper's Magazine*, 'The Great Leap, scenes from China's industrial revolution', December 2005.

30. Dean Calbreath, *San Diego Union-Tribune*, 'As US trade gap balloons, China soars with more high-tech products and leaves behind its cheap export reputation', 20 March 2005.

CHAPTER 6

1. ABN Amro, *Overnight Report*, 'Warning flares', 2 May 2005.
2. Charles T. Maxwell, *Barron's*, 'The gathering storm', 15 November 2004.
3. Simon Haley, Capital Economics, *Global Economics Daily*, 'Commodity prices: current highs are not sustainable', 5 May 2006.
4. Jim Rogers, *Hot Commodities: How Anyone can Invest Profitability in the World's Best Market*, Chichester: John Wiley & Sons Ltd, 2005, p. xvii.
5. <http://www.cbo.gov/ftpdocs/71xx/doc7128/04–07-ChinaOil.pdf>.
6. <http://www.gold-eagle.com/editorials_02/chapmand062902.html>.
7. Robert C. Beckman, *The Downwave: Surviving the Second Great Depression*, London: Pan Books Ltd, 1983.
8. Rogers, *Hot Commodities*, p. 6.
9. Gerard Minack, *Downunder Daily*, 'Base jumping' (date unknown).
10. Population Reference Bureau, World Population Growth from 1750 to 2150, <http://www.prb.org/PrintTemplate.cfm?Section=Population_Growth&Template=/ContentManagement/HTMLDisplay.cfm&ContentID=5602>.
11. Michael T. Klare, *Blood and Oil: The Dangers and Consequences of America's Growing Petroleum Dependency*, London: Penguin Books, 2003, 3rd edn, p. 9.
12. Klare, *Blood and Oil*, p. 94.
13. George Magnus, *Financial Times*, 'The world is heading for a shock over the high price of oil', 15 August 2005.
14. Malcolm Moore, *Daily Telegraph*, 'High oil prices pose serious risk, says IMF', 8 April 2005.
15. World Energy Outlook 2005, 'IEA Projects Growth in Middle East and North Africa Oil and Natural Gas Sectors through 2030 but a Lack of Investment would Push up Prices and Depress GDP Growth', <http://www.iea.org/Textbase/press/pressdetail.asp?PRESS_REL_ID=163>.
16. Harry Stourton, *Moneyweek*, 'What Jim Rogers is buying now', 25 November 2005, <http://www.moneyweek.com/file/5067/jimrogers-2511.html>. Accessed 17 July 2006.
17. Joseph Nocera, *New York Times*, 'On oil supply, opinions aren't scarce', 10 September 2005.
18. World Energy Outlook 2005, 'IEA Projects Growth in Middle East'.

19. Klare, *Blood and Oil*, p. 122.
20. Carola Hoyos and Kevin Morrison, *Financial Times*, 'US drivers face higher prices for new petrol', 16 March 2006.
21. Stefan Weiser, *Commodities Now*, 'Commodities – too late to invest?', September 2005.

CHAPTER 7

1. <http://www.predecimal.com/p4norman.htm>.
2. Alan Greenspan, 'Gold and Economic Freedom', in Ayn Rand, Nathaniel Branden, Alan Greenspan and Robert Hessen, *Capitalism: The Unknown Ideal*, New York: New American Library, 1967, pp. 96–102.
3. James Turk and John Rubino, *The Coming Collapse of the Dollar and How to Profit From It: Make a fortune by Investing in Gold and Other Hard Assets*, New York: Doubleday, 2004, p. 57.
4. Niall Ferguson, *New York Times Magazine*, 'Our currency, your problem', 13 March 2005.
5. Jack Weatherford, *The History of Money: From Sandstone to Cyberspace*, New York: Three Rivers Press, 1997, p. 195.
6. Irving J. Janus, *Psychology Today*, 'Groupthink', November 1971, <http://www.stanford.edu/group/scie/Career/Wisdom/groupthink1.htm>.
7. James Ashton, *Daily Mail*, 'Brown counts cost of bullion sale', 30 November 2005.
8. World Gold Council Press Release, 'Investment Demand for Gold Soars During Volatile First Quarter', 23 May 2006.
9. Kevin Morrison, *Financial Times*, 'Investors look to central banks for signs of gold sales policies', 28 June 2006.
10. World Gold Council figures for mining costs in 2005, <http://www.gold.org/value/markets/supply_demand/mine_production.html>.
11. Jonathan Compton, Bedlam Asset Management, *Mid-Quarter Review*, 'In God We Trust', November 2005.
12. Ambrose Evans-Pritchard, *Daily Telegraph*, 'Beijing whispers push gold to $700', 10 May 2006.
13. Morrison, 'Investors look to central banks for signs of gold sales policies'.
14. ABN Amro, *Overnight Report*, 'Going for gold', 25 May 2005.
15. The World Gold Council's website provides some alternative choices, <http://www.gold.org>. Also recommended is the website of leading gold consultants GFMS, <http://www.gfms.co.uk>.
16. Lawrence Dune, *Bloomberg News*, 'Exchange traded funds help boost gold, silver prices', 11 May 2006.

17. John Hathaway, Tocqueville Gold 2005, Year End Review and Outlook, 26 January 2006, <http://www.gold-eagle.com/editorials_05/hathaway012606.html>.
18. Investec Asset Management, *Managers Update*, Global Gold Fund, March 2006.
19. Max King, Investec Asset Management, *e-View*, 10 October 2005, <http://www.investecfunds.co.uk/uploads/eview1005.pdf#search='gold%20shares%201934'>.

CHAPTER 8

1. Gerard Minack, *Downunder Daily*, 'Four lessons', 22 May 2006.
2. Benjamin Graham, *The Intelligent Investor: A Book of Practical Counsel*, 4th edn, New York: Harper & Row, 1973.
3. Jeremy Lang, *The Lang Approach* (in-house brochure of Liontrust Asset Management, London, n.d.).
4. Martin Wolf, *Financial Times*, 'Why a long-term bet on the stock market may disappoint', 22 March 2006.
5. Gerard Minack, *Downunder Daily*, 'Live by the E, die by the E', 30 May 2006.
6. Brown Brothers Harriman, *Technical View*, '10year yields on the brink', 5 April 2006.
7. ABN Amro, *Overnight Report*, 'Pie fight', 31 March 2005.
8. Brown Brothers Harriman Monthly, *Financial Markets Outlook*, 'Evolving from bull to bear market', 23 March 2006.
9. Gerard Minack, *Downunder Daily*, 'Sirens singing you to shipwreck', 4 April 2006.
10. ABN Amro, *Overnight Report*, 'Inversion therapy', 19 June 2006.
11. Jack D. Schwager, *Market Wizards: Interviews with Top Traders*, New York: HarperBusiness, 1993.
12. Brown Brothers Harriman Monthly, 'Evolving from bull to bear market'.
13. Brown Brothers Harriman Monthly, 'Evolving from bull to bear market'.
14. Gerard Minack, *Downunder Daily*, 'Apollonic investing', 11 April 2006.
15. Andrew Hill, *Financial Times*, 'Portents aplenty as investors find reasons to be fearful', 23 May 2006.
16. Gillian Tett, *Financial Times*, 'Derivatives activity linked to share falls', 19 May 2005.
17. Gerard Minack, *Downunder Daily*, 'Not the Bernanke put', 22 July 2006.

18. John Cassidy, *Dot.con: The Real Story of Why the Internet Bubble Burst*, London: Penguin Books, p. 289.
19. For a detailed study of such markets see Russell Napier, *Anatomy of the Bear: Lessons from Wall Street's Four Great Bottoms*, Hong Kong: CSLA Books, 2005.

CHAPTER 9

1. <http://history.uchicago.edu/faculty/MaeNgai/ngai.htm>.
2. Robert Beckman, *The Downwave: Surviving the Second Great Depression*, London: Pan Books Ltd, 1983, p. 26.
3. See Jim Mellon and Al Chalabi, *Wake Up! Survive and Prosper in the Coming Economic Turmoil*, Chichester: Capstone Publishing Ltd, 2005.
4. <http://esa.un.org/unpp/p2k0data.asp>.
5. Richard Russell, *Daily Newsletter*, 26 May 2006, <http://www.cia.gov/cia/publications/factbook/rankorder/2067rank.html>.
6. David White, *Financial Times*, 'China courts Africa in quest for commodities', 20 June 2006.
7. William Bonner, *Empire of Debt: The Rise of an Epic Financial Crisis*, Hoboken, NJ: John Wiley & Sons, Inc., 2006, pp. 66–7.
8. Michael T. Klare, *Blood and Oil: The Dangers and Consequences of America's Growing Petroleum Dependency*, London: Penguin Books, 2003, 3rd edn, p. 71.
9. <http://news.bbc.co.uk/2/hi/business/3970855.stm>, 1 November 2004.
10. Allen T. Cheng, *Bloomberg News*, 'Ahmadinejad calls for closer ties with Shanghai group', 15 June 2006.
11. Irwin Stelzer, *Sunday Times*, 'Opening shots in a new style of trade warfare', 5 June 2005.
12. Bill Deedes' column, *Daily Telegraph*, 4 August 2006.
13. Christopher Adams, *Financial Times*, 'Planning shake-up to aid push for N-plants', 6 July 2006.
14. Carola Hoyos, *Financial Times*, 'Energy watchdog to back N-power', 21 April 2006.
15. Christopher Adams and Rebecca Bream, *Financial Times*, 'Investment spread over decades proves difficult to cost', 18 May 2006.
16. Fiona Harvey, *Financial Times*, 'Onshore wind farms profitable even without subsidy, says Carbon Trust', 6 July 2006.
17. Bjorn Lornborg, *The Skeptical Environmentalist: Measuring the Real State of the World*, Cambridge: Cambridge University Press, 2001; James Lovelock, *The Revenge of Gaia: Why the Earth is Fighting*

Back – and How We Can Still Save Humanity, London: Penguin Books, 2006.

18. <http://www.bbc.co.uk/sn/tvradio/programmes/horizon/dimming_prog_summary.shtml>.

19. Martin Wolf, *Financial Times*, 'Do we need to cry now that the climate wolf is at the door?', 12 July 2006.

20. Bob Carter, *Daily Mail*, 'World "not warming up"', 11 April 2006.

21. Edward Robinson, *Bloomberg News*, 'VCs bet on solar, biofuel money-losers in green energy frenzy', 29 June 2006.

22. <http://www.chesapeakeclimate.org/news/news_detail.cfm?id=102>.

23. Charles Clover, *Daily Telegraph*, 'Alternative ways to generate power', 13 March 2006.

24. Fiona Harvey, *Financial Times*, 'Black clouds gather over EUs carbon dioxide permits', 19 May 2006.

25. Alan Beattie, *Financial Times*, 'Ethanol puts power in Brazil's tank', 16 May 2006, and Jonathan Wheatley, *Financial Times*, 'Brazil prepares to grow the next world fuel', 9 March 2006.

CHAPTER 10

1. Jack Weatherford, *The History of Money: From Sandstone to Cyberspace*, New York: Three Rivers Press, 1997, pp. 175–7.

2. Robert Beckman, *The Downwave: Surviving the Second Great Depression*, London: Pan Books Ltd, 1983, pp. 178–9.

3. Warren Giles, *Bloomberg News*, 'WTO six-way talks collapse, jeopardising global pact', 24 July 2006.

4. Joseph Stiglitz, *The Roaring Nineties: Why We're Paying the Price of the Greediest Decade in History*, London: Penguin Books, 2004, p. 22.

5. For further informatin one should look into sustainable solutions such as permaculture: see Patrick Whitefield, *The Earth Care Manual: A Permaculture Handbook For Britain & Other Temperate Climates*, East Meon: Permanent Publications, 2004. See also <http://www.permaculture.co.uk/main 2.html>.

6. For guidance on the topic and helpful tips to avoid unnecessary spending see Rebecca Ash, *The New Spend Less Revolution: 365 Tips for a Better Quality of life While Actually Spending Less*, Petersfield: Harriman House Ltd, 2006.

7. Beckman, *The Downwave*, p. 183.

8. Consultant Derek Arden produces handy booklets, rather than hefty tomes, on negotiation skills, <http://derekarden.co.uk/store/index.asp>.

9. For some intriguing suggestions in this field which involve monetary reform and social credit see Michael Rowbotham, *The Grip of Death: A Study of Modern Money, Debt Slavery and Destructive Economics*, Charlbury: Jon Carpenter Publishing (second printing, 2000), 1998, pp. 216–36. Frances Hutchinson likewise proposes a return to decentralised, community-based solutions: Frances Hutchinson, *What Everybody Really Wants to Know About Money*, Charlbury: Jon Carpenter Publishing, 1998. See also Michael Woodin and Caroline Lucas, *Green Alternatives to Globalisation: A Manifesto*, London: Pluto Press, 2004.
10. A more detailed discussin will be provided in my next book.
11. Stiglitz, *The Roaring Nineties*, p. 48.

SELECT BIBLIOGRAPHY

Beckman, Robert, *The Downwave: Surviving the Second Great Depression*, London: Pan, 1983.

Biggs, Barton, *HedgeHogging*, Hoboken, NJ: John Wiley & Sons, 2006.

Bonner, William, *Empire of Debt: The Rise of an Epic Financial Crisis*, Hoboken, NJ: John Wiley & Sons, 2006.

Calverley, John P., *Bubbles and How to Survive Them*, London: Nicholas Brealey Publishing, 2004.

Cassidy, John, *Dot.con: The Real Story of Why the Internet Bubble Burst*, London: Penguin Books, 2005.

Eichengreen, Barry, *Capital Flows and Crises*, London: MIT Press, 2004.

Gladwell, Malcolm, *The Tipping Point: How Little Things Can Make a Big Difference*, London: Little, Brown & Co., 2001, reprinted 2005.

Graham, Benjamin, *The Intelligent Investor: A Book of Practical Counsel*, 4th edn, New York: Harper & Row, 1973.

Greenspan, Alan, 'Gold and Economic Freedom', in Ayn Rand, Nathaniel Branden, Alan Greenspan and Robert Hessen, *Capitalism: The Unknown Ideal*, New York: New American Library, 1967.

Harrison, Fred, *Boom Bust: House Prices, Banking and the Great Depression of 2010*, London: Shepheard-Walwyn, 2005.

Hills, Richard, *Hedge Funds: An Introduction to Skill Based Investment Strategies*, Leighton Buzzard: Rushmere Wynne, 1996.

Hutchinson, Frances, *What Everybody Really Wants to Know About Money*, Charlbury: Jon Carpenter Publishing, 1998.

Kindleberger, Charles P., *Manias, Panics and Crashes: A History of Fancial Crises*, 4th edn, New York: John Wiley & Sons, 2000.

Klare, Michael T., *Blood and Oil: The Dangers and Consequences of America's Growing Petroleum Dependency*, 3rd edn, London: Penguin Books, 2003.

Lomborg, Bjorn, *The Skeptical Environmentalist: Measuring the Real State of the World*, Cambridge: Cambridge University Press, 2001, 17th printing, 2006.

Lovelock, James, *The Revenge of Gaia: Why the Earth is Fighting Back – and How We Can Still Save Humanity*, London: Penguin Books, 2006.

Mellon, Jim, and Chalabi, Al, *Wake Up!: Survive and Prosper in the Coming Economic Turmoil*, Chichester: Capstone Publishing, 2005.

Napier, Russell, *Anatomy of the Bear: Lessons from Wall Street's Four Great Bottoms*, Hong Kong: CSLA Books, 2005.

Rogers, Jim, *Hot Commodities: How Anyone Can Invest Profitability in the World's Best Market*, Chichester: John Wiley & Sons, 2005.

Rowbotham, Michael, *The Grip of Death: A Study of Modern Money, Debt Slavery and Destructive Economics*, Charlbury: Jon Carpenter Publishing, 1998.

Rowbotham, Michael, *Goodbye America!: Globalisation, Debt and the Dollar Empire*, Charlbury: Jon Carpenter Publishing, 2000.

Schwager, Jack D., *Market Wizards: Interviews with Top Traders*, New York: HarperBusiness, 1993.

Shiller, Robert J., *Irrational Exuberance*, 2nd edn, Princeton, NJ, and Oxford: Princeton University Press, 2005.

Simmons, Matthew R., *Twilight in the Desert: The Coming Saudi Oil Shock and the World Economy*, Hoboken, NJ: John Wiley & Sons, 2005.

Stiglitz, Joseph, *The Roaring Nineties: Why We're Paying the Price for the Greediest Decade in History*, London: Penguin Books, 2004.

Talbott, John R., *The Coming Crash in the Housing Market*, New York: McGraw-Hill, 2003.

Todd, Emmanuel, *After the Empire: The Breakdown of the American Order*, London: Constable & Robinson, 2004.

Turk, James, and Rubino, John, *The Coming Collapse of the Dollar and How to Profit From It: Make a Fortune by Investing in Gold and Other Hard Assets*, New York: Doubleday, 2004.

Weatherford, Jack, *The History of Money: From Sandstone to Cyberspace*, New York: Three Rivers Press, 1997.

Woodin, Michael, and Lucas, Caroline, *Green Alternatives to Globalisation*, London: Pluto Press, 2004.

INDEX

Compiled by Sue Carlton